Harvey and Jessie

Jessie Lloyd O'Connor

Harvey O'Connor

and Susan M. Bowler

HARVEY and JESSIE

A Couple of Radicals

TEMPLE UNIVERSITY PRESS

Philadelphia

Temple University Press, Philadelphia 19122
Copyright © 1988 by Temple University. All rights reserved
Published 1988
Printed in the United States of America

The paper used in this publication meets the minimum
requirements of American National Standard for Information
Sciences—Permanence of Paper for Printed Library Materials,
ANSI Z39.48-1984

Library of Congress Cataloging-in-Publication Data

O'Connor, Jessie Lloyd, 1904–
Harvey and Jessie : a couple of radicals / Jessie Lloyd O'Connor,
Harvey O'Connor, and Susan M. Bowler.
        p.   cm.
Includes bibliographical references and index.
ISBN 0-87722-519-2 (alk. paper)
1. O'Connor, Jessie Lloyd, 1904–   . 2. O'Connor, Harvey, 1897–1987.
3. Labor and laboring classes—United States—Biography.
4. Radicals—United States—Biography.   I. O'Connor, Harvey. 1897–1987.
II. Bowler, Susan M.   III. Title.
HD8073.A1025   1988
322'.2'0922—dc19
        [B]   87-21737
                    CIP

Contents

Foreword
Dave Roediger

The words to the labor anthem "Solidarity Forever" end this superb dual autobiography almost with a pun. The story of Jessie Lloyd O'Connor and Harvey O'Connor is that of two American radicals who have persisted through long lifetimes in trying to "bring to birth a new world." They have likewise sustained a marriage based on solidarity with each other for more than half a century. In a nation in which ex-radicals far outnumber radicals and in which golden anniversaries are an endangered species, theirs is a remarkable political story and a remarkable love story. That they represent such different backgrounds—the Western proletarian radicalism of Harvey and the Midwestern millionaire socialism of Jessie—makes the story still more incredible and still more instructive with regard to that which is enduring in the American tradition of dissent. Indeed both as separate threads and as a wonderful tapestry, the two stories told here ought to cause historians to reevaluate how we study radicalism in the twentieth century. If these stories are not typical—would that they were—they are nevertheless as instructive as they are engaging.

The best point of departure for understanding the durability of dissent in the lives of the O'Connors lies in a self-description by Jessie's grandfather, Henry Demarest Lloyd, recalled in a 1957 article by Harvey. The elder Lloyd saw himself, O'Connor explained, as a "socialist-anarchist-communist-individualist-collectivist-cooperative-aristocratic-democrat."[1] The same list, with "feminist" substituted for "aristocratic," applies well to Harvey and Jessie, as does the same sense that various strains of radicalism need not always and everywhere be at war with each other. Significant here is not only the direct influence of Henry Demarest Lloyd, which is clear in the labor journalism of both Harvey and Jessie and in the many exposés of monopoly written by Harvey with Jessie's assistance,[2] but also the heritage of a many-sided late nineteenth- and early twentieth-century radicalism whose advocates often admitted that different paths to the "cooperative commonwealth" could be pursued in good faith. Bill Haywood and Gustavus Myers, Alice Paul and John Reed, a young William Z. Foster and Rosika Schwimmer, Edward Bellamy and Florence Kelley—all of these walk together in the later prose of one or both the O'Connors, and the sense is that they walked toward a common goal, however different the byways they chose to explore. More than three decades ago, Harvey was already describing himself as an "old graybeard . . . brought up in the old Socialist Party and the IWW." There was much of value in such an upbringing.[3]

But the disinterest in sectarian quarrels, so evident in this dual autobiography, stems from more than heritage and is not merely nostalgic. After all, many radicals and ex-radicals active in the early twentieth century have left memoirs that are exceedingly interested in setting straight the record of struggles over the correct line.[4] Part of what sets the present work apart is undoubtedly the experience of the O'Connors as top labor journalists whose work sought to convey human drama. Thus even where tactical differences in the labor movement are explored in this book, the points are carried through intimate character sketches—of Jay Lovestone or Michael Tighe, for example—rather than through theoretical discussion. To put it another way, Jessie's and Harvey's sensibilities and writing style lead them to locate political opinions in real settings and real persons and to admit a fair amount of ambiguity.[5] In that sense, their work in this book and in earlier writings on the Gastonia strike, the Seattle General Strike, and steel industry organizing captures many of the concerns raised in the past two decades by writers of the "new labor history."[6]

Finally, in accounting for the absence of a sectarian edge from these memoirs, we must recognize that the independent socialism professed by the authors represented a distinctive politics rather than a lack of politics. The O'Connors *chose* to nurture a variety of left-wing projects—especially industrial union organizing but also anti-fascism, civil liberties, and opposition to imperialism and war—

without generally belonging to an organized political tendency. This makes their politics difficult to characterize. Staughton Lynd's excellent study of pre-C.I.O. steel industry organizing in the Great Depression, for example, settles for typing Harvey as merely a "partial exception," who did not quite fit in under the "Social Democratic intellectual" label that Lynd uses to characterize the writers and researchers advising rank-and-file union leaders.[7]

It may well be that political wisdom lay with being a "partial exception." Certainly a political logic did. One key to that logic is Harvey's reflection on the 1919 strike in Seattle, in which Lenin's pamphlet "The Soviets at Work" played a role in radicalizing strikers. O'Connor, both a participant in the strike and one of its major historians, wrote:

> The extraordinary influence of this pamphlet was to be felt in subsequent events in Seattle as workers pondered the problems of "management" in a workers' state. There was of course an initial problem not considered in Lenin's speech—how to seize power to create a workers' state in the first place. For Lenin's purposes that was not necessary— that problem had been solved in front of the Winter Palace. . . . Not many Seattleites . . . had much of an answer to Lenin's initial problem of winning power.[8]

O'Connor learned from the general strike and subsequent developments in Seattle both the possibilities of mass action and the possibilities of defeat. In his later years, he avoided both pessimism and revolutionary posturing. Gastonia held similar lessons for Jessie. One result was a shared politics, which held that the fostering of institutions to empower workers and the encouragement of general leftward movement in American political life was more important than party building.

Of course, to be an independent Socialist in the United States meant to be called a Communist or a "fellow traveler." Such was the case not only during the early Cold War but also during the Depression. Elizabeth Dilling's 1934 anti-Communist classic, *The Red Network*, for example, counts Jessie as "wife of communist Fed. Press corres. Harvey O'Connor,"[9] before listing her participation in four "front" organizations. During the same year, A.F. of L. unionists exchanged a round of correspondence red-baiting Harvey, branding him, in Michael Tighe's words, as the "communist-inclined . . . mastermind in our convention" and characterizing both Harvey and

Jessie as supporters of " 'outside influences' . . . determined to wreck [our] organization."[10]

Tighe's comments came at a time when the O'Connors' work in the steel industry cut squarely against the Communist Party line of dual unionism,[11] and it would be easy to show other instances, from the thirties to the support for Yugoslav socialism in the fifties and beyond, that demonstrate that the fullest recent history of American communism is correct in calling Harvey O'Connor a "non-Communist."[12] The same label applies to Jessie.

The more interesting question is that of fellow traveling. Indeed this book, along with the recent collection of the writings of Mary Heaton Vorse,[13] makes clear the urgent need for histories of modern American radicalism that refuse to consider the Communist Party in isolation from its periphery. A fixation on the Party, in both memoirs of members and ex-members and in the work of historians, has left enormous gaps in our knowledge of the radical past. Harvey O'Connor, for example, goes unmentioned in Bert Cochran's *Labor and Communism*.[14] Moreover, the assumption of too many Communists, ex-Communists, and historians is that those labeled "fellow travelers" were superficial, easily misled, and reactive in their politics and were seekers of vicarious pleasure through identification with the Russian Revolution. Where those outside the Party, but supportive of some of its campaigns, are discussed, the urgency of moral condemnation often overwhelms any sense of history and any attempt to disentangle varied motives for their support, let alone how those motives may have changed over time. Oddly, a historical literature bitterly denouncing fellow travelers coexists with a growing body of scholarship sympathetic to longtime Party leaders.[15] Perhaps one way to move the history of communism beyond the rather arid current debates within the field would be to focus on the tens of thousands of fellow travelers, rank-and-file workers in Communist-led unions, and persons who left the Party without great hostility. This periphery, far larger than the Party, voted with its feet by supporting some Party activities in some periods and refusing to support other causes at other times.[16]

The case of the O'Connors illustrates the complexities involved and the inadequacies of existing scholarship on anti-anti-Communists. Jessie and Harvey supported Communist-led strikes, and

Harvey wrote for the *Daily Worker* (where for a time he was city editor). They visited the Soviet Union during the early Stalin years and worked for the *Moscow Daily News*,[17] writing largely uncritical accounts of the changes occurring in Russia. During McCarthyism, Harvey was instrumental in mounting an important First Amendment challenge to anti-Communist witch-hunts.[18]

Such activities fit the profile hostile historians have drawn of fellow travelers, but Harvey and Jessie do not. Complications abound, not the least of which are that in the Soviet Union Jessie sought out critics of the regime in the Tolstoy circle and that in the United States the O'Connors embraced some aspects of Communist policy while rejecting others. Their writing shows not a jot of the affected proletarianism or heavy didacticism characteristic of too much *Daily Worker* journalism—a style Harvey briefly critiques in the pages below. Howard Fast's characterization of fifties fellow travelers as admiring from a distance the hard discipline of the Party[19] applies poorly in this case. Jessie explicitly justifies anti-McCarthyism on the grounds that an end to attacks on the civil liberties of Communists would militate against an atmosphere that bred authoritarian socialism.

Most fundamentally, the charge that fellow travelers embraced a fantasy of Socialist progress in the Soviet Union in order to avoid fundamental change at home—a charge insistently made in David Caute's sometimes useful *The Fellow Travellers*—falls flat in explaining the careers of the O'Connors.[20] The Soviet Union was simply never at the center of their political universe. Even their defenses of the Russian Revolution, such as the one reprinted in this volume, take the form of attacks on the absence of civil liberties, of the rights of labor, and of food at home during the Depression. The O'Connors joined Communists to fight for racial justice, better housing, and trade unions in the United States. Harvey, in the pages below, praises American Communists chiefly as courageous labor organizers capable, under the right circumstances, of contributing to the empowerment of American workers.[21] Indeed from the Seattle General Strike, Harvey seems to have seen the benefits of Soviet power as lying largely in enabling American workers to glimpse the possibility of a worker-managed society, much perhaps as the Socialist settlement of the state of Washington was for a time projected by Eugene

Debs to be capable of showing all of America the possibility of non-capitalist rule.[22] This stance did not make those who shared O'Connor's perspective the most perceptive observers of Soviet realities, but it certainly does not establish them as dilettantes seeking to bask in Sovietism's reflected glory.

But the term "fellow traveler" may have a more human and personal application to the stories of Jessie and Harvey. In Russia, where the political use of "fellow traveler" originated, the usage exists in both genders (the feminine *poputchitsa* and the masculine *poputchik*), and the words are very commonly used in a non-political way to mean "companions on a journey."[23] Perhaps the greatest virtue of this book is that it gives so strong a sense of its authors as individuals and as companions. With little space taken up in polemics, there is ample room for the personal, and both authors have a sense of the importance of personal matters. In contrast to many radical autobiographies whose interest in class forces and parties so predominates ("The Party Made Me To Be Come What I Am What Ever It Is," wrote the Alabama Communist Hosea Hudson to historian Nell I. Painter as the two collaborated on his autobiography[24]), this book richly lingers over two very different childhoods. It shows unfolding radicalization born of human experience and exposure to movement culture rather than conversion to a political logic. It features splendid digressions on old Wobblies, on dance, and even on John Reed's swimming suit.

Most vitally, it gives us the story of a couple of radicals achieving solidarity at home while on an exciting political journey. We can appreciate the hesitations that the authors must have felt in marrying, hesitations stemming from much more than radicals' ambivalence about the institution of marriage. We can wonder at a match bringing together great wealth and poverty, a man who matured in lumber camps and labor strife and a woman who matriculated at Smith. We might note affinities in the youthful hardships of each and the superb education, gotten quite differently, of both. Did the feminist, radical, and aristocratic upbringing of Jessie and the hard realities of Harvey's childhood both tend to produce fierce independence? Some mysteries will remain as to why this love story has a happy ending. Perhaps, as Basil Davidson has recently written in discussing the ability of the late and great British intellectual Thomas Hodgkin to combine intellectually aristocratic traditions and radical politics, it has been possible for the O'Connors to live with opposites without reconciling them.[25]

The shelf of primary documents from which we can begin to write a social history of American radicalism is an exceedingly slender one. This is a major addition.

Notes

Acknowledgment: Thanks to Mikhailina Karina for research assistance in preparing this Foreword and to Jean Allman, Steve Rosswurm, and Jim Barrett for comments.

1. Harvey O'Connor, "Henry Demarest Lloyd: The Prophetic Tradition," in Harvey Goldberg, ed., *American Radicals: Some Problems and Personalities* (New York, 1957), 79, quoting from Caro Lloyd, *Henry Demarest Lloyd* (New York, 1912), 1:112.

2. Compare Henry Demarest Lloyd's *A Strike of Millionaires Against Miners* (Chicago, 1890); *Wealth Against Commonwealth* (New York, 1894); and *Men: The Workers* (New York, 1909) with the writings of Harvey O'Connor and Jessie Lloyd O'Connor described in this volume.

3. Harvey O'Connor, "Needed: To Spread the Idea of Socialism," *Monthly Review* 2 (May 1950), 17. See also Harvey O'Connor, "Rebel Voices," *Monthly Review* 16 (February 1965), 624–26, and Jessie Lloyd, "One Woman's Resistance," appended to Harvey O'Connor, *Revolution in Seattle* (Seattle, 1981), 261.

4. See, e.g., such very different works as William Z. Foster, *From Bryan to Stalin* (New York, 1937), and David Dubinsky and A. H. Raskin, *A Life with Labor* (New York, 1977).

5. Remarkable in this connection is the capacity for self-criticism and criticism of left tactics by O'Connor. See Harvey O'Connor, "Idea of Socialism," 16–17, and "What Price Socialism?" *Monthly Review* 6 (April 1955), 451–53.

6. See especially Harvey O'Connor, *Steel-Dictator* (New York, 1935), a neglected classic, and *Revolution in Seattle*.

7. Staughton Lynd, "The Possibility of Radicalism in the Early 1930s: The Case of Steel," in James Green, ed., *Workers' Struggles, Past and Present: A "Radical America" Reader* (Philadelphia, 1983), 195.

8. O'Connor, *Revolution in Seattle*, 120.

9. Elizabeth Dilling, *The Red Network* (Kenilworth, Illinois; and Chicago, 1934), 301.

10. "Michael Tighe to William Green" (April 23, 1934, and May 2, 1934) in the microfilm edition of the *American Federation of Labor Records: The*

Samuel Gompers Era on Reel 141, "National and International Union Correspondence." I am indebted to Professor J. Carroll Moody of Northern Illinois University for this reference.

11. Lynd, "Possibility of Radicalism," 195–96.

12. Harvey Klehr, *The Heyday of American Communism: The Depression Decade* (New York, 1984), 74.

13. Dee Garrison, ed., *Rebel Pen: The Writings of Mary Heaton Vorse* (New York, 1985).

14. Indeed, Harvey O'Connor and Jessie Lloyd O'Connor, falling between the fields of history of reform and history of communism, are seldom mentioned by historians. See Bert Cochran, *Labor and Communism: The Conflict that Shaped American Unions* (Princeton, 1977). There is a single mention of Harvey in Klehr, *Heyday of American Communism*, 74, and two brief mentions in David Caute, *The Great Fear: The Anti-Communist Purge under Truman and Eisenhower* (New York, 1978), 149 and 180. Exceptional in this regard is the work of Lynd, especially "Possibility of Radicalism," and Staughton Lynd, ed., "Personal Histories of the Early CIO," *Radical America* 5 (May–June 1971), 52–55.

15. See, e.g., Howard Fast, *The Naked God: The Writer and the Communist Party* (New York, 1957), 63–65; William L. O'Neill, *A Better World: The Great Schism* (New York, 1982), especially 102–3, 173–83, and 206–11; David Caute, *The Fellow-Travellers: A Postscript to the Enlightenment* (New York, 1973); William Wright, *Lillian Hellman: The Image, the Woman* (New York, 1986); Francis Broderick, *W. E. B. Du Bois: Negro Leader in a Time of Protest* (Palo Alto, 1959), written before Du Bois joined the Communist Party; Stephen J. Whitfield, *Scott Nearing: Apostle of American Radicalism* (New York and London, 1974). Nearing was briefly a Party member.

16. Good beginnings in this direction are Mark Naison, *Communists in Harlem During the Depression* (New York, 1983), and George Lipsitz, *Class and Culture in Cold War America* (New York, 1981). See also Vivian Gornick, *The Romance of American Communism* (New York, 1977), 251–52. On the current state of the history of American communism, see the exchange between Maurice Isserman and Phyllis Jacobson in *New Politics* 1, second ser. (Winter 1987), 220–26; Maurice Isserman, "Three Generations: Historians View American Communism," *Labor History* 26 (Fall 1985); Theodore Draper, "The Popular Front Revisited," *New York Review of Books* (May 30, 1985).

17. On the *Moscow Daily News*, see Sylvia R. Margulies, *The Pilgrimage to Russia: The Soviet Union and the Treatment of Foreigners, 1924–1937* (Madison, 1968), 100–2.

18. Caute, *Great Fear*, 149, briefly treats the 1954 case, which is best followed in the pages of *Monthly Review*.

19. Fast, *Naked God*, 63–65.

20. Caute, *Fellow-Travellers*, 6-7 and passim.

21. See Harvey O'Connor, "From Wobblies to CIO," *Monthly Review* 22 (April 1971), 49–50.

22. O'Connor, *Revolution in Seattle*, 1. See also Tracy B. Strong and Helene Keyssar, *Right in Her Soul: The Life of Anna Louise Strong* (New York, 1983), 77. Similarly, O'Connor's many writings on imperialism do not portray the Soviet Union as a model, let alone *the* model of Third World development, but as a force sometimes contributing to the weakening of colonial and neocolonial rule.

23. Caute, *Fellow-Travellers*, 1, treats the origins of political use of the term. I am indebted to Professor Charles Timberlake of the University of Missouri for help with the Russian translation.

24. Nell Irvin Painter, *The Narrative of Hosea Hudson: His Life as a Negro Communist in the South* (Cambridge, 1979), 34. The excellent narrative quite transcends the quote.

25. Basil Davidson, "Thomas Hodgkin: An Appreciation," *Race and Class* 28 (Spring 1987), 2.

Preface

Beth Taylor contacted me the week before Memorial Day, 1985. Beth had just finished editing a manuscript, *The Contumacious Couple*, which she described as the joint memoir of Jessie and Harvey O'Connor, Socialists and labor journalists. The O'Connors' son, Stephen, had first urged them to record their memories and David Green, a Ph.D. candidate in American Civilization at Brown University, had developed a chronology of Jessie's and Harvey's lives while organizing their personal papers for deposit at Smith College and Wayne State University.

With a six-month-old child to raise and a Ph.D. in literature to complete, Beth did not feel she had the time to reshape the manuscript for publication. After a few conversations, she asked if I would take over the project. As Beth described the manuscript and Jessie and Harvey, I became more and more interested. The idea of being compensated for historically valuable and politically congenial work recommended itself to me. I asked to see the 612-page manuscript and read it in a little over a day. I found it revealing and often touching. Jessie and Harvey danced and doubted, wrote and organized, loved and fought, and they chronicled noble acts and petty deeds, euphoric highs and abysmal lows, and virtually everything in between.

Yet, I could not overlook the problems. Harvey had produced the terse, sharp outline of a book, alluding to many critically important people and events that he barely discussed. Sections in this book on the logging camps and Industrial Workers of the World, the Seattle

General Strike, and the early days of the C.I.O., did not appear in *The Contumacious Couple*. Jessie, typing blind, had depended on those around her to read the last sentence of her developing manuscript aloud each day so that she could "pick up where [she] had left off," as she once put it. She wrote an effusive and richly detailed account. Jessie described her parents' Texas house in minute detail while failing to discuss her life as a Federated Press reporter and mentioning events in Gastonia and Harlan County only in passing. Her Russian diary had been dropped without integration into the text and her unpublished autobiographical novel about Russia did not inform the manuscript at all.

When I met and talked with Jessie and Harvey, however, their spirit and courage settled the issue for me. I agreed to take on the job when I could and, in the meantime, to solicit critiques of *The Contumacious Couple* from historians. We received generous, thoughtful, and extremely demanding reviews from Mari Jo and Paul Buhle, Sara Evans and Harry Boyte, Dave Roediger, Mary Cygan, Jacquelyn Hall, and Theodore Rosengarten.

Most decisive in shaping the book, however, were Jessie's and Harvey's own sense of what the book should say and my growing understanding of their personalities, politics, and history. Jessie and Harvey took an active role in every phase of this manuscript's creation, reading or hearing every draft of every chapter, correcting errors, fine-tuning language, directing me to rework any portion that did not resonate with the reality of their lives. This work reflects the O'Connors' clear agenda. Topics they chose to discuss are included. Topics they consciously left aside are not. More than once, Jessie or Harvey said, with gentle finality, "That is a question for my biographer, if there is one." I have made no effort to camouflage or obscure these lacunae. The integrity of this work lies in the silences it keeps as well as those that it breaks.

I tried, however, to keep the silences as few as possible. I argued in favor of including much that the reviewers and I considered important. Generally, Harvey and Jessie went along; sometimes they did not. Some days were easier and more harmonious than others. Most of the lacunae in *The Contumacious Couple* were caused by bad memory rather than any reluctance to discuss the topic in question. In this regard, their personal papers were crucial. The thousands of personal papers Jessie and Harvey so lovingly maintained kept all three of us honest. I constantly referred to the diaries, songs, letters, articles, pamphlets, and books, discussing significant or revealing passages with Jessie and Harvey, weaving portions of these documents and Jessie's and Harvey's insights into the text. Jessie and Harvey lived by their pens, and their papers yielded descriptions that brought the feel and detail of past years back to their minds. More than once, these papers brought me up short, revealing without ambiguity what Jessie and Harvey thought at a particular moment or about a particular thing—which was not necessarily what I had thought they would have thought or, perhaps, would have wanted them to think. The papers also surprised Jessie and Harvey several times. "Did I really say that?" Jessie once asked as I read her the drafts of some Federated Press stories on Harlan County.

I do not mean to suggest that these papers eliminated my influence on this work. It was simply impossible to read all of Jessie's and Harvey's papers to them. Ultimately, I chose the ones that they heard. Though I strove mightily to remain faithful to their lives in these choices, the process was inevitably interpretive. I believe this book captures the essence of Jessie's and Harvey's personalities and politics, and still more important, so do they. But this book is only an introduction—we encourage others to complete the story. Copies of an annotated version of this work are available at Smith College and Wayne State University, which house Jessie's and Harvey's papers, for any who want more information on how the manuscript was developed. *The Contumacious Couple* and transcripts of interviews used in writing this book can also be found at Smith and Wayne State. Those personal papers still in Jessie's and Harvey's hands will, I hope, soon find their way into these archives. Jessie's family papers can be found in the New York Public Library and at the University of Wisconsin. The splendid archives of the Federated Press are housed at Columbia University.

With all its ups and downs, this has been a labor of love for me, and I will always be grateful to Jessie and Harvey for the opportunity they gave me to work with them. Jessie and Harvey have their warts, as all of us do, but few of us have their strengths. They and their colleagues struggled heroically to remake the world, and I believe that they succeeded—more, perhaps, than they realize. The world I was born into was a far better place as a result of their efforts, which create a still deeper debt—one that I proudly acknowledge but can never hope to repay. Solidarity, Jessie and Harvey.

Susan M. Bowler
Providence, R.I.
June 1987

Acknowledgments

I would like to thank the Industrial Workers of the World (3435 N. Sheffield, Room 202, Chicago, Illinois, 60657) for permission to quote "Write Me Out My Union Card," "Hold The Fort," and "Solidarity Forever," song titles from various editions of its *Little Red Song Book*, as chapter titles in this work. I also thank them for letting us quote the lyrics to "The Preacher and the Slave" and "Solidarity Forever."

I also thank MCA Music Publishing for their permission to quote lyrics from "Magic Penny" (words and music by Malvina Reynolds, © Copyright 1955, 1959 by Northern Music Company. Copyright renewed. Rights administered by MCA Music Publishing, A Division of MCA Inc., New York, N.Y., 10022. Used by permission. All rights reserved.)

I thank Columbia University's Rare Book and Manuscript Library for permission to use their Federated Press papers.

Finally, I am deeply grateful to Susan Boone, who administers Jessie's collection at Smith College. Without her help and cooperation, this book would never have been finished. I thank Smith College for permission to quote freely from Jessie's personal papers.

Harvey and Jessie

Write Me Out
My Union Card

I was born, presumably, on March 29, 1897, in Minneapolis, Minnesota. Since I was picked up as a toddler from a foundling home for which no records remain, I'll never know for sure. Many years ago, Jessie and I went prowling around Minneapolis trying to open this Pandora's box, but fortunately we failed. In any event, I am grateful to my unknown parents for a sound constitution and normal mind.

My adoptive parents, to whom I shall refer as my parents, were James J. O'Connor and Jessie Kenney O'Connor. My father was born in St. Charles, Illinois, and worked the Mississippi river boats out of Clinton, Iowa. He became a chef on the Northern Pacific Railroad between St. Paul and Seattle, and apparently a good one for he "cheffed" the famous Japanese Admiral Togo across the country. The company thought well of him and he was able to get two or three of his brothers-in-law berths on the Northern Pacific. My father boasted that he was on the first diner that crossed over the Cascades through the tunnel. (Before that the trains had been switched-backed up one side of the Cascades and switched-backed down the other side. The company left heavy cars, such as diners, below.)

My father, a slight, rather thin man, showed all the marks of his unhealthy work environment. I would think that working in the kitchen of those diners must have been a hell of a job. The kitchen crew, on duty from 6:00 A.M. to 10:00 P.M., had only a couple of hours off in the afternoon. Every few trips my father came home with the seat of his pants burned out—an inescapable hazard in the

3

cramped quarters of the narrow kitchen. Three cooks and a dish-washer shared that hot little galley. The setup of the dining cars caused Northern Pacific to integrate the work force long before it became a fashionable subject of conversation: the black waiters and the white kitchen crew "bunked" together in the diner after about 10:00 P.M. when the last patrons had left. The crew laid thin mattresses with sheets and blankets on the tables of the diner and slept, black and white together, with no terrific fuss.

Of my father's relatives I know little. I remember my father's sister, a Mother Superior, from a successful wake in which the company told ghost stories (inspired by worldly spirits) between visits to the parlor, an awesome room dimly lit by candles and smelling of incense, to pray for the soul of the late departed. Father had a brother, a soldier in Yellowstone Park, and, perhaps, a ne'er do well—we regarded soldiers as riffraff whom you wouldn't want your sister to marry.

I knew far more of my mother's than my father's family. I dimly remember her grandmother in a rocking chair on the lawn smoking a clay pipe. Her father came from around Augusta, Maine, and spoke in a soft, downeast way. He had worked the woods in northern Minnesota and settled down in what was then St. Anthony Falls, now Minneapolis, where he met and married my grandmother. During the Civil War, he served with the First Minnesota Volunteers and, I believe, was a captive at Andersonville prison. Later, he hunted down the dread Sioux in the Minnesota River valley and helped to push them westward. I remember "Dadda," a fine old gentleman with a white mustache, quite fondly. He had retired on a pension of some twenty dollars a month, a good figure in those days, and worked a small farm on the outskirts of St. Paul where my parents lived. They grew mostly potatoes and corn. Many a day I rode the harrow to give it weight, gathered potato bugs in kerosene cans, and shucked what seemed to be endless ears of corn. Every Decoration Day, Dadda dressed up in his uniform and marched in the Grand Army of the Republic parade and then took me out to a nearby cemetery on Edgerton Street to scatter flowers on veterans' graves.

My grandmother, "Gaga," was spare of frame like my mother, cheerful, and always busy around the house. She came from the Miramichi country in New Brunswick; just how she got to Minneapolis I don't know. Her only dissipation was sniffing snuff; after a pinch in each nostril a beatific expression spread over her face—quiet joy. These grandparents had seven children, all of whom I knew as aunts and uncles; they were, in many ways, a well-knit family group. Indeed, one of my earliest memories is of joining a procession of mother and aunts to the outhouse. It was quite a social occasion and a good time was had by all.

I have very dim memories of living in Minneapolis, but when I was three or so my parents moved to nearby St. Paul, perhaps to be nearer the Northern Pacific commissary department where dining cars were cleaned and stocked. We lived a block from the end of the Mississippi Avenue trolley on Edgerton Street in a place primitive by current standards: no electricity—of course—kerosene lamps. No running water but a pump outside that, when I was older, I primed with boiling water in winter freezes. No central heat or radiators—rather, a big wood stove in the kitchen and a coal stove in the living room that meant a lot of lugging water, wood, and coal. The ample outhouse had three large holes for adults and a small one on the side for children. I decorated the interior with cigar box lids I obtained from the grocery store next door. They were not only decorative, but useful in blunting the wintry blasts through the chinks.

We lived in an extended family, as they say nowadays, which included my maternal grandparents and usually a couple of aunts but none of my father's family. My father was nominally a Catholic but never went to church. Neither did anyone in my mother's family, who were Scotch-Irish and hated Catholics, but otherwise did not let religion bother them much. Nevertheless, at marriage my mother had agreed to bring me up in the bosom of Holy Mother Church. So I went to Sunday School at St. Patrick's, down by the railroad tracks, where I was drilled in the catechism but never permitted a glance at Holy Bible. In being prepared for Confirmation I ran across the Holy Trinity. This three-in-one doctrine troubled me, the more so because my mother made me shine my shoes with three-in-one shoe polish. I asked the Father down at the church to explain this to me. He answered that the Trinity was a divine mystery that transcended human understanding—you believe it. I can't recall any discussion of this at home. I never thought to question my elders and betters—a child didn't do that then.

A few dramatic incidents occurred in those early years. One fine Sunday afternoon a monster came roaring up Edgerton Street—an automobile. People rushed out of doors to witness the apparition. The car came back more slowly later, drawn by horses: the carbide tank that powered its lights had exploded. In addition, once or twice in summer we would make a grand excursion to Lake Minnetonka on the outskirts of Minneapolis. We took the trolley near home, changing for the interurban downtown—a nickel for each parent's fare with me riding free. Automobiles roared along the lake, folks rowed in small boats, and vendors in Crackerjack booths sold candied popcorn.

Though humble, much about our new home attracted my interest as a child. The house had been part of a beer garden. A large dance pavilion, a bandstand, and many smaller structures provided endless sources of delight for me. On rainy days I operated a railroad system in the sand under the pavilion, using engines and cars made of shingles, spools, and whatever was at hand. The property came with horses and chickens. I developed an oratorical proficiency by lecturing the chickens. They would gather around me spellbound; who knows what I was saying—they didn't care. I had one deformed little rooster that had only pin feathers. He followed me around like a puppy and even wanted to go to school with me. I had to pen him to prevent that.

The Ulysses S. Grant school was a mile or more away—a long trudge, particularly in the Minnesota winters. I got along well in school despite my mother's apprehension. She wouldn't let me start until I was seven because she feared I was slower than other lads. But by then I had figured out how to read simple stories by myself. I was an A-B student, good at English, history, and geography but indifferent in math and scientific subjects. I was so good in spelling that I represented the school in the citywide spelling bee. I was the last boy to be spelled down—but several girls outlasted me. My downfall was "epitaph," which I heard as "epitah"; anyway, I didn't know what it meant.

My mother thought I should learn to play the piano, but my father was quite aghast. "No son of mine is going to be a piano player," he said, apparently because the only men piano players he ever knew played in saloons. I took lessons from Sister Pancratia at a convent across town. The piano was in the parlor of a big old house and through the open doors I saw other nuns busy ironing and sewing in the next room. Sister Pancratia was a sweet young thing, though I doubt that she knew much about music. My fare was the "Burning of Rome," Ben Hur's "Chariot Race," "Beautiful Star of Heaven," and similar tripe by E. P. Paull. On the martial stuff I would bang away at the old upright until it began to sway back and forth while my mother listened transfixed with joy. Occasionally Sister Pancratia would break down and weep as she tried to tell me her life story. I was too young and dumb to understand what she was saying—perhaps like many other Catholic girls who had loved too well, she was told to hie herself to the nunnery.

One of the most disconcerting aspects in reviewing my early life is that I was totally unaware of the various big decisions that were being made. I don't know why we moved from the old beer garden up on Edgerton Street down to 409 Jessamine, near the schoolhouse. Possibly, since some of our extended family had left for the West Coast, we had to move to smaller quarters. Perhaps my father's failing health was an important consideration. The new house was fairly modern with electricity and running water.

After moving, perhaps around 1909, I was graduated from grade school and went to John A. Johnson High School for several months before we moved again, this time to Tacoma, Washington. I remember one thing of my brief stay at this high school that causes me a good bit of distress to this day. When a black girl came to school, we chased her down the street hollering, "Nigger girl, Nigger girl." I never saw her again after that introduction to racial hatred.

I

After twenty years as a chef, my father had contracted tuberculosis—known then as consumption—and was no longer able to stand the heat in the kitchen. Since he couldn't work on the dining cars anymore, the Northern Pacific, out of the goodness of its heart, put him on a commissary car. Heavy traffic flowed out of Chicago and the Twin Cities—before the age of jet liners and superduper highways—to the Pacific coast and way points. Most travelers were poor and were going west to benefit themselves. They couldn't afford to eat in the diner where a meal would cost two or three dollars, an extravagant sum. So they ate at restaurants all along the railroad route; the trains made three meal stops a day of about thirty minutes.

Everybody would pile out of the cars and dash into the large restaurant that was equipped to serve a main dish—probably for fifty cents—and get the animals fed. The commissary car supplied these restaurants from the central supply depots in St. Paul and Seattle.

We made the move to Tacoma around 1910 or so. We went out on a pass, issued by the Northern Pacific to employees as a kind of bonus against low wages. As a dining car chef my father had earned about ninety dollars a month—fairly good money, but the commissary car paid less. We traveled to the coast in a tourist sleeping car, a poor man's Pullman. This car differed from the usual Pullman in having a kitchen at one end where people boiled water for tea and coffee and cooked light meals from big packages of food brought aboard. Three trains ran each day. The first-class train, the North Coast Limited, the one my father worked on, all first-class Pullman, pulled one or two diners and an observation car. A slower train carried coaches and tourist sleepers. The third train made all the stops for passengers dropping off at various points along the route. In addition, the railroad operated special immigrant trains that must have been rather primitive in accommodations.

When we got to Washington, we stayed at the sylvan home of Uncle Frank and Aunt Shirley near Milton, a suburb of Tacoma. To me their home was a fairy land with a brook running through a grove of great Douglas fir, flowers, ferns, and everything green, green, green—and usually dripping from the famed Puget Sound mist. Uncle Mone, as we called him, was a big, rawboned, cheerful fellow who worked on the Northern Pacific diners and was one of the first members of the tribe to move from Minnesota to the coast. Very likely because of the hostility of his sisters to his wife, Uncle Mone had moved his family to Tacoma rather than to Riverton, near Seattle, where the rest of the Kenneys lived. Aunt Shirley was very much disliked—even despised—by the rest of the family because they accused her of being part Indian or black. But as I recall, she was fat and most amiable; she really seemed to me quite a wonderful person.

After our move west, I saw more of my mother's family, the Kenneys. My mother, Jessie, was the eldest. Aunt Susan (Toot) was next on the family tree. A slender, rather gaunt woman, she was married to Bill Ploof, an ex-pugilist and a kind of hard luck character. A blacksmith by trade, he had a hefty torso and a tendency to fight outside the ring. They had a raft of children whom I didn't know very well. Next was Aunt Meade (Amelia), a robust, quite auntly woman who had a son and an adopted daughter. Her husband, H. L. Evans, had been a Nonpartisan League lecturer. The Nonpartisan League was a farmers' organization, particularly strong in North Dakota. Many considered the league quite radical in a Populist way. I don't remember ever meeting him, but he seemed well regarded in the family. I was named for their son and he became Big Harvey and I, Little Harvey. On a subsequent trip to Chicago, we stayed with Aunt Meade out in Edison Park where I was introduced to the nefarious ways of big-city life by my cousin and mentor. His favorite hideaway was in back of a Chinese laundry where he smoked cigarettes—a new vice to me for my father chomped cigars.

Uncle George, a thin, anemic man, and his wife, Aunt Josephine, lived in Riverton in the first of three, small, two-bedroom, one-story houses built cheek by jowl on the same street. Aunt Hance (Blanche) occupied the second and Aunt Dell (Della), the third. The children of the latter two were forbidden to associate in any form with those of Uncle George for fear of "papist contamination" from Aunt Josephine. Even in rainy weather they were not to ride together to or from school. Aunt Josephine was a redhead and a good-natured woman with several children. I am happy to report that my mother did not share the prejudices of her sisters.

Uncle George, an amiable fellow, also worked on the Northern Pacific diners where my father had gotten him a job. Aunt Hance was a tall, robust person with a good sense of humor. She married Ed Kinney (the name a source of endless confusion in the Kenney family), who was also a cook, and they adopted a girl. Adoption was a common occurrence in this Kenney family as infertility seemed to have been a problem for most of the Kenney women. Aunt Dell, the youngest, was the best-looker in a family not noted for beauty. She had been a cashier at the Sherman House in Chicago, about as high on the totem pole as any member of the family ever climbed. She married Ed Coulter and they had a son, also adopted, I believe. At least three of the sisters were great believers in law and order and Aunt Dell, in particular, was a strict disciplinarian as my sister found out when she went to live with her after my mother's death. My sister, Jessie, was at the nubile age and Aunt Dell watched hawklike over her morals much to Jessie's distress. Moreover, Jessie had been raised Catholic, which offended my aunts, who wouldn't let her play with their children. While Aunt Dell acted generously in taking over the trials of parenthood, my sister was never able in later life to forget or forgive her troubled girlhood.

After our move to the coast, my mother headed the family for my father was too ill to be of much use. When he was too weak for the job in the commissary car, the Northern Pacific fired him. No pension, severance pay, or social security. After having pawned the few valuables she had accumulated in her married life, my mother decided to rent a house in Tacoma to take in roomers. The house was near the corner of Ninth and E streets, not far from the business district and on a slope of the hill on which Tacoma was built. Cable cars ran up Ninth to the top and then down Eleventh Street to downtown—the only practicable way to get around that hilly town. Down the street two blocks was C Street, the red light district, which could be interesting to a very young man. Ladies, with real red lights in their windows, sat inside begging one to accept their hospitality. I really didn't know much about what was going on, but my mother told me to avoid C Street.

We were living in rather heroic poverty. In the early 1910s, depression hung like a pall over the city. The roomers were nearly as poor as we were; I went to work delivering for a bakery after school hours and on weekends. My five dollars a week supplied the food for our hungry house, while the roomers' rent went for the monthly bill to the landlord. I never knew how my mother made the rent. Most of the furniture was at the disposal of the roomers and we sat on apple boxes. We would go down to the public market Saturday evenings to pick up cheap food, which would not hold over till Monday.

My father got worse and worse. I had never known him well, but I got along with him famously. His work on the cars had kept him away so much. The Seattle–St. Paul run took seven days out and back, and he only got two or three days off between runs. I can remember my mother wanting him to discipline me once. He took me out behind the barn and we just talked, much to my mother's chagrin. As my father got weaker, I saw him less and less. He would disappear in daytime and come home nights. I must say my mother wasn't very sympathetic, but would mock him as to whether he had gotten a job or not. When my father saw he was becoming a drag on the family, he disappeared. I suppose the Northern Pacific gave him a pass to get back to St. Paul. I think that we got word from the railroad that he had died about 1912. The police found his body in some kind of coal shed in an alley in the winter where he had died of pneumonia. The good old days—no welfare state then! The spectre of insecurity—whether from joblessness, accident, disease, or old age—was a constant companion in working-class homes. Prosperity was fleeting; the industrial system lurched forward by fits and starts; the progress of the nation was built on the broken lives of millions, like my father. He died and was buried alone. The Ancient Order of Hibernians took care of the funeral; my mother apparently had paid up in the Degree of Honor, the ladies' auxiliary.

I went to Tacoma High School, which was known as Stadium High and housed in a splendid building. The Northern Pacific had decided to build a great hotel in Tacoma on a high bluff overlooking Commencement Bay, the Olympics, the Cascades, and Mount Tacoma (Rainier to you). Came the panic of 1907 and the Northern Pacific went broke, leaving the hotel practically finished. The school board bought the building for a song and made a high school out of it, certainly one of the most splendid schools in this country, in a kind of French chateau style. A deep ravine ran alongside the building and here one of the first stadiums in the country was built—a great athletic field, plus concerts in the evening with the stars shining overhead and the moon glittering on the bay.

This excellent school offered me an opportunity I appreciated fully only as an adult. I would not have been there but for my mother. I hardly understood my mother's sacrifices to keep me in school— most poor boys worked, or looked for work. High schools were for the upper strata of society; for most working-class parents, it meant real hardship to send their children to high school, still more for a widow. But my mother was very conscientious and made of pretty stern stuff. I think when she looked around her and saw the conditions in which she and others lived, she wanted me to have a better break. I give her a lot of credit for that.

In spite of my job and the tenuousness of our finances, I did fairly well in school. As in grammar school, I was good in history, English, and languages, poor in science and math, and a flunker in physics. I regret that I did not appreciate the splendid sciences. The curriculum was elective although somewhat bound by university entrance requirements. So I was able to take two years each of Latin, German, and French, which, perhaps, was not as silly a course for a working-class boy as it sounds. I never regretted knowing something of three foreign languages. Though I couldn't speak any of them, having some understanding of pronunciation and grammar was a great help to me later.

Indeed, my writing and speaking career began in high school. I edited the German page and the debating society page in the school paper, the *Tahoma*. The head of the German department used to go over my copy with many an "*Ach Weh*" and "*Was bedeutet das?*" My public-speaking career got off to a disastrous start. The Daughters of the American Revolution held an annual contest devoted to orations on patriotic themes, and the theme that year was "The Bill of Rights, the Palladium of Our Liberties." I submitted a paper that rated second, which made me feel pretty good. But Mr. Rogers, our dramatics and elocution teacher, believed in learning things by rote and I was never good at memorizing. Halfway through my oration I lost the continuity and stood there mute and dumb before a large audience. My mother was so overcome she got up and left the auditorium. After a while something flicked and I continued to the miserable end and, of course, I won nothing in that contest.

I did much better in the debating society Mr. Rogers organized where we touched on all the hot issues of the day. The debating society had a fundamental influence on my life. Poverty and the curse of unemployment were so prevalent that I accepted them as the natural order of the world, a fate to be endured by those not favored by fortune. In this high school debating society, however, I fell upon socialism. Gene Debs was running for President on the Socialist Party ticket in 1912 and he was to get almost a million votes. His candidacy was the subject of one of our debates. (Nobody objected to our debating socialism in high school. In other times what an uproar the McCarthy types would have raised!) In preparation for the debate, I got a book from the library entitled *Elements of Socialism*, by John Spargo. It was rather a dull book on a fascinating subject, a kind of textbook. I brought the book home, but it didn't stay there for long. My mother had a great fear of radicalism and unions; once my father had been tempted to join a newly organized union of dining car workers and she was frightened out of her boots for fear he would be fired. As she was a strong-willed woman, he yielded. (Sure enough, she was right—the organizers were fired.) In this case, my mother looked at the title of my library book and said, "Young man, you turn around and take that book back where you got it and never let me see another book on socialism in this house." Well, that whetted my interest—I felt the book must be pretty hot stuff. I was an obedient son: I took the book back to the library and read it there.

Later, on the way to school, I noticed a graphic on the window of a cigar shop run by an old Swede named Frans Bostrom—the emblem of the Socialist Party, two hands clasped over the globe, just like the emblem on the cover of the Spargo book. I decided to take a look inside the store and introduced myself to Comrade Bostrom, quite a friendly fellow. In the rear behind swinging doors was a coal stove where the old Socialists got together to discuss the prime points of Marxism and debate what Marx really meant in chapter five, page 186. Bostrom invited me to a meeting of the Young People's Socialist League (Yipsels), where he introduced me to his niece, Herma, a red-haired girl just down from a logging town, Kapowsin, up on the road to Mt. Rainier. She was also quite friendly, which made my introduction to socialism pleasant.

Through the Yipsels and the old boys in the back of the tobacconist shop, I tapped into the local radical and Socialist movement. Washington's radicalism was deep and long-standing. When, in 1912, the Socialist Party reached the summit of its electoral success nationally, Washington demonstrated its radicalism. Of Debs's nine hundred thousand votes for President, forty thousand were cast in Washington, and, in addition, Socialists ran well in local races. In Seattle, Hulet Wells got 11,000 votes for mayor against 14,500 for George F. Cotterill, the winner, and one Socialist candidate for a county office amassed 21,000 votes. Several smaller communities elected Socialist mayors, as well as two state legislators. Moreover, both the Washington and Seattle Socialist parties were "Red"—that is, left-wingers within Socialist ranks—by a wide margin.

Meanwhile, I polished my writing skills, though none of my published work was political in nature. I wrote passably well and high school, like the radical movement later, gave me opportunities to develop my skills. I learned hunt-and-peck typing at Stadium High. After hours I would sneak into the typing room and learn to type my handwritten stuff—much to the relief of my teachers, I imagine. In any case, I began reporting on sporting events for a local newspaper. Sports was not my main interest but that is all the *Tacoma Times* was concerned about up at the high school. The *Times* was a little

Scripps-Howard operation, eight to twelve pages and hardly any staff. The city editor was also managing editor and city hall–police reporter. Sometimes I would show up early with a story from the day before and he would be jumping into his coat to race to the police station to pick up the night's news on murder, mayhem, and larceny. The operation was rather ridiculous by present-day standards of journalism but the *Times*, nevertheless, was a profitable business then. The only pay I got out of reporting school sports was the by-line that appeared on all my stories. The competition up the street got to sniffing about my writing for the *Times*, so the *News-Tribune*, the big conservative Republican business paper that ran twenty-four or so pages, lured me away by actually paying for my stuff. I became a stringer, which meant that I clipped my stories, not all of which carried my by-line. The *News-Tribune* paid me in cash, not fame. But my mother was a hard-nosed person and she thought I was getting in with the rough crowd around the stadium and so she forbade me to do any more reporting even for pay. That ended my newspaper career for the time being. I continued to work at the bakery tending the store and delivering bread and pastries. I would open up Sunday morning while the baker slept off his Saturday night.

My mother's concerns were just; speaking of rough company, I was in on it alright. There at the high school was Hays Jones, at that time mostly concerned with sports. And Ernie Hover, the brightest boy in his class, president of the class, topnotch debater, and a real intellectual. My little bedroom was on the first floor and all I had to do to escape was to climb out the window and drop to the ground. I would go out with Hays Jones and Ernie Hover for a night on the town. After a while my mother got wise to my trick and one night she hauled me down to the police station where the desk sergeant gave me a real lecture. "The next time," she told me, "it's the reformatory for you." On fine summer days, the three of us would go out to Point Defiance park—a wonderland of virgin forest, ferns, and flowers lapped by the waters of Puget Sound. We would rent a rowboat and row across the sound to Maury Island with a few provisions but depending mostly on fish, clams, and goeyducks that we could get off the lonely beach. On one occasion we did something that would classify us as juvenile delinquents. Instead of returning the boat to the park we stashed it under the docks downtown so that we could have it rent-free next weekend. But when we went to retrieve our boat, the harbor police had removed it.

I was graduated from Tacoma High in 1915 and soon after we moved to Vancouver. My mother opened a rooming house there, too. I tried to enter King Edward VII High School but the headmaster, a Scotsman with a distinct burr, quizzed me and found me wanting in academic excellence. "Bah, you Americans and your wretched schools," he said. Instead, I spent many a happy hour on the shores of English Bay, marveling at the enormous tangles of kelp, the shells and marine life, and downtown Vancouver fascinated me. British Columbia was in the throes of a railroad boom. Boosters promised that the new railroad being built across the mountains in the northern part of the province would make Prince Rupert, its terminus, a Pacific metropolis. Every way station along the route had been platted into town lots and fortunes were to be made, many suggested, if only a person would venture $100 or so. Granville Street, the main stem of Vancouver, bustled with real estate stores peddling the wilderness to the unwary. Maybe the boom was part of the reason for our move to the city. In any case, later the bubble burst and all the projected great cities along the route of the Canadian Northern remained mere flag stops in the wilderness.

After a short time, we moved back to Washington, this time to Seattle. My mother's health was getting worse—tuberculosis, probably caught from my father. She was no longer strong enough to be running a rooming house. The responsibility for supporting her and my sister became mine. Many of my classmates from Tacoma High were going to the University of Washington—Ernie Hover, Hays Jones, Icy Bulman, and others. But I got a job working as a bill collector for five dollars a week, tramping up and down the business district dunning delinquents, an unpalatable job, but I lacked training for anything better, and jobs were hard to come by. The European war had not yet become a roaring financial success for the United States.

On the social side, I transferred from the Tacoma Yipsels to the Seattle branch. Our meetings were serious and also fun. We were obliged to read and discuss the works of Karl Marx and Friedrich Engels—mostly pamphlet extracts from *Das Kapital* such as "Value, Price and Profit," "Wage Labor and Capital," and stories by Jack London and Upton Sinclair. Others, older members, expounded on socialism. But the expounders were apt to know little more than their students about the profundities of Marxist theory, and talk easily drifted away into news of the latest strike, arrest, deportation, or atrocity. Action was the watchword. There was much to be done and theory could wait. It was a weakness, but preferable to the arid debates that went on in the musty little Socialist Labor Party hall in an old rookery down on Second Avenue. We sang labor and revolutionary songs, and attended occasional dances and jollifications. Cultural life around Seattle was lively—the I.O.G.T. (Good Templars) center, the hangout of temperance Swedes, had strong coffee and delicious pastries. As we progressed in Marxism we were graduated into the Socialist Party, of which there were a dozen locals in Seattle, some in working-class districts, others organized in foreign language sections, all under the leadership of the downtown local.

II

I soon realized that my five dollars a week would not support the family. In my rounds of bill-collecting I had occasion to go down to the skid road south of Pioneer Square and Yesler Way, also known as the slave market. The job sharks operated storefront employment agencies listing jobs in the various logging camps of the Puget Sound area on blackboards. The war business was beginning to boom by 1916. Orders poured in for replacements for wooden ships sunk by the German subs, which put a premium on lumber. Most of the jobs posted meant little to me; I knew nothing of logging and was too spare of frame to be much use in work that required a strong back and weak mind, as they said. But sharks also hired flunkeys (waiters) and dishwashers, positions for which my mother had fully prepared me. These paid around forty dollars a month, bed and board—quite a step up from five dollars a week, the more so as there would be only two mouths to feed at home. So I hired out, for which camp I can't remember but that doesn't matter—they were much alike. I worked at around two dozen camps during my logging career. Only one stands out. The camp at Pysht was so bad that I couldn't wait for the logging train to get away, so I walked down the tracks. It was a stormy night and the boat to Seattle from Neah Bay arrived late. I took a tug to the boat for Pysht had no dock. Waves swept over the deck and confined us to the engine room; I got as nearly seasick as I ever did in my life.

Generally workers got to and from the camps by the logging railroad. The companies strung their camps out along these railroads, which were the only mode of transportation into the wilderness. The funny little Shea locomotives, their boilers set at an angle because of the steep grades, did very well sliding down the mountainsides fully loaded with brakes screeching; they climbed the trip up with flatcars empty. The camp consisted of bunkhouses of a size to be hoisted onto flatcars and moved from site to site. Such bunkhouses also served for eating and cooking. The larger ones could accommodate forty to sixty men seated on long benches at tables made of rough lumber, three or four to a shack. A wood stove gave heat; a couple of kerosene lamps flickered dimly in the smoke and vapor. A little ventilation was afforded by the door and, in any wind at all, by the chinks in the walls. Some camps had "muzzle-loading" bunks that required men to creep in at the foot of the bunk and inch forward. The system had the great virtue of packing more men, sardinewise, into a small bunkhouse.

At 5:00 A.M., we were up and doing, getting the tables set for the mad rush at 6:00 A.M., when we would go outside and pound on a triangle made of an old rail. Within fifteen or twenty minutes the loggers consumed breakfast. The central dish for breakfast was always hot cakes. The cook greased the range with a rind of a slab of bacon, then he dipped, dipped, dipped the pitcher with the batter and at the end hurried to turn the early lot. Then flip, flip again onto the plates, which we rushed to the tables, holding a half dozen of them on outstretched arm. Fast as we could run, we never could keep up with the gargantuan appetites of the loggers. Meanwhile, coffee pots—two half-gallon pots to a table—would be empty and we'd make another dash to the pantry between the eating shacks and the cookhouse, to fill them again. In addition, loggers ate any eggs, ham or bacon, doughnuts, and various pastries left over from the night before. Suddenly all was quiet as the men left en masse; we cleaned up the debris, washed tables, and hosed the floor down, the water draining out through holes.

Lunch was a real meal and dinner ditto. We would be through about 8:00 P.M. with time out in the late morning and midafternoon. My favorite camp was the Snohomish Logging Company, where we had a decent cook and food and reasonable time off. With one flunkey to each sixty-man shack, we stayed on the run. The whole crew consisted of the head cook, a vegetable man, a dishwasher, a baker, and three flunkeys. The bull cook, some wounded veteran of the woods, limped around from bunkhouse to bunkhouse with his broom and hose, built the fires at 4:30 A.M., and kept them going through the day and into late evening.

The bigger camps had a baker; the companies held to the theory that starches were cheaper and more filling than any other grub. Generally, though, the food wasn't half bad. After all, logging was hard work, ten to twelve hours on a crosscut saw, and even the lumber companies believed that the slaves, like horses and mules, had to be well fed if work was to be done. In some camps the cook and the commissary company conspired to make profits by shortchanging loggers, but the loggers set a limit to belly robbing—if things got out of hand, they quit in waves. Nevertheless, at one camp a notorious belly robber dubbed T-Bone Slim operated. Legend said that he could make a T-bone out of the toughest piece of meat. Over the meat and the potatoes he poured a concoction of burnt flour, lard, and water known as "monkey." On the whole, the companies provided fresh meat hauled up as sides of beef and pork on the logging railroad.

Each camp had its "bull of the woods," the head man, who kept pushing the work. His job was speeding up the work—the "bulls" were notorious for their willingness to take chances with other people's lives if necessary to meet their daily quota. Often loggers died of minor injuries for lack of medical attention. The bull of the woods always refused to allow the trains to pull out until fully loaded. If an injured logger needed the train to take him to a doctor quickly, it was his misfortune. A whistle punk watched the throttle at the steam engine when logs were being hoisted on the highline and onto the flatcars. And, of course, the loggers—sawyers, choker men, high tree toppers, train operators—rounded out the crew.

That the companies refused to provide bathhouses was one of the scandals of such work. In summer the loggers were sweat-sodden; in winter soaked to the skin. Between fall and spring, 160 inches of rain fell annually in the rain forest of the Olympic peninsula. The constant downpour, hour after hour, day after day, simultaneously made the magnificent Douglas fir forest possible and the loggers' lives more difficult. The men would take off their sodden clothes at night and drape them around the pot-bellied wood stoves. Imagine the fumes that arose, aggravated by clouds of tobacco smoke, not to mention the mess caused by numerous tobacco chewers. The companies also failed to make provision for recreation in the camps, but that mattered much less; who wanted recreation after a hard day's work in the woods? All the loggers wanted was a hot dinner and a flop. Before the union won the eight-hour day, the men worked from sunup to sundown in the winter and ten to twelve hours in summer.

Men worked only a few months at a camp, in part because of the tense nature of the dangerous work. Occasionally the huge trees wouldn't fall just right and God help anybody in the way. Then there was the highline—a steel cable from one tall tree on the logging site to another near the donkey engine and railroad. Huge hooks grappled the log that was hoisted by the highline and swung along to the waiting flatcar. Sometimes the hooks did not hold or the log would begin to swing crazily—another desperate chance for the men below. The mayhem was enormous; in any sizable operation rarely a month passed that the little Heisler locomotive did not go down the line with one flatcar carrying only a solitary object—a body carelessly covered with a tarpaulin. No government safety official inspected the highly dangerous highline. The injured could not rely on workmen's compensation; the bigger camps, such as Puget Sound Timber on the Olympic peninsula, sometimes had arrangements with the nearest hospital. Once I got what seemed to be laryngitis and lost my voice. They shipped me down to the hospital in Port Angeles; after a few days the voice seemed better and I went back to work, but others were not so fortunate.

A man could stand only a few months of this kind of work and then he headed for the skid road, usually in Seattle. Unlike most of the loggers who were single men without family, I had a mother and sister to support. I couldn't carouse on the skid road. Nevertheless, loggers not only frequented, but named this district. The skid road was a constant feature of many logging camps where logs could be skidded down the mountain on a flume, heavily greased with what was known as pig fuck. When they reached a millpond at the bottom, the logs could be rafted down a river to the sawmill. A variant was a flume down to the railroad siding. The term "skid road" is commonly construed as skid row—but there was no such thing as a skid row in logging camps. The loggers' garb, among other things, confined them to this district. Because the loggers wore caulked shoes with steel studs, they were barred from the more respectable parts of town where their boots would ruin floors.

In town in a burst of release, the logger got drunk, whored, gambled, and spent his stake. Within a week he was down on the slave market looking for another job, another few months of work in a camp. Such was the logger's life. That the men who produced the fundamental wealth upon which the economy of the region rested should be regarded as pariahs, condemned to backbreaking toil and to animallike existence whether on the job or away, that in the city they should be consigned to a skid road pale that existed only to rob and debase them—this was the supreme confirmation to the Industrial Workers of the World (I.W.W.) and Socialists, like me, of the fundamental truth of Marxist theory. It gave point to the line in the "International," "We have been naught; we shall be all"; from this arose the revolutionary determination to wipe out a system that inverted values and condemned the most useful members of society to the most repugnant existence. The I.W.W. welcomed the loggers, as no one else did; at the Wobbly hall we found education and enlightenment.

In the dreary degradation of the skid road, the Wobbly hall became the haven of hope. This was a huge second-floor hall near the center of the skid road. Apart from the small space roped off for the office, the Wobblies dedicated most of the big hall to the needs of the migratory worker. Here the worker found benches, chairs, a space in which to check his bindle, the latest radical papers, books, but most of all the confraternity of fellow workers from all parts of the West. Every evening there was a program—first, the Wobbly songs, then speakers on industrial unionism, firsthand reports from hot spots of the class struggle, songs and sketches presented by the foreign language fraternal, choral, and literary societies, and then more songs. These were our people, they spoke our language, their ideas reflected the hard facts of our lives. We were at home.

Confined to the skid road, the logger also found entertainment along the streets where itinerant vendors, missionaries, radical orators, and the Salvation Army competed for attention. Each evening near O'Hanrahan's newsstand, which sold more copies of the *Industrial Worker*, *Solidarity*, the *Masses*, the *International Socialist Review*, and the local Socialist paper than of all the local dailies, the I.W.W., the Socialists, and others brought out platforms and started speaking. Young apostles of industrial unionism and socialism then mounted the platform to warm up the audiences for the main speakers. Such could be James P. Thompson, the I.W.W.'s most fluent spokesman, J. T. "Red" Doran, Walker C. Smith, Bruce Rogers, Kate Sadler, and a dozen others, as ready in handling hecklers as in expounding their doctrines. Here, too, came the news, at firsthand from participants, of the latest outrages against the working class in California, Arizona, Montana, or from wherever the itinerant radical hailed.

The penchant of the Wobblies for song arose, in some measure, from the activities of the Salvation Army across the street. A lively competition there, with the Army's brass band blaring out hymns to the beat of a big bass drum and the Salvation lassies in their bonnets screaming at the top of their voices, sometimes drowning out the best efforts of capable Wobbly speakers. Gradually, across the West, the need to answer the Salvation Army noises with a countervailing force grew. Wobbly versifiers made up their own words for the favorite hymns and for the tunes of popular songs. The Wobblies collected these, with classic songs of the labor movement, in the famous *Little Red Songbook*, which has since run through some thirty editions. The early editions have become collector's items. Through many of the songs ran the typical Wobbly humor—ironic, biting, reflecting the reality of life as seen by the migratory worker:

> Long-haired preachers come out every night,
> Try to tell you what's wrong and what's right;
> But when asked how 'bout something to eat
> They will answer with voices so sweet:
>> You will eat, bye and bye,
>> In that glorious land above the sky;
>> Work and pray, live on hay,
>> You'll get pie in the sky when you die.

These songs told of their lives, their ideas, and their hopes, and constituted for most Wobblies as much theoretical knowledge of the principles of the I.W.W. as they were likely to be able to express.

The Wobblies were also the most successful organizers of migratory workers. The Forest and Lumber Workers, in 1912, was the second national union, after the textile workers, to be formed by the I.W.W. The Wobblies' main strength, at first, was in the Louisiana-Texas "piney woods," where, in 1910, I.W.W. and Socialists had formed the Brotherhood of Timber Workers. The Brotherhood was a "people's organization"—lumber workers, preachers, merchants, doctors—united against the outside lumber interests. The Timber Workers counted white workers and black, native-born including the Cajun French, and Mexicans and Italians in their ranks. In 1911, the Brotherhood sent fraternal delegates to the national I.W.W. convention and a year later Secretary William D. (Big Bill) Haywood addressed the Timber Workers convention, which then affiliated with the I.W.W. This militant union struck often and encountered a rather unusual impediment to meetings held near the sawmills and camps. The managers would begin "tin-panning," beating upon circular saws, to drown out the union speakers. At such a meeting in Grabow, Louisiana, in 1912, shots rang out from the lumber office and three unionists fell dead. Fifty-eight Timber Workers were held in the "Black Hole of Calcasieu," but the state later failed to convict them. The state and the bosses succeeded in breaking up the union, but many members drifted on to the oilfields of Oklahoma and helped to organize the I.W.W. Oilworkers Union around 1916.

Closer to home in the squalid Grays Harbor, Washington, mill towns—Aberdeen, Hoquiam, Raymond, and Cosmopolis—the I.W.W. had shut down the mills in 1912 to get a fifty-cent increase on wages of two dollars a day. The authorities and bosses responded in what was becoming classic style. Vigilantes sprang up to attack strikers, the government deported foreign-born strikers, en masse, and 150 men were loaded into boxcars at Hoquiam to be sent away. Fortunately, the mayor and the railroad workers stopped that, and the workers and bosses compromised with a $2.25 scale. Strikes broke out sporadically from then on, a kind of guerrilla warfare conducted by an organization not strong enough to enforce a general shutdown. In this period the American Federation of Labor (the A.F. of L.) chartered the International Union of Timber Workers, with which the shingle weavers affiliated. This union had some strength in the sawmill towns where other A.F. of L. unions could lend support, such as in Ballard, a suburb of Seattle, in Tacoma, Everett, Bellingham, and Aberdeen. But Timber Workers couldn't reach out to the logging camps. Although an industrial union, the Timber Workers' concept of collective bargaining, which included contracts with the employers, and membership of "home-guards," men living in towns, were worlds apart from the I.W.W., which scorned truces with the class enemy as embodied in contracts, and whose members for the most part were rootless.

On March 5, 1917, the I.W.W. union, which had become Lumber Workers Industrial Union 500, convened in Spokane. A month before the declaration of war against Germany, the growing shortage of labor was putting workingmen in a better bargaining position. The platform framed by the convention centered on the eight-hour day, six-day week, and abolition of bindles. These rather modest demands reflected the wretched conditions in the camps: the men wanted single beds with springs, clean mattresses and bedding, good lighting, not more than twelve to a bunkhouse, and, of course, no double-tier bunks. In the kitchens they asked for porcelain instead of enamel dishes. A drying room for wet clothes, a laundry room, showers, free hospital service, hiring on the job or from the union hall, free transportation to the job—these, with a minimum wage of sixty dollars a month with board, completed the union program. The union soon claimed six thousand members, organized in three autonomous districts left free to tackle the boss whenever they felt so inclined. The Wobblies rejected the leadership principle, believing instead that all workingmen were leaders. Therefore, the I.W.W. left members free to act on their own initiative. The Duluth, Minnesota, division had three branches; those in Spokane and Seattle, seven each.

In the short-log country—eastern Washington, Idaho, and western Montana—the job delegates fanned out and by April a strike wave eliminated the twelve-hour day prevalent there in springtime, and boosted wages from $3.50 to $5.00 a day in the "river drives" when the logs cut in fall and winter were floated downstream in the spring freshets. Strikes spread throughout the Inland Empire and to the Pacific slope. I was a Union man and the general strike in the woods was my first labor action. The strike went on sporadically for months. We loggers would advance our demands, and when a camp was obstinate, we'd strike. The boss would fire us, and another crew would come up, and the same thing would happen, over and over, again and again, until the company gave in.

With the mounting shortage of labor and the I.W.W. strikes, my wages went up to fifty and sixty dollars a month. I managed to hold on to fifty dollars in the winter of 1916, above what I contributed to my mother's household. I took a break from logging and I decided to enroll at the University of Washington in February 1917. Tuition was free but books and supplies gobbled up my money. I found myself in a French class with fifty others, in English lit with a hundred, real mass production education. In April came the declaration of war and they closed down most of the university, telling us either to work or fight. So that ended my academic career. I left without too many regrets. If the war hadn't come, I couldn't have afforded to stay anyway. Imagine my surprise years later, however, when I visited the new library at the university. In the large lobby there were niches all around the room dedicated to books by U. W. alumni. And there in one niche were copies of my books! A two-month alumnus!

Around this time—late 1917, early 1918—I made my first trip to New York. We youngsters in the radical movement regarded New York as the center of our universe, what with *The Masses*, the swirling Bohemian life, the powerful Socialist and anarchist movements. I had staked out some spare cash for my mother and had five dollars in my pocket to make the trip. You supported yourself on the road by shipping to jobs across the country. I shipped to the Volta dam in Montana, a good thousand miles with fare paid. I worked the dam several weeks to make a stake for the next move. I was wearing my Wobbly button when an old fellow gave me some good advice—take it off before the deputies get you. So I reversed the emblem in my buttonhole. I tried a few days in the freight yards of the Great Northern at Great Falls, decided it was too arduous for my taste, and bought a ticket going east. I landed in Milwaukee and reported to the slave market, where I found a job in a slaughterhouse. I shoveled like mad at the foot of the chute where the fertilizer came down. Dust flew everywhere—what a mess! But the worst of all was the Polish boardinghouse where I rented a room. For breakfast: blood sausage!

I quit after a few days and drifted down to Chicago and holed in at the Y.M.C.A. An earnest counselor said I shouldn't be wasting my time on odd jobs, but I explained I was on my way to New York and needed a road stake. He sent me to a job in a big cafeteria—Wigman or some such name. This was a grand, two-story operation and I had to pile up the used dishes and take them down a broad staircase to the kitchen. Things went along fairly well for several days until on one trip I missed a step and down came the loaded tray of dishes in a crash that reverberated through the palace of eatery. That finished me.

Being broke, as usual, I sought refuge in a two-bit flophouse on West Madison Street. I arrived in the evening and the manager gave me a candle—there was no electricity in the place—and escorted me to a cell barely large enough to contain a cot. The walls, cardboard with a wire netting toward the top, kept neighbors from pilfering the guests' belongings. Within a few minutes the majordomo returned demanding that I snuff out the candle, and I went to bed. Almost immediately the bedbugs attacked. I got up, lit the candle, and lifted the gray sheet. Along the side of the mattress a festering mass of vermin of various colors squirmed and writhed in the pale light. I spent the rest of the night on the chair and escaped with the dawn's early light.

Before I left Chicago, though, I went to the national I.W.W. headquarters at 1001 West Madison, on Chicago's version of the skid road. I asked to see Fellow Worker Bill Haywood, the national secretary. As a Wobbly, I knew that the most important national officer would see any rank and filer without question. A young woman waved me down the hall, and in a small office with an open door, I saw the great man. I introduced myself and Big Bill asked me a lot of questions about Seattle, the woods, the Lumber Workers Industrial Union 500 of which I was a member, and my trip across the country. As his desk was heaped with correspondence and he was obviously a busy person, I thanked him for his courtesy and left after ten minutes or so.

I shipped out to Akron to a rubber factory, but one look at the place cured me of any desire to work there so I went up to Cleveland and shipped out to the Hog Island shipyard in Philadelphia. They handed me a pail to catch hot rivets from a forge twenty feet away. I perched on a girder some twenty or thirty feet above the bottom of the hull. On the whole a risky business and I decided not to test fortune anymore, and called for my time. While in Philadelphia I visited the I.W.W. hall down by the waterfront. The Wobblies there were a strange lot, a mixture of anarchists and old-line unionists. They had a contract with the boss, something most Wobblies, who believed in guerrilla warfare, despised. I took the train up to New York, landed on the New Jersey side, and ferried across to lower Manhattan. With my tin suitcase in hand, I marched up Broadway, the entire distance to Times Square, witnessing the sights of this strange Mecca of radicals.

In New York I went to the Wobbly hall and introduced myself. Someone caught mention of my name and urged me to join him in going to an Irish Republican Army meeting. Well, my Irish is skin-deep and I had never concerned myself with the problems of the Auld Sod, so I declined. I must confess that little stands out in my memory about my stay in New York. Perhaps I found it all rather confusing, after the class struggle certainties of Seattle and the logging camps. I worked my way back home in much the same way I came, by shipping with fare paid to various jobs en route. My longest stretch was from Montana back to Seattle when I had to pay my own way. I landed home with the same five dollars, more or less, that I had when I left. I was happy to be back in familiar surroundings and among the kind of people not torn by the ferocious internecine wars that raged in New York.

III

I had some experience with political writing and reporting. Between logging camp jobs I would go to Seattle where, among other things, I helped Walker C. Smith, editor of the *Industrial Worker*, the Wobbly weekly. Smith was a working-class intellectual: a hard, earnest worker who turned out a paper read all through the West, in hundreds of logging, railroad, construction, and farm camps. The Wobblies had taken an antiwar position so things were rather touchy with the Department of Justice, and Walker had to walk a tightrope between good I.W.W. ideas and the second-class mailing privilege. Like many Wobblies he was somewhat scatological. He was having some trouble with his wife, a woman with ideas of her own. "No need," he said, "to idealize women, they don't shit through their ribs!" Walker would throw copy at me for editing and typing. The Wobblies valued the ideas of the migratory workers and printed what they submitted. Most came in from the camps, hand-written and often rather illiterate. The stuff was so lively that it was a pleasure to handle even the worst scrawls that came along. And I got good training in editing.

The *Seattle Daily Call* really wound up my logging camp career. A Norwegian little-magazine type of fellow named Thor Mauritzen, who had come up from L.A., decided to start a Socialist daily in Seattle. Mauritzen was a short, stocky fellow who described himself as "a cowboy, hobo, rancher, soapboxer, editor, publisher and rebel who wouldn't stay put." He went around to Hulet Wells, a Socialist leader, and others with his seemingly preposterous idea and most of them told him he was crazy. New York and Milwaukee could have Socialist dailies, they believed, but not a jerkwater town like Seattle. Mauritzen went to see Henry C. Piggott, an independent sort of fellow, more Populist than Socialist, and a printer, who had himself always thought that Seattle needed a fearless paper. Piggott said, "If you get together five hundred dollars, I'll consider printing your paper"—a risky proposition both financially and from the point of view of a hostile Department of Justice. Well, Mauritzen got together his five hundred dollars and began printing stock certificates for this venture. So the first issue of Mauritzen's dream appeared, to everybody's astonishment. He rented a full floor of a loft built on a steep hillside off First Avenue with access only by a boardwalk, but only a block away from Piggott's printshop. Carpenters made rough tables and benches, Mauritzen procured some nondescript typewriters, and charged a Mr. Wheeler, aged seventy-five, with the responsibility of producing a daily paper all by himself. Wheeler, who wrote under the piquant name of *Bertuccio Dantino*, naturally busied himself with shears and pastepot to keep the linotypers busy. Fortunately, Wheeler could clip articles from the Socialist press, the New York papers, and especially the *New York Call*, the Socialist daily. Mauritzen named the Seattle paper for its older brother in Manhattan (presumably no one in the Socialists had ever heard of the old *Daily Call* of 1886–1887, the spokesman for the Knights of Labor and the Seattle Labor Party). The *Call* subscribed to a pony service from United Press for five hundred words of copy and counted on the telegrapher to slip Mauritzen the entire daily report. The first issue numbered five thousand copies, and nearly all were sold. Within a few weeks the skid road was good for several thousand copies: newsboys hawked other thousands on the streets, docks, and at the shipyard gates. Soon orders for bundles began flooding in from other towns and from the logging camps. They were hard up for staff when I came back to town and inasmuch as I was mildly literate and could handle a typewriter, I joined up. I swept out the office, helped the stereotyper pour metal for the plates, and wrote editorials.

The *Call* came out early in the afternoon to catch workers coming off shift. Newsboys peddled the paper up and down the main downtown streets but the principal circulation was at the gates of the shipyards and factories and on the skid road south of Yesler Way. We didn't deliver to private residences. Down on the skid road Will

"Red" O'Hanrahan included five hundred or so copies of the *Call* among the labor and radical papers from all over the country he sold at his newsstand. Mounting his soapbox, he would paraphrase the leading articles and editorials in the *Call*, as he had long done those in the *Industrial Worker* and other papers, in a rich vernacular. O'Hanrahan ranked as a speaker with any of the radicals who, as I said earlier, followed him on the soapbox. His summaries of the *Call's* articles were great advertising. O'Hanrahan, a popular educator, often opened the radical soapboxing with his evening commentary on the day's news in which he dissected, to the merriment of his audience, the stories in the local dailies. To their satisfaction he analyzed the oddities, barbarities, and ludicrosities of capitalism. Scores and hundreds would gather around him for what was a virtuoso performance better than a vaudeville show. O'Hanrahan was ecumenical; he was for the Socialists, the Wobblies, for any working-class movement. He reflected the Seattle labor movement that had little or no room for animosity among unionists, Socialists, and Wobblies in spite of the vast differences in the lives of the Socialists, mostly petitbourgeois home guards, and the Wobblies, mostly migrants.

As the paper developed, people began to sit up and take notice. Along came a former member of the school board, just recalled for her pacifism. She had fled to the snow slopes of Mt. Rainier to organize the first alpinist society in the region. Somehow a copy of the *Call* got to her and she deserted the slopes—Anna Louise Strong. She became a leading editorial and feature writer and accumulated a devoted following, a story that she tells in her *I Change Worlds*. Then an English lady, Mrs. Marguerite Remington Carter, gave the paper a whiff of social grace and literary elegance perhaps not appreciated too much on the skid road. She had winsome daughters on whom she kept a tight rein, because she feared the free love inclinations among some young radicals. Her knowledge of French allowed us to translate and reprint articles from *L'Humanité*, the great Parisian Socialist daily. Charles Ashleigh, the English poet and the only Wobbly without overalls, publicized attacks on the Wobblies and the progress of conscription cases. Paul Bickel, a high school math teacher, wrote scientific and educational articles. Joe Pass, our literary guide, broke all precedents by actually going up to a Central Labor Council meeting and writing a report on it. As an active Yipsel, he was also a link to young Socialists. This was about the first local reporting that appeared in the *Call* and opened up new vistas. Like other small leftist papers, we had no conception of local news gathering. With a top wage of twelve dollars per week, all worked more for love than money.

Our circulation soon ran over ten thousand a day, which, at a penny for the paper and a penny for the newsboy, netted Mauritzen more than $100 a day. Additional revenues came from Chinese herb doctor ads and paid announcements of meetings and suchlike. That barely covered expenses. In fact, the story goes that when Mauritzen couldn't scrape together the money to pay the printer, he would appeal to his friend Sam Sadler. Sadler, who had a way with dice, would return in a few hours with enough money to make the bills. We always balanced on razor's edge with the Department of Justice, which had an embryo F.B.I. in operation. We never got second-class mailing privileges, which didn't matter too much as most of the sales were on the streets and in bundles. John McGivney, who had drifted down from Nome, Alaska, where he had been editor of the *Nome Daily Industrial Worker*, the miners' paper, soon became our first real editor. A man of distinction, he had been trained in an Irish Jesuit college, knew his literature, and wrote thoughtful editorials. One day I saw him out on the boardwalk staring over the railing down some fifty feet or so and looking mighty glum. Seems that Anna Louise had written an editorial that went far over the line and he was sure the Department of Justice would be coming to close us down—not that the cops would have arrested McGivney. In anticipation of precisely this sort of thing, I, the most expendable staff member, had been named the editor. My name appeared on the masthead; therefore, I was the person responsible to the gendarmerie and prime candidate for the hoosegow. Though nothing happened, getting out a daily in wartime continued to be a delicate adventure in tightrope walking.

Certainly the *Call* was one of the most remarkable ventures in Socialist journalism to appear in this country. True, the times were with Mauritzen. The acquittal of the Everett I.W.W. members, who had been charged with murder for defending themselves from a brutal and unprovoked attack by local lawmen and vigilantes, had sent a thrill through the radical movement from coast to coast, and nowhere more so than in the Puget Sound country. Membership in the I.W.W. shot upward. Thousands of workers were flooding into Seattle to escape the draft by working in the shipyards, and among them were few admirers of Wilson and his war. They flocked into the A.F. of L. shipyard unions. The regular Wednesday night meetings of the Central Labor Council drew 250 delegates or more from constituent unions; the gallery in the Labor Temple's auditorium where the council met was filled with unionists and radicals, listening to the dramatic debates and to speeches by visiting luminaries. The suppression of ordinary rights of free speech added zest and exhilaration to the scene as people struggled, in guarded and Aesopian terms, to express the ideas that burned within them. Above and beyond all that, something had happened in the world that drew Seattle labor out of its provincial isolation—the overthrow of the Czar in Russia. In Petrograd the Council of Workers, Soldiers and Sailors Deputies—the Soviet—was in constant session, building unions and workers' parties, and eying with ill-concealed distrust the maneuverings of the various bourgeois ministries that struggled with the chaos left by war and autocracy in a ravaged land. The Seattle radical movement, and with it the *Call*, which had been in-looking all its life, suddenly became world conscious.

The *Call* managed to keep within the bounds of legality in reporting these stories: our readers recognized the code words and the editors didn't have to spell out ideas that would allow the government to put the paper out of business. We weathered attacks of vigilantes determined to succeed where the government had failed. Finally, however, the local draft board decimated the ranks of staff members. Even Mauritzen had to go to the shipyards to avoid the draft. Still Seattle did not lose its labor daily—the *Union Record*'s staff stepped into the void.

The *Union Record* was the weekly paper of the Seattle Central Labor Council—A.F. of L.; Harry Ault, editor of the *Union Record* since 1912, had built its circulation and had always dreamed of making it a daily. The *Call* proved that a labor daily was practical; if a tiny Socialist-I.W.W. daily could survive so long in wartime, a paper backed officially by the mainstream union movement would have to do even better. Ault had long been committed to socialism and the Socialist press. He came from a Socialist family that moved to Puget Sound in response to Eugene Debs's fleeting enthusiasm for colonizing the new state of Washington and turning it into the first Socialist commonwealth with the Red Flag flying over the state capitol in Olympia. If the colonies did not succeed in their ultimate goal, they certainly had an important influence on the Pacific Northwest. Some forty years later, in 1936, Postmaster General James A. Farley alluded to the movement when he proposed a toast "to the American Union—forty seven states and the Soviet of Washington." Moreover, whatever the fate of these colonies, their voices reached out far and wide; many a rebellious working man, fed up with factory slavery in the east, headed west as a result, not always, perhaps, to join a colony but to be in a section of the land where the voice of dissent could be heard.

So the Aults wound up at Equality colony up near Bellingham— only one of the many such colonies along Puget Sound. Equality eventually busted up because too many Socialists insisted on arguing about Marx instead of working. And the colony attracted too many chiefs and not enough Indians. Finally, the old man (Ault's father) stipulated on his deathbed that he be cremated on a bed of pine boughs, which was too much for neighbors who already regarded the colony as a nest of free lovers and anarchists. Harry, who learned the printers' case on the Equality paper, continued to work for Socialist sheets like the *Seattle Socialist*, and others in Idaho and Toledo. The strong Socialist influence on the Central Labor Council in 1912 made Ault the logical candidate to edit the *Union Record*.

The war and the demise of the *Call* gave him his chance to transform the *Union Record* into a daily. The Boilermakers and Iron Shipbuilders had twelve thousand members, the Machinists five thousand, and other shipyard unions many thousands more. If each member kicked a dollar into the kitty, labor would have enough to buy a press and start a daily to compete with the reactionary, antilabor *Times* and Scripps-Howard *Star*. The unions duly voted such an assessment, and Ault's dream came true. With the Feds breathing down their neck, the staff of the *Seattle Daily Call* agreed to cease publication on a Saturday. The next Monday the daily *Union Record* appeared—the only trade union daily in the country. Sam Sadler, a board member of both the *Call* and the Central Labor Council, was the intermediary who helped arrange the transition. Hulet Wells, the Socialist leader and president of the Labor Council, which was rapidly being radicalized by the shipyard workers, favored the changing of the guard.

At that time Seattle was a principal shipyard center, both for wooden and steel ships. German subs and the United States shipyards raced to see which side would win the war. Seattle did not have thirty thousand workers to man the shipyards, so they were recruited from all over the country. That such work won exemption from the draft attracted thousands of young men who preferred to work than fight. Among them, a leaven of Socialists and Wobblies soon converted the unions to militancy—a way of blowing off steam inasmuch as strikes were forbidden for the duration of the war.

I did not participate in the early days of the daily *Union Record*. The draft board was after me and I had no more taste for the Army and the war to end all wars than the shipyard workers. My union, the I.W.W., abandoned the field of antiwar propaganda after the declaration of war. The Wobblies preferred to fight the boss directly. They took no part in the No-Conscription League, disdaining to appeal to a President and a Congress owned by "the class enemy." True to form, the Wobblies didn't presume to tell members like me what course to take. They left registering for or refusing what was euphemistically known as "selective service" to the conscience of the individual. Just in time I found the escape hatch, the Merchant Marine, a quasi-military outfit where one manned the hundreds of new ships being launched. Actually it was hardly an escape from the rigors of war for the fatality rate was higher in the Merchant Marine than in the Army, what with the German U-boats torpedoing anything afloat on the seven seas. Moreover, the wooden ships, built with green timber and liable to self-destruction, were menaces to navigation and one's health.

I came out of the West Seattle Merchant Marine training school a petty officer, and I had a dreadful uniform that I had to wear when taking the ferry over to Seattle after the day's work. On the whole my first assignment was a soft berth, but I had to go and blow it. I'd go up to the Socialist Party headquarters in my uniform, and as this was opposite the Federal Building, the snoops soon spotted me. The commandant called me in to his office to tell me very paternally that, since I had kept the wrong company, I was going out on the next ship. Thus ended what might have been a cushy way of sitting out Mr. Wilson's war. He assigned me to the *Wishkah*, a wooden boat recently out of the shipyard. She had gone to Nanaimo on Vancouver Island to load coal but when she got out in the broad Pacific past Cape Flattery, her pumps couldn't keep up with the inflow of water. Prudently the skipper backtracked to Seattle, where the tub was drydocked. Then she was loaded with box shooks—crates knocked flat for use in packing pineapples, which seemed to be essential for winning the war. So, with me aboard, we headed out into the Pacific bound for Hawaii.

On this trip, a lot of the green crew were seasick from the huge swells common on the Pacific. I cleaned the black gang's messroom, a little cubbyhole at which only six could sit. For some odd reason the walls were whitewashed, a headache to scrub each day after the greasy engine crew had eaten. But the skipper paraded at 11:00 A.M. every day with his white gloves seeking out traces of dirt and grease. One day as I sat on the poop deck enjoying a seegar in the afternoon I noticed that the ship was describing a circle in the sea. The steering gear had broken down, and only the captain and the bosun, of the entire crew, had ever been to sea before. Had this happened in a storm it might have been lethal. A similar accident caused a ship to founder in a typhoon off the Philippines, with all hands lost.

Fortunately, the pumps kept ahead of the bilge water and we got to Honolulu, barely. After unloading the cargo we waited for a chance to get into the port's only drydock, to caulk up our leaking seams. A half dozen leaky wooden tubs lined up ahead of us, so I had a month to take advantage of Waikiki beach. Little Japanese butterflies in kimonos tripped along their ways in back streets. The other Japanese in port manned a big warship with the rising sun flag swung at anchor in the stream. Occasionally the tide would bring her about so that her big guns aimed straight at the city. For the time being the Japanese were our allies. At dawn the crew lined up on the foredeck to salute the emperor and do their calisthenics. Their sons would give a different kind of salute at Pearl Harbor a generation later. We set out for San Francisco after being caulked and en route the armistice was declared, although we didn't know that until we hit port, for we had no radio. The *Wishkah* never went to sea again. The Merchant Marine beached her somewhere in the bay and burned her.

IV

I returned to journalism after my hitch in the Merchant Marine. Whenever three Socialists get together, they always talk of getting out some kind of propaganda material. So it was after the war and the demise of the *Daily Call*. Several of us collaborated and pretty soon

the *International Weekly* hit the street. This time I was the real editor
with quite a staff—Hays Jones, Joe and Morris Pass, Paul Bickel,
and others. We ran a hot little paper—four pages standard size. Labor and capital locked horns in Europe in 1919 with the war over.
Germany, France, Italy, and Hungary experienced the rising tide of
radicalism; the Soviets battled counterrevolutionaries and Allied intervention; the Labour Party in Britain aimed at reconstruction of
society. In the United States great strikes broke out in steel, focus of
industrial feudalism, in the coal mines, and in the railroads. I
thought the Revolution was just around the corner. We gathered all
these reports together for a sizzling page-one story. I concocted the
headline out of the biggest type in the shop—CAPITALISM TOT-
TERING! Shortly after this issue hit the streets, the cops came and
padlocked the printshop, which was a joint Socialist-Wobbly enterprise. The *International Weekly* tottered. Ever since, I have been
chary of predicting the end of capitalism.

If the *International Weekly* folded, the restiveness of the Pacific
Northwest grew. The foremost cause of the unrest that swept the
country was the constantly soaring cost of living, up 50 percent in
three years. Wages in the basic industries had been held under governmental control but few countervailing controls held down prices.
Huge shipments of food and supplies were being sent to starving
Europe, and the shortages resulting in this country led enterprisers
to charge all that the traffic would bear. At the same time profits also
soared. Thinking workers couldn't stand the fact that the costs of the
war would be piled on them while their employers prospered as never
before.

In Seattle the high cost of living was an especially exasperating
prod. The Pacific Northwest had always been a high-price region, far
off the beaten track of American commerce; shipping and railroad
companies padded the costs of transport to extract extra profits. The
Pacific Northwest regarded itself as a colonial possession, exploited
by the Eastern captains of industry. The influx of thousands of workers during wartime strained the city's housing and public facilities to
the breaking point and inflated already rising prices. Landlords re-
aped a bonanza by heaping men and families into the scant housing
available. Seattle was exceptional also because of the advanced organization of labor. Almost a quarter of the working population belonged to unions flanked, as in few other communities, by radical

wings of the Socialists and I.W.W. We, on the left, knew that Seattle was the most likely site for a speedy reaction to the release of wartime controls on strikes.

No one was surprised, therefore, that after the war all hell broke loose in Seattle. The struggle began in the shipyards where the workers went out for higher pay. The thirty thousand shipyard workers in the city had been bound by the national A.F. of L. agreement with the War Labor Board, which exchanged union recognition for the right to strike in wartime. While the Metal Trades Council held an overall agreement with the yards, neither that Council nor its twenty-one constituent unions had any final authority in wartime over the wage scales. That authority rested with the Shipbuilding Labor Adjustment Board, usually called the Macy Board, after its chairman, V. Everit Macy. The Macy Board twice authorized wage increases in 1917. The unions better organized before the war won an average raise of sixty cents a day; those representing mainly the unskilled and semiskilled, much less. The increase for some of around 12-1/2 percent didn't keep pace with a rise in living costs during the period of 31 percent. The top wage for shipyard laborers was $4.16 a day, or a little under $100 a month. The Board's scales were said to be the minimum but in practice they became the maximum and employers were discouraged from paying more. The Board also tried to equalize wages nationally, which operated to the detriment of the Pacific Northwest, where both wages and prices were traditionally higher than on the East and Gulf coasts.

Immediately after the armistice, the Metal Trades Council demanded a general wage readjustment. Its president, James A. Taylor, went to Washington to confer with Charles Piez, director of the Emergency Fleet Corporation, and with the Macy Board. When the Board's appeal committee split on the Seattle wage issue, Taylor returned to Seattle confident that he had permission to negotiate directly with the shipyards, provided that wage increases did not increase the price of shipping to the government. A strike vote, preliminary to negotiations, was authorized by the Metal Trades Council in November 1918, and majorities were received in most unions. On January 16, 1919, negotiations opened on demands for an $8 scale for mechanics, $7 for specialists, $6 for helpers, and $5.50 for laborers. The Council calculated that its wage demands would leave a profit of $200,000 on each ship, as against the existing

$286,000 profit, based on an 8,800-ton ship costing $1,350,000 and sold to the government for $1,636,000. The owners offered increases to the skilled trades but nothing to the unskilled. The skilled trades joined with the mass of the workers in rejecting the splitting tactic.

A Western Union messenger boy helped to precipitate the strike. He bore a telegram addressed to the Metal Trades Association, the employers' body; by mistake he took it to the Metal Trades Council. Its contents were explosive. Director Piez of the Emergency Fleet Corporation had cut through any hope of further negotiation by informing the employers that they would get no more steel if they agreed to any wage increases. On January 16, 1919, the Council authorized a strike, to begin five days later. On January 21, thirty thousand men downed tools, augmented by fifteen thousand in nearby Tacoma. The yards made no effort to reopen; the unions banned demonstrations, parades, or gatherings, and an unearthly quiet enveloped the yards. To scotch the rumor that many of the men were opposed to the strike, Local 104 of the Boilermakers, which comprised nearly half of all strikers, called a meeting to which six thousand members responded. Dan McKillop, an official, denounced the shipowners who had taken the credit for the ships built by the workers. "If they think they can build ships, let them go ahead and build them." As for the threat to build ships only in the East, "Well," said McKillop, "let them try it. If they want to start a revolution, let 'em start it."

The Retail Grocers Association decreed a no-credit policy to put pressure on strikers. The Cooperative Food Products Association, a cooperative formed by unions and the Grange, answered that food would be available to any striker. Thereupon the "dry squad" raided the co-op on a liquor warrant, which provided the cops an excuse to go through the co-op's correspondence and business files. The squad duly confiscated the records in an effort to put the co-op out of business. The stalemate was complete. The men were adamant; many of the yard bosses had gone to California for a vacation; the government, far from being eager for a settlement, bombarded the yards with messages to stand firm and resist labor's demands.

The idea of a general strike swept the ranks of organized labor like a gale. If the general strike was labor's ultimate weapon as the syndicalist wing of the I.W.W. believed, certainly here and now was the time to use it, to break the impending assault on unionism. Surely if all workers folded their arms, capitalism would collapse—or at least the capitalists would accede to the workers' demands. Never had a more dramatic meeting of the Central Labor Council been held than that which convened January 22; delegates from some 110 local unions jammed the floor and unionists filled the gallery. The delegates cheered to the echo every reference to the general strike and hooted down the cautions of the conservatives that such a strike violated many international union rules. On February 2, the special meeting of three representatives from each union voted to set the strike date for Thursday, February 6. This group constituted itself the General Strike Committee and took over from the Central Labor Council complete authority for the strike.

Almost immediately the relevancy of Lenin's speech on management, which had aroused so much discussion among workers, became apparent. If the strike were to be completely effective, the life of a city of three hundred thousand would grind to a sudden halt, with catastrophic consequences. If essential services such as light and power, fire protection, and hospitals were to continue, the Committee of Fifteen, the watchdog of the General Strike Committee, would have to cope with the problem of civic management. Thousands of single workers ate in restaurants; were they to starve during the strike? How about milk for babies? And who would police the strike? Certainly, the unionists had little faith in the impartiality of the custodians of law and order.

An even more crucial question came up at the February 4 meeting of the Committee of Fifteen. How long would the strike last? Was this a demonstration of sympathetic support for the shipyard unions, to be ended as soon as labor had shown where its heart was? Or should the strike continue until the shipyard owners and the government agreed to confer? As a matter of cold fact, just what were the aims of the strikers? Most unionists saw the action as a demonstration of sympathy, calculated to strengthen the arm of the shipyard unions. Others felt that the first general strike in America would be so conclusive in its show of strength that the walls of Jericho would come tumbling down—not the walls of capitalism, but the walls of pitiless hostility to the earnest demands of the shipyard workers. Unfortunately, the Committee made no clear decision on these critical questions.

As if to answer questions about the strike, the *Union Record* published the most famous editorial of its entire history, excerpts of which were read by millions across the country, who by now had their eyes riveted on what some were already proclaiming to be a revolutionary situation. The editorial, written by Anna Louise Strong and approved by Editor Ault and the Metal Trades Council, read, in part:

ON THURSDAY AT 10 A.M.

There will be many cheering, and there will be some who fear.
Both these emotions are useful, but not too much of either.
We are undertaking the most tremendous move ever made by LABOR in this country, a move which will lead—NO ONE KNOWS WHERE.
We do not need hysteria.
We need the iron march of labor.

LABOR WILL FEED THE PEOPLE.
Twelve great kitchens have been offered, and from them food will be distributed by the provision trades at low cost to all.
LABOR WILL CARE FOR THE BABIES AND THE SICK.
The milk-wagon drivers and the laundry drivers are arranging plans for supplying milk to babies, invalids and hospitals, and taking care of the cleaning of linen for hospitals.
LABOR WILL PRESERVE ORDER.

The strike committee is arranging for guards, and it is expected that the stopping of the cars will keep people at home.

A few hot-headed enthusiasts have complained that strikers only should be fed, and the general public left to endure severe discomfort. Aside from the inhumanitarian character of such suggestions, let them get this straight—

NOT THE WITHDRAWAL OF LABOR POWER, BUT THE POWER OF THE STRIKERS TO MANAGE WILL WIN THIS STRIKE. . . .
The closing down of Seattle's industries, as a MERE SHUTDOWN, will not affect these eastern gentlemen much. They could let the whole northwest go to pieces, as far as money alone is concerned.
BUT, the closing down of the capitalistically controlled industries of Seattle, while the WORKERS ORGANIZE to feed the people, to care for the babies and the sick, to preserve order—THIS will move them, for this looks too much like the taking over of POWER by the workers.

Labor will not only SHUT DOWN the industries, but Labor will REOPEN, under the management of the appropriate trades, such activities as are needed to preserve public health and public peace. If the strike continues, Labor may feel led to avoid public suffering by re-opening more and more activities,

UNDER ITS OWN MANAGEMENT.

And that is why we say that we are starting on a road that leads—NO ONE KNOWS WHERE.

We could always depend on Anna Louise Strong to get things going in a situation like this. The last line of the editorial raised a frenzy among the capitalists. Many assumed that we were headed for the Revolution, although the editorial didn't say that. The Department of Justice had been waiting for just such an editorial. The leadership of the Central Labor Council, owners of the *Union Record*, along with the editors were indicted for sedition, the business press went wild, the Chamber of Commerce frothed at the mouth, and Mayor Ole Hanson called in the United States Army to suppress the Revolution.

At 10:00 A.M. that Thursday the general strike began. Streetcars headed for the barns, trucks for the garages, transportation ceased. Second Avenue, then the main thoroughfare, was silent and empty from the Washington Hotel down to Yesler Way. A few minutes before, the pressmen at the *Times* and other papers had begun covering the presses with tarpaulins. Silence reigned over the city. Here and there small groups of unarmed men with armbands—the Labor Guards—patrolled the streets with orders to disperse any gatherings of union men. But no one had gathered to disperse. Public transportation had ground to a halt and, in any event, unionists had been advised to stay at home for the duration.

The peace that had descended was disturbed only by Mayor Ole Hanson. From City Hall he thundered a proclamation on Friday, the second day of the strike:

I hereby guarantee to all the people of Seattle absolute and complete protection. They should go about their daily work and business in perfect security. We have 1,500 policemen, 1,500 regular soldiers from Camp Lewis, and can and will secure, if necessary, every soldier in the Northwest to protect life, business and property.

The time has come for the people of Seattle to show their Americanism. Go about your daily duties without fear. We will see to it that you have food, transportation, water, light, gas and all necessities.

The anarchists in this community shall not rule its affairs.

All persons violating the laws will be dealt with summarily.

The proclamation was all huff and puff. People stayed home.

The exhilaration from the marvelous display of solidarity experienced Thursday and Friday began by Saturday to give way to apprehension. The most clearly stated and widely accepted purpose of the strike was to help the shipyard workers get an honorable settlement of their wage demands. But nobody on the other side seemed inclined to negotiate anything. While Mayor Hanson's fulminations helped to keep up the backs of unionists, the ominous silence in Washington dismayed many. Workers believed the general strike would shock officialdom into action and negotiation. No one had questioned that the government would insist on a settlement of some kind. The country needed ships and the government would come to terms. That's where we made our major miscalculation. The war was over and while more ships were needed to replace the tonnage sunk by German submarines, the capitalists felt no great urgency about it. The shipyards along the East and Gulf coasts and in California continued operating. The dismal truth began to break through to the workers: Despite its record-breaking speed in delivering ships in wartime, Seattle was expendable. For all Washington cared, the Seattle yards could remain closed; the unions had to be taught a lesson. The reactionary Citizens Committee, headed by a distinguished divine and an eminent banker, informed the Committee of Fifteen that no bargain could be struck with revolutionaries: call off the strike, and then, perhaps. . . . Mayor Hanson took his cue from the Citizens Committee. Friday evening he ordered the Committee of Fifteen to end the strike Saturday morning, or else. His "or else" was an empty threat and tended to stiffen opposition among unionists.

Far more effective were the threats of international union officials to revoke local union charters, particularly in the printing trades. The failure of the strike leaders to decide under what conditions and by whom the strike would be ended now became a weakness. Small editions of the dailies began to appear. On Saturday, a few unions returned to work; that afternoon the Committee of Fifteen voted thirteen to one to end the strike at midnight. Although several more unions had voted the same day to return, the General Strike Committee, with final authority, voted to continue the strike by seventy-six to forty-five. In late afternoon most thought that the vote to end the strike was assured; but after a dinner recess several unions changed their position upon the urging of the metal trades and longshore unions. The strike was ending with far less unity and discipline than it had begun. The General Strike Committee met again Monday morning and then adopted the motion to end the strike. More unions had gone back to work, but others that had returned Saturday voted to resume the strike and bring it to an end with united ranks at noon Tuesday, February 11. The strike had lasted five working days.

The majority of Seattle unions felt no sense of defeat as the strike ended. They had demonstrated their solidarity with their brothers in the yards, and the memory of the great days when labor had shown its strength glowed in their minds. Not until many years later, in a very different climate of opinion, did some of the leaders begin apologizing for what they excused as a momentary aberration by an otherwise solid body of citizenry. They wanted to rewrite history, to blame the general strike on "radicals" or "the I.W.W. element." Forgetful of the evident fact that some three hundred delegates chosen for the purpose from a hundred local unions voted the strike almost unanimously, some have described the great general strike of Seattle as merely an incident to be forgotten, glossed over, or explained away. But I am not one of them. I thought then and think now that the action was one of American labor's proudest moments.

Seattleites read with some astonishment the bizarre accounts of the general strike that appeared in local papers and in the nation's leading magazines. On the home front, the *Star* produced the most extraordinary expression of reactionary thought. Though the New York *Tribune's* correspondent reported "absolutely no violence" and the commanding general of the United States troops brought in said he had never seen such a quiet and orderly city, the *Star* got out a bobtailed edition (with a few scab printers and truck drivers) reporting that clubs, revolvers, rifles, carbines, automatics, and machine guns were distributed among the fearful and that trucks, sandbagged and carrying machine guns able to sweep the streets, lumbered up the main avenues of the town during the strike. The *Saturday Evening Post* announced that "bolshevism has put forth its supremest effort in America and has failed." A curious tale, typical of that hysterical period, followed. "The I.W.W. themselves," said the *Post*, "openly boast that the Russian revolution was planned in the office of a Seattle lawyer, counsel for the organization, during those three overheated days wherein Lenin and Trotsky tarried in the city's midst, en route to Russia; and that an American revolution was planned or at least discussed at the same time." The *Post* referred to "an especially illuminating little treatise in booklet form entitled *Russia Did It*, by an ambitious young Bolshevik author who, alas, now languishes behind prison bars in lieu of $10,000 bail. Two and a half tons of this booklet alone were distributed. Equity [the Socialist-I.W.W. print shop] ran its presses frantically day and night." Alas, too, for the truth: it wasn't a booklet but a rather small leaflet.

We Yipsels, the pride and joy of the Socialist Party, had leafletted the shipyards just before the strike. Morris Pass, the cartoonist who later drew for the Yiddish daily *Freiheit* in New York, drew a cartoon of a brawny worker shoving a fat little capitalist into a coffin. So no one would mistake it, the box was labeled "coffin." I drew up the appropriate screed. At the time there was a Victory bond issue with the slogan "The Yanks Did It." What more fitting than to label our leaflet in big type, "Russia Did It!" We counseled the shipyard workers to take over the yards—after all they, not the capitalists, built the ships!

The forces of law and order really blew their tops over that one. The police spread a dragnet out to trap some twenty of us, who had been indicted and charged with criminal anarchy. We felt rather proud of ourselves for criminal anarchy was the postgraduate crime of those days—the garden variety was criminal syndicalism. Nevertheless, the situation was serious, with twenty years in the pen facing us. We counseled with George Vanderveer, the favorite attorney of the labor and radical movements, and a most able lawyer. He gathered us all in his office and after a discussion he turned to a little Wobbly newsboy, who wasn't too bright, and asked him if he would go down to the district attorney's office and surrender with the proviso that bail would be furnished immediately. "Certainly, Fellow Worker Vanderveer," the newsboy responded. Turning to the rest of us, Vanderveer said, "Get out of town and out of the state as fast as you can." That so many radicals could gather at that meeting with no stoolpigeon present was remarkable, but the F.B.I. was just a gleam in J. Edgar Hoover's eye then.

After several months the little Wobbly newsboy who had surrendered came to trial. The spectacle was so ludicrous that the jury voted acquittal; the state eventually dropped the charges in the other cases and one by one we drifted back to our old stomping grounds in Seattle. Getting out of Seattle for California caused me a few qualms.

The train was ferried across to the Oregon shore since no bridge spanned the Columbia. I got off at the ferry to meet a bunch of deputy sheriffs lined up on the platform to give us all the once-over. I felt sure my time had come, but nothing happened. Police work was rather slapdash. No photos and descriptions wired from one city to another—no wonder none of those indicted was ever caught.

My return to Seattle and to journalism made me painfully aware of the country's first Red Scare. In spite of vicious repression, radicalism persisted for some time after the general strike. Anna Louise organized a Russian Information Bureau that spread the word about the Bolshevik Revolution. The *Union Record* ran a series of articles on the Revolution and published Lenin's "Letter to American Workers" in a pamphlet, the first copy to be published in this country. The *Record* also published a pamphlet containing the best of Anna Louise's "Ragged Verse."

Soon after I got back I went to see Anna Louise in her little cubbyhole of an office. In addition to her other assignments, Anna had the title of associate editor and handled the editorial page. "How about a job?" I asked her. "I'll have to see Harry about that," she said. I came back a day or two later and sure enough, I had become a member of the staff. Anna Louise introduced me to Joe Corbett, the city editor. He was the nervous type who invariably pulled out a cigarette when confronted by a problem, and these came every few minutes. He was a Canadian from Winnipeg, well educated, quite elegant in manner and dress, and always courteous. Now I may have been an editor on Socialist papers but I was strictly a cub reporter here. Joe pulled out a cigarette and said he had always wanted to interview a horse that wore a straw bonnet down at Prefontaine Place near City Hall, but had never been able to find time. Would I like to do the interview? "My God!" I said to myself, "interviewing a horse, and for a labor paper!" However, I didn't have much choice—I'd sink or swim on my first assignment. Well, that horse, I found, had some remarkable ideas. I came back with the story and it turned out that the horse had ideas quite similar to a *Daily Call* editorial. The *Record* accepted my story, running it as a funny feature.

I had my foot in the door. I was assigned to City Hall. My chief contact was Bob Hesketh, a leader of the conservative faction in the Central Labor Council. When I came into his office, tucked away in City Hall near an exit, Bob would dive into his desk drawer for the bottle, an excuse for his morning nip. A few years later he became International Secretary of the Hotel, Restaurant and Bartenders Union in Cincinnati, an appropriate job that he held until the Great Spirit called him for a final drink. I owe a lot to Joe Corbett, who was always most patient and, wonder of wonders for a city editor, always polite. "Now Harvey, you just split a paragraph at the end of a page," he would remonstrate repeatedly. How was I to know when the page would end in the middle of a paragraph? In off-hours I aspired to be a music critic and wrote enthusiastic reviews about the Seattle Symphony Orchestra although I didn't know a bass note from a tenor. Fortunately, nobody else on the staff knew any more about symphony music. What stuff!

On the extracurricular side, I joined the Seattle Workers Theater, an amateur group that tried to do serious plays. I was trapped into Gorki's *Lower Depths*. My part was in a low dive with the hero, drunk as usual and telling his life story—Russian type. I would say, "And what then," "how awful," and similar come-ons. The hero was a revolutionary dentist who pulled out most of my teeth at a tender age. On one memorable occasion he was supposed to commit suicide, but the gun clicked, again and again, until mercifully someone dropped the curtain on the dreadful anticlimax. On another occasion the gun sure enough went off and ignited his shirt. The curtain dropped again.

A leading force in the Workers Theater was Nan Havel, wife of Joe Havel, the bookkeeper and de facto treasurer and payroll keeper at the *Record*. He was a fine character, quite correct in speech, manners, and dress. Joe got into a tangle at the Central Labor Council, where he was a delegate of our Newswriters Local 13 of the International Typographical Union. The printers had decided to organize reporters—a precursor of the Newspaper Guild. I must say we were a cross for our publishers to bear—demanding wages and conditions far superior to those on the business press. Some right-wing labor people discovered that Joe was a member of the Communist Party. In the aftermath of the general strike in Seattle, the conservatives had recovered control of the Central Labor Council. They put Joe on trial and expelled him, although the vote was quite narrow. The Havels left for San Francisco, where I saw them many years later. They had prospered. Joe owned several apartment houses and had an elegant suite atop one of them with a sparkling view of San Francisco. He had become a billiard expert, with a fine billiard room, and had grown quite conservative—not unusual for many who had had a rough time for their convictions.

Day by day, things got harder for the Socialists and Wobblies. So fiercely did the flames of persecution lick around the I.W.W. late in 1919 that only two halls in the entire state of Washington remained open, in Seattle and Centralia. Continued police raids on the Seattle hall had led Lumber Workers Industrial Union 500, representing some twenty thousand loggers in the Pacific Northwest, to canvass its membership on methods of protecting that hall, the nerve center of the union and its central means of contact with the men as they moved in and out of the camps. Active members, passing through the Seattle hall, voted 1,021 to 233 to call a general strike in the woods if the hall were closed.

Wobbly attempts to defend halls in other cities were unsuccessful and sometimes tragic. Centralia is midway between Seattle and Portland, the mercantile center for the lumbering and farming interests of Lewis County, which stretches up to Mt. Rainier. On Armistice Day, 1919, the American Legion organized a parade in such a way as to pass by the I.W.W. hall. The Wobblies, some dozen or more then in town, gathered with Secretary Britt Smith to consider what to do. They saw three choices before them: Close the hall on Armistice Day and allow it to be sacked, as the earlier one had been in the previous year. Stand by in the hall and be beaten up by the Legionnaires and deported—the Everett treatment. Or they could defend their hall. They chose the third possibility. When the parade came to the hall, the Legionnaires broke ranks and attacked, breaking in doors and windows. The Wobblies met them with a hail of rifle fire, not only from the hall but from adjacent rooming houses and a hill. The Wobblies were prepared because the Legion had passed out handbills that they were going to chase them out of town. Three Legionnaires were killed, and all the Wobblies but one were rounded up and jailed; Wesley Everest escaped by the back door.

Everest fled down an alley, pursued by rifle bullets, and gained the bank of the Skookumchuck River, which he attempted to ford. The river was too deep and swift, and he came back up the bank, revolver still in hand. Dale Hubbard, nephew of F. B. Hubbard of the Eastern Railway and Lumber Company and former president of the Employers Association of Washington, headed the mob. Everest shouted that he would surrender to an officer of the law, but not to the mob. He fired and Hubbard fell, mortally wounded. His revolver hot and empty, Everest was seized by the mob, his teeth were knocked out, and he was led to jail with a belt around his neck. "You haven't got the guts to lynch a man in broad daylight," he jeered through bloody lips. He was right. That night at 8:00 P.M. the lights went out all over Centralia. Soon thereafter a group of men drove up to the jail, smashed in a door, and dragged Everest out. They threw him into a car that headed a procession to the Chehalis River bridge on the outskirts of town. The lights then went back on in Centralia.

Badly beaten again, Everest would not give up. From his position on the floor in the back of the car he hit out at his assailants. Someone in the back seat then proceeded to castrate Everest as the others held the screaming man. "For Christ's sake, men," he pleaded, "shoot me—don't let me suffer this way." Years later a visiting Legionnaire who was looking into the events of that horrid night interviewed the castrator. Every few minutes, the visitor said, the man got up and washed his hands. In any event his business shrank, for self-respecting workers said they'd rather die than have anything to do with *him*.

At the bridge the mob dragged out Everest, knotted a rope around his neck, and flung his body over. Everest clutched at a plank; Legionnaires stamped on his fingers, and he fell. Dissatisfied with the knot, the lynchers pulled the body back up and used a longer rope, and hurled the body over again. Still dissatisfied, they hauled Everest's body up a third time—by then he must have been dead—and tied a more professional knot on a longer rope and flung the body over. Then, with car lights playing on the scene, they amused themselves by shooting at the swaying body. Satiated at last, the mob left and darkness returned. Next morning somebody cut the rope and the body fell into the Chehalis River.

Fearful that friends of Everest might rescue the corpse, a posse searched the river and recovered it. Then they dumped the horribly mutilated body on the floor of the jail in the sight of the other Wobblies, where it stayed for two days. Finally the deputies gave shovels to a detail of four imprisoned I.W.W.s, took them to a field on the outskirts of town, and forced them to dig a grave into which the body was flung. Such was the end of Wesley Everest, who died grim, game, and staunch in his principles.

Elmer Smith, a local attorney who had advised the I.W.W. on their rights, defended the surviving accused Wobblies, all charged with murder. He was a tall, rugged kind of man, more Populist than radical but indignant at the way workingmen were treated. His was a hard case to plead in the trial over at Montesano in neighboring Grays Harbor County. The trial attracted national attention but little could be done to avoid the guilty verdict. Many of the jurors later said they would have voted for acquittal on grounds of justifiable self-defense if the Wobblies had confined their defense to that of the hall. The presence of armed men in houses across the street and on a nearby hill was the determining factor for them. The Wobblies stayed in prison until the thirties; only after a long and persistent campaign in their behalf were they freed.

The decision on how to defend the hall was a typical Wobbly operation. The men did not consult regional headquarters in Seattle or national in Chicago. The rank and file made the decision on the spot with no idea of what the consequences might be nationally—a real syndicalist strategy and also a sign of the times. What with the decline in the lumber industry, the I.W.W. turned more and more into a defense organization—defending the hundreds of jailed and indicted members from coast to coast.

I met Smith after the trial in 1920 when he came to Seattle to see Harry Ault at the *Union Record*. Smith wanted someone to start a weekly newspaper for the Farmer-Labor Party in Lewis County, and Harry pointed the finger at me. I went and found the memories of the Everest affair still vivid. Elmer had decided to run for prosecuting attorney of Lewis County so that workers could get a fair shake from the law. Elmer had bought the equipment of the Toledo *Messenger*, but we had to move it to our office. Hays Jones came down to help in the big moving job—a flatbed press not much bigger than a sizable table, a linotype, and some cases of type. We got an itinerant printer to run the linotype. Hays and I handled the flatbed, whose arm turned page after page; after that we fed in sheets to get the other side printed. The *Farmer-Labor Call* carried Elmer's message to all the settlements in Lewis County and, when the votes were counted, Elmer had carried all the rural precincts. Unfortunately, he lost in Centralia and in the county seat. After the November election he had little further need for the *Farmer-Labor Call*, so I lightened cargo by going back to Seattle, leaving the printer to carry on for a few more months.

It's about time to turn to domestic affairs. I was no longer living at my mother's place. I couldn't even if I had wanted to—she had accumulated all her worldly possessions in the small apartment, leaving only paths from the kitchen to her bedroom. Though in increasingly bad health, she kept an eye on me. One day, when I was in my early twenties, she surprised me by mentioning that Blanche Quick, a Yipsel girl from a Socialist family, was in love with me. Blanche, it seemed, had worshipped me from afar and when that did her no good, she got in touch with my mother. Well, marriage had never occurred to me as a winning proposition; it was a bourgeois trap to hang a family on you, to enslave you to a steady job for the rest of your life, and to hell with it.

Of course, I had known Blanche for some time and had visited her parents' house. Memory fails me but I must have weakened and met with Blanche and agreed to the fate worse than death. Certainly my mother's failing health influenced me. Alone, I could support her financially, but I couldn't really nurse her. A wife could be helpful with the latter. Both women, my mother and Blanche, were amenable—it was, in fact, their idea—and so it happened. Still, I emphasized that I wanted no children and would not be tied down for the rest of my life. Love being what it is, Blanche agreed, even to the point, eventually, of a hysterectomy. I have often wondered whether that was what she really wanted, but she never raised any doubts with me. We went down to City Hall and for five dollars got hitched. Blanche, a brunette on the well-rounded side, agreeable, quiet, efficient, supported herself as a bookkeeper. I suppose if I had stayed in Seattle and settled into the groove, I'd have been married to this day to Blanche, living a comfortable life in some dumb newspaper job.

Blanche did help with my mother, who was getting to the point where she could no longer be left alone in the apartment. We rented a largish house near the University district and opened up a boarding house to help support us. I had started on the *Union Record* at twenty dollars a week and then was getting thirty perhaps, so we needed the extra cash. We had a room for my mother, and someone around all the time to care for her while we worked. After a year or so she became so weak that we put her in a T.B. sanitarium out near River-

ton and soon after she died. She deserved a better break in life than
she got.

The *Union Record* fell upon unhappy years. Circulation, which
had been as high as seventy thousand with presses running day and
night, declined to twenty thousand or so. The paper moved to a loft
building on First Avenue where the staff was lodged in the barnlike
second floor, impossible to heat in the winter. When I returned from
Centralia I became labor reporter, which I preferred to the city hall
beat. Wages went up to forty, fifty, and eventually sixty dollars a
week when I became city editor.

I supplemented my income by serving as correspondent for International News Service, the Hearst operation. For ten dollars a week I
filed duplicates of some of our police and other splashy or sensational
stories. I corresponded for Chicago-based Federated Press, the labor
news service that had been organized in 1919 by Socialist, I.W.W.,
Farmer-Labor, cooperative, and farmers' papers. In its early days
Federated Press had many high-powered staff people, who later became noted foreign and national reporters. In reporting the nation's
labor and left-wing activities it was doing a valuable service. Federated Press was much more to my liking than Hearst, for sure!

The *Union Record* died a protracted, humiliating death in which
everything was lost including honor. A lot of feeble labor-capitalistic
enterprises destroyed the credibility of the paper. The most notorious of these was Deep Sea Salvage, which used gullible unionists'
money for a fatuous enterprise doomed to bankruptcy. People began
to doubt that the paper was an honest sheet. It reflected little credit
on me that I remained as city editor on a dying daily, in an atmosphere of corrupt decay, in what had, so few years before, been the
most vibrant labor movement in the country. Hays Jones, on a swing
West in 1924, saw the situation in correct perspective and advised me
to get the hell out of Seattle. I was weary of the times, the years of
Harding, Coolidge, and Hoover, the most depressing decade I was
ever to suffer through. My hopes rose in 1922 when the Farmer-
Labor Party, which had succeeded the defunct Socialist Party, elected
quite a few legislators. By 1924 the new party had all but disappeared. The juice had gone out of the Labor movement. The Communist Party was barely noticeable—composed mainly of Russian
nationalists. The I.W.W., justly preoccupied with self-defense, no
longer counted for much in the lumber industry. In 1925, I followed

the advice of Hays Jones and of Bill Douglas, also a Washingtonian, to "go east, young man." To what, I had no idea, but anything was better than festering in Seattle.

V

When summer came, Blanche and I prepared for our move to the East. Years before I had learned to drive in an ancient Chevrolet. For the big trip East, I got a new Willys Overland. A cratelike affair on wheels, its front seat folded back to make a bed. I added a cabinet that fit the left side running board that had shelves for storage and a leaf that we could open and use as a table. So off we went, Blanche and I, into the wild blue yonder, on the road that led "no one knows where." We had no particular objective, no jobs in sight, only enough money to see us through the trip, barring accidents.

We traveled the asphalt out of Seattle and hit a bit more around Spokane, but that was all until deep into Minnesota. We navigated without numbered highways or road signs, relying on yellow bands around occasional telephone poles that indicated the Yellowstone Trail. We came to the Grand Coulee in eastern Washington, a canyon worn by the Columbia ages ago, miles across, and quite deep. Though not as spectacular as the Grand Canyon, descending into the old riverbed of the Grand Coulee and then puffing up the other side to the rim thrilled Blanche and me. We came to the Bitterroots just after a freshet had strewn rocks and boulders across the pitiful road making driving rather difficult. We passed a sheep herder near Billings on a misty morning who beckoned for a ride into town. After he got into the backseat I noticed he carried a long iron rod. He didn't use it, but politely asked for a dollar bill to buy breakfast when we left him in Billings; accommodating him seemed the better part of valor. In many parts of Montana we got off the deeply rutted road and drove along the prairie. We ate by car side and bedded down in it at night. Motels or even guest houses didn't exist, for few people did cross-country driving except as a feat or sport.

We hit civilization again at Minneapolis, continuing on the paved road to Chicago. We entered from the north by Sheridan Road, passing Wayside (the Lloyd house) utterly oblivious of the part it was to play in our later life. By the time Blanche and I got to Chicago, we were nearly broke. I went to see Carl Haessler, the managing editor of the Federated Press, for which I had corresponded in Seattle. Carl was a wiry specimen, full of a wry humor, a resolute atheist, one of the best friends I would ever have, and a thoroughly remarkable character. Jailed for draft resistance during World War I, he had organized the first general strike in a military prison, Leavenworth; the authorities responded by building a barbed wire stockade of barracks outside the prison to hold the agitators. Undaunted, Haessler organized, published, and smuggled out a radical newspaper, the *Wire City Weekly*, which described life and brutality within the prison. He ran the Federated Press, a labor news service similar to Associated Press, which counted a hundred or so labor, radical, and progressive papers, including the sheets of many international unions, as clients. Many of the editors and correspondents on papers that subscribed to the service also submitted stories to the Federated Press. Consequently, Carl tended to know just about everyone in labor-leftist circles and operated something of an unofficial employment agency for radicals. When I asked for a job, Carl had one on tap with the Brotherhood of Locomotive Engineers *Journal* in Cleveland. The Engineers paid sixty dollars a week, which was what I had been getting on the *Union Record*.

We proceeded with all deliberate speed onward to Cleveland to meet up with Albert F. Coyle, the dynamic editor. A graduate of Yale Divinity School, animated by the highest ideals, he was, nevertheless, willing at times to use devious means to achieve his object all sublime. Coyle had been a Y.M.C.A. secretary and shipped out as a chaplain with the United States forces at Archangel, where presumably the Army was to safeguard big supplies of armaments from seizure by the Bolsheviks. Before long he crossed the lines and joined the Bolsheviks, who sent him straight to Moscow. He greatly admired Lenin and returned to the States as a strong proponent of recognition of the Soviet regime. Somehow he came to the attention of Warren Stone, Grand Chief of the Engineers, who wanted to expand his journal along progressive social and political lines. Stone supported Senator Bob LaFollette of Wisconsin, who was running for President on the Progressive Party ticket against Coolidge and some nondescript Democrat. So Albert Coyle with his progressive ideas was the man Stone needed to expand the *Journal*, and, at that moment, I was the man Coyle needed to relieve him of the burden of writing run-of-the-mill stuff on the inside of the paper and handling copy for the printer. Coyle, a darter, always loped at a half-run, overwhelmed by the weight of the affairs resting on his slender shoulders. Since he traveled constantly—to Chicago, to New York, to Washington, to God knows where—I came in handy. Typically Albert grabbed a briefcase and overnight bag, summoned his secretary with her notebook, and raced down to the Union Station, dictating along the way, reaching the platform with only a minute to spare. Albert would dash off some editorials between trips and I filled the remaining pages with labor and political articles.

Albert believed the *Journal* should solicit and publish articles by leading authorities around the country. Unfortunately, not all wrote well, so I cleaned up some of what they sent in. As I had previously worked on dailies with hourly deadlines, the monthly schedule of the *Journal* was a relief. When I wasn't editing I did some campaigning. Coyle was running for Congress in the eastern part of Cleveland and in Geauga County, a rural section to the east. I chauffeured him around on his campaign, making forays into the wilds of Geauga, hardbitten Republican territory, with him. LaFollette carried Cleveland and Milwaukee, but Coyle didn't make it to Congress. The campaign was an education for me in some ways, particularly the aftermath. The Progressive Party, LaFollette's personal organization, collapsed and disappeared almost immediately after he lost interest in it outside of Wisconsin. I understood LaFollette's withdrawal; he had had little support from the A.F. of L. hierarchy and the pitiful remnants of the Socialist Party didn't do much for him either. However, I couldn't help but note how LaFollette's party differed from the old Socialist Party, whose locals dug into many a working-class district and which cheerfully survived many an electoral loss. LaFollette left adrift the five million or so who voted for him; the railroad brotherhood executives who had been a mainstay in the Progressive campaign found other things to occupy them. The death of the Progressives did nothing to strengthen morale in the dismal twenties.

Neither did the disarray of the left. Sometimes radicals seemed to fight each other as much as the class enemy. While at the *Journal*, I witnessed one such battle. Coyle believed in the cooperative movement, by which workers would acquire mines and divide all profits between them—eliminating wages, as such. But he went about it in a manner that undermined the United Mine Workers, who regularly fought losing, rearguard battles in West Virginia. When a group of forlorn men banded together to open a small mine, Coyle and the Locomotive Engineers Grand Chief helped. However, these non-union mines often undercut the prices charged by organized mines, giving management an excuse to reduce wages or threaten the Union. John L. Lewis of the United Mine Workers raged at these efforts that threatened the Union scale. He denounced Warren Stone and Coyle as scabs and consigned the Locomotive Engineers to perdition as a scab union. Stone and Coyle, for their part, had little respect for Lewis, whose lackluster organizing campaigns, they believed, crippled labor. In the end, both lost. The "co-op" movement petered out as West Virginia went nonunion.

The attitude of the rank and file toward the *Journal* did not inspire me. Only a few working engineers ever showed up in our office. Our section of the paper was isolated from the rest of the outfit on a separate floor. The associate editor, a bitter foe of Coyle, controlled the back section of the magazine. But this section contained information of immediate concern to engineers, especially the page with the monthly insurance premiums. I heard that many engineers in small towns got their magazine at the post office, tore out the insurance page, and tossed the rest of the magazine into the wastebasket. Most of the engineers were impervious to the progressivism of the Grand Chief.

All in all, it was a dull job in 1925–1926. The Socialist Party and the I.W.W. barely existed and I had never had any contact with the Communists. When Art Shields of the *Daily Worker* blew into town and told me about a big textile strike in Passaic, New Jersey, in which the Communists were active, I was impressed and decided to look into the local variety. I met Rumanian-born Ike Amter, the Communist organizer, a good-natured hulk of a man. In winter he wore a peajacket with one pocket devoted to lettuce and the other to nuts, his main nourishment away from home. At that time the Communists put out mimeographed shop and factory papers, written for the most part by underground members, some of whom very vividly described the real lives and misery of ordinary people on the much touted Coolidge-Hoover never-ending high plateau of prosperity. I'd whip the material into shape and run it out on the mimeograph, but I wasn't at the factory gates at 6:00 A.M. distributing it. As I look back

I realize the importance of these shop papers. They began the work of organizing and educating the core of workers who later formed the backbone of the young C.I.O. industrial unions.

In 1927 something happened that was to be decisive in my own life. I had noted a tall, lanky fellow passing my office door occasionally. He, having made suitable inquiries about me, dropped in for a chat one day. He was none other than Jay Lovestone, secretary of the Communist Party. He was consulting with Coyle from time to time about organizing a trade union delegation to go to Moscow for the tenth anniversary of the Revolution. Coyle had promised to recruit various dignitaries of the railroad brotherhoods to go on the delegation—the A.F. of L., relentlessly and vociferously anti-Red, were hopeless in this adventure. I came to know Lovestone as a fascinating and devious person for whom maneuvering was the chief joy of life. It was a deeply ingrained habit with him—so much so that some of his antics made little sense. For instance, he would pay my fare to Albany on the Twentieth Century Limited to keep him company, and I would get off at Harmon, where engines were changed from electric to steam, and all for what purpose? To show off his importance? Was he so in need of the company of an unsophisticated young man? He did tell me that once, when the train stopped in Cleveland, he seized the opportunity to stand under an open window where William Z. Foster, the Party chairman, was conferring with local Party people. Lovestone got an earful, he boasted. He was always in the money, traveling first class. I thought that rather peculiar for the leader of a working-class organization, but Jay explained that he had good friends in the fur industry who saw to it that he wanted not.

Lovestone and Coyle often cooperated, though, and I ultimately benefited from that. When Coyle's secretary resigned, Lovestone had just the woman for the job, Betty Gannett. Coyle hired her as a matter of course. About the same time I was getting restive on my job and hankering for the excitement of the big city. I must have told Lovestone this for he was most obliging. Would I like to write articles on the labor movement and economic matters for the Soviet Union press? I had been a fervent admirer of the October Revolution back in 1917, and little happened thereafter to lessen my admiration. It was before the worst days of Stalin. I had written, and would continue to write, stories describing Bolshevik advances in labor and social organization, and exposing baseless rumors in the American commercial press and various other papers. So I was definitely interested. I offered several samples to Lovestone—which he liked. Jay said I should quit the *Journal* and come to New York to devote full time to the writing for him. Albert didn't object—probably because Jay provided a replacement for me in the bargain. When I went to New York, Len DeCaux, who had been working on Oscar Ameringer's *Illinois Miner*, took my place.

My new job was softer than that on the *Journal* but after a time I became dissatisfied. I never knew how my stuff was used, or specifically just what was wanted. And never seeing the results of my handiwork made me uneasy. When I told him of my frustrations, Lovestone had another idea. He had wanted to Americanize the *Daily Worker*. He installed me as city editor to carry out his plans. I lasted six weeks on that job. The *Worker* had two editors, a custom then on Communist papers, one editor to watch the other. One was Bill Dunne, a union stalwart from Butte, a splendid fellow with an unfortunate penchant for the bottle. The other was Harry Wicks, the poison pen artist, whose editorials dripped with vitriol. He would look over my shoulder and demand more blood and guts in my copy. I didn't like the style of the *Worker* much, and the staff was inadequate. As city editor I had one reporter to cover the whole metropolis. I liked Sender Garlin, my reporter, a most capable chap, but it was all quite futile. Though we worked hard to cover city news, Party politics got in the way. For example, we would hear of a garment union story, hot news, and we'd work on it. Then we had to send the story to the Party's union office for approval. If the piece didn't follow the Party line, it got squelched. If it came back a week later with an "O.K.," the story was long dead.

Albert Coyle came to my rescue this time. Having the official delegation to Moscow for the tenth anniversary pretty well organized, he was now organizing an unofficial delegation—kind of garden variety. Coyle invited me to be secretary of the delegation. My chief responsibility would be to prepare a report for the United States union people. Carl Haessler, my friend on Federated Press, was also on the delegation as was Ernest Lundeen, later a Farmer-Labor Congressman, and many others from labor federations and local unions, including quite a few women. My wife Blanche came along and both of us encountered the insidious side of Party practices. Most of the women were Party members, to balance the fact that nearly all, if not all, the men delegates were non-Party. Once Blanche, a Socialist, came to me crying, saying that the Party women were meeting and refused to let her in. It was one way of encountering the Party cell. For my part, whatever was decided in the cell was never told to me—I was just the secretary.

In spite of it all, we had an exciting trip. We landed in Helsinki and took the night train to Leningrad. Breakfast in the Leningrad station came as a most unpleasant surprise to my provincial taste. Instead of hot cakes, bacon, and coffee, the Russians offered us cold fish, black bread, and tea. We spent several days in Leningrad—visiting the Winter Palace, the Smolny Institute, headquarters of the Bolshevik Revolution, and the battleship *Aurora*. On to Moscow for one of the world's great spectacles, the immense parade of workers, soldiers, and sailors through the enormous Red Square. The United States delegation had preferred seats on the platform overlooking the square. After the anniversary we went down into the Ukraine and saw the enormous Dnieprostroy dam then under the supervision of American engineers. Before heading back to Moscow we visited Nizhni Novgorod (Gorki now). While touring an enormous textile factory we had an experience I've never forgotten. A woman broke away from her machine and rushed toward us shouting and crying. Since our guides quickly ushered us out, we never learned what she was trying to tell us. The incident unnerved me, but the progress that I'd seen at all of our stops—especially compared with conditions in the United States—convinced me the Revolution was improving the lives of the Russian people. I came back to the States more enthusiastic than ever.

On our return to Moscow we got into the funeral cortege for Rayna Prohme, who had been an organizer with Mikhail Borodin and others in Shanghai before the Chiang Kai-shek takeover. We trudged along on a cold, sleety day behind a brass band blaring out the funeral march in horrible cacophony—to the warm Novodevichij monastery, where Rayna's coffin rested on a hydraulic lift. Though I spoke briefly for our delegation, I had never heard of the woman before. Afterwards, we were bussed back to town. Sometime later I realized that a funny thing had happened on the way to the monastery. A young woman from Chicago quit marching in the procession at one of the boulevards to keep a dinner engagement at the Quakers, so she said. I never met her that day. Her name: Jessie Lloyd.

I prepared a report on the Soviet experience that was duly amended by the group and published as a pamphlet upon our return to New York. On the whole the year 1927 had been quite a contrast and a dramatic improvement over the business in Cleveland; I should thank Jay Lovestone for getting me to New York. For others, things didn't work out as well. Albert Coyle lost his job on the Locomotive Engineers *Journal* as a result of the trip. While on the boat going over he got a curt message from the Engineers' Grand Chief who had just heard the details of the trip—"You're fired." The press had nosed out the true purport of the delegation, which was too much for the Grand Chief.

My experiences with the Party in Russia and the United States had soured me on the Party's concept of democratic centralism. The demise of Jay Lovestone completed my disillusionment. Lovestone's belief that America was an exceptional country got him into trouble. When the news hit Moscow, orders came down to get rid of Jay. The man who had just been reelected with great applause suddenly found himself on the outside looking in, his former supporters now vehement in his denunciation. I continued to have great respect for the Russian Revolution and the role of the Communists in many strikes in the United States. Indeed, among the engineers of revolution, I found myself in agreement with them as often as any others. Like the Communists I believed that educating a steadfast corps of worker-leaders in the labor fight would come only with and in struggle. The pure academic reading that the Socialists seemed to rely on more and more didn't move me, though I knew that the Communists believed in backing up fighting with intelligence. I thought as they did, that ten miners in a camp continuing to read Lenin after their strike was declared lost represented a major victory for the strike and the miners—or any other group of workers. Some of the rank and filers in the Party were among the finest people I have known, courageous and self-sacrificing, but some of the leaders were another story. I cooperated with the Party on many occasions afterward, but could never bring myself to join.

As Blanche and I headed back to New York, our concerns were quite pedestrian. We had left our jobs to take the Moscow trip and neither of us had any hot irons in the fire. Our top priority when we returned had to be job-hunting—the Revolution would have to come later.

Discovering
The World

My great grandfather, Samuel Augustus Maverick, one of the first settlers in San Antonio, Texas, was more a lawyer and land speculator than a rancher. He wound up with cattle almost by accident when a buyer in one of his land deals paid up with his herd in lieu of cash. Maverick had cattle but no ranch, so he put the animals on an island in the Gulf and hired a man to tend them. This man neglected to brand some of the new calves at birth and occasionally the cattle would straggle over to the mainland. Folks who saw them remarked, "Oh, there's a Maverick without any brand." Soon, many people came to refer not only to unbranded cattle but also to any quite independent people as mavericks. Independence of thought was also one of the hallmarks of my upbringing.

I

One of my earliest memories of my mother, Lola Maverick Lloyd, is from our little summer cottage on the lake bluff in Winnetka. Mother was carrying Bill, my brother, to our big tin outdoor bathtub. She wore a dress of a Japanese cotton crepe that you don't see now, the color of raspberry ice cream. Her hair was wavy and brown, her cheeks and chin delicately modeled, her eyes dark and shining, sometimes pensive, sometimes mischievous. Mother never bothered me or my siblings with the routine womanly arts. She enjoyed the creative side of cooking tasty meals. An artistic woman with a profound appreciation for beauty, Mother kept the living room straight because she wanted it to look attractive. But to dust for dusting's sake didn't appeal to her.

In 1902, after Mother had taught mathematics at Smith, her college friend Amey Aldrich invited her down to the seashore in Rhode Island and introduced her to the household of Watch House on Sakonnet Point. Watch House was the home of Jessie Bross and Henry Demarest Lloyd and their four sons. A thirty-room ocean front property, Watch House hummed with activity. Henry and Jessie entertained a continuous stream of guests of diverse backgrounds, interests, and professions. These included family, their sons' friends, people working for reform causes, and sometimes tired factory workers sent for a rest by Jane Addams of Hull House. My mother's brief diary captures the spirit of the house. The inexhaustible sociability and endless plays, charades, games, and sailing at Watch House captivated her and she fell in love with one of Henry and Jessie's sons, William Bross Lloyd. Her diary recorded the most important event in her summer: "Will asked me to marry him. I went all to pieces."

The relationship between my parents grew in these joyful surroundings, but was also based on a common vision of human potential. Dad's grandfather, Lieutenant Governor Bross of Illinois, helped found the *Chicago Tribune*, then the organ of a small third party, the Republicans, which wanted to stop the spread of slavery. Dad's father, Henry Demarest Lloyd, published *Wealth Against Commonwealth* in 1894, exposing the corrupt, monopolistic policies of Standard Oil and articulating a new vision of American life. The productive power of the machine, my grandfather believed, could free the human spirit and foster the development of a society that valued cooperation as much as his own favored competition. Secure in the necessities of life, human beings could divert their energy to creative endeavor to benefit all. Henry Demarest Lloyd died before I was born, but my parents and their guests often discussed his ideas and personal example in our home. Grandfather had an aphorism: "Labor may be often wrong, but it is always on the right side." He meant, I thought, that regardless of errors, the goal of creating just conditions for the vast majority is good for the human race. He contracted the pneumonia that killed him because he refused to let a cold

keep him from giving a union-sponsored speech on public ownership
of street cars to a group of workingmen. He backed up his words
with action.

Dad shared his father's ideals. Devoted to socialism, he joined the
party in 1906. He stood as the Socialist candidate for various local
offices and ran for United States Senator on the Socialist ticket right
after World War I. He continued his father's struggle for public ownership of the Chicago street railways when I was a child. Though he
served as director of the *Chicago Tribune* Company for a number of
years, Dad finally became disgusted with the paper's increasingly
reactionary stance and resigned. Max Eastman once told my father,
"Your mind is diabolical in its lack of compromise and opportu-
nism." And, in those days, Dad stood firmly against the ruthless
capitalist exploitation that turned America's workingmen into wage
slaves. In fact, for a while after the Russian Revolution, he joined and
gave financial support to the Communist Party.

Mother had attended Smith when women struggled against public
opinion to go to college. Perhaps that is why she couldn't be bothered
with petty detail. In a world in which women could not vote, men got
the country into war, and poverty beat down millions, she felt that
those who cared about humanity should not waste time on work anyone could do. As a teenager, I saw Mother picket with garment workers demanding better conditions for labor; help feminists like her
friend, Alice Paul, secure political rights for women; and support
pacifists trying to avert the horrors of a bloody war. After her marriage to my father, a man of considerable wealth, she could afford
these pursuits better than most.

My parents were married in November of 1902 and I arrived in
February of 1904. My sister Mary followed two years later and brother Bill, two years after that. Because of my father's money, we grew
up in one of the biggest houses in Winnetka, a wealthy suburb of
Chicago. Though my father professed and believed Socialist ideals,
his household ran on a very traditional basis. Indeed, he was a demanding, and often difficult, employer. Hired help, which always
included a cook, upstairs and downstairs maids, a chauffeur, a gar-
dener, and generally a governess, did most of the work in the house.
Our wealth gave us a great deal of freedom. My father, a lawyer, went
to his office most days, but never worked long hours after he came

into his inheritance at age thirty. When we were small children, Mother stayed strictly at home expressing her politics mainly by the interesting visitors she entertained. Consequently, as children, we saw a great deal of our parents.

Ideas about how to make life better for people have always seemed of vital, immediate importance to me. All kinds of company visited us and we often heard their social and political discussions with our parents. Fascinating people of exciting experience, our parents' guests stimulated our imagination, and provided a portion of our political education. When I was six, I saw a woman with a short, mannish haircut in our dining room. She stayed with us a while to rest up because she had been doing a man's work in the stockyards. Ella Reeve Bloor put on overalls and passed for a man to get information on the most dangerous and unsanitary parts of the yards. The fact that women were forbidden from those sections didn't stop her. I noticed that she did not eat meat on that visit. My parents told me that she had become a vegetarian in response to the filth and brutality she had seen. John Reed came through on his way to Moscow to swim on our beach and talk to my parents about the revolution that had just deposed the Czar. I never forgot Reed's wonderful physique and beautiful diving—or his semitransparent and very modern turquoise silk bathing suit. I was also taken by his description of the Revolution. The friends that Mother and Dad disagreed with were generally their oldest friends from the early years, and the ones they agreed with most were strangers, like Reed, lately met in common struggles for better ways of living. Through heated and often witty discussions, I discovered my own family's history: that concern for the deprived and commitment to bettering their lot had long been a family concern.

That same year, I got an idea why my parents had such unusual beliefs—by Winnetka's standards. While riding into town with my father on the Northwestern, I saw a group of pale, grimy children playing on a garbage-strewn lot beside the railroad tracks. I asked Dad why the children played in the dirt instead of the grass. He told me that their parents had no money. I didn't understand and wouldn't drop the subject. "There's lots of empty land, I've seen it." Dad explained that to live far from industrial jobs cost money that workers just didn't have. When I told him I thought it was unfair, he agreed and said, "That's why I'm a Socialist."

Both of my parents taught me a healthy suspicion of the main-line media. We called one portion of the Hearst paper the "whale section" because anyone who believed it could swallow a whale. Dad and Mother put their trust in the reports they heard from progressive friends and the alternative papers and magazines to which they subscribed. When I was old enough to read, I often chose the leftist sheet, *The Liberator*, the radical magazine, *The Masses*, or the feminist, *The Forerunner*, all of which could be found in the house. Socialist politics and progressive ideas were always in the air when I was growing up. No wonder all of us children imbibed them, to a greater or lesser extent.

Dad was a brilliant, witty, and genial man and I learned much from him besides politics; he held advanced views on politics and society as a matter of conviction, but he also got a lot of fun out of being unconventional. For example, both Dad and Mother believed in taking human skin as casually as any other feature of life. On hot days when we were little they would turn on the sprinkler and let us dance naked in the spray: even down on the beach near our house Bill swam without a suit long after some of our neighbors expressed shock. Dad used to laugh when he heard about them and he would tell one of his favorite stories. When he was in high school, he and some of his friends swam on a lonely beach without suits in off-hours. One old maid complained to his father that she could see them. Next day, they went further down the beach. The old lady called up Grandfather Lloyd again indignantly exclaiming, "You'll have to do something about these boys because I can still see them— with field glasses."

Another story, told of my father by a family friend, is one of my merriest memories. Dad scorned limousines, though he had the money for them, because he didn't want to be boxed in a showcase. He loved his open touring car and even in the dead of a Chicago winter would drive it eighteen miles to the opera, with whatever hardy guests would accompany him. Though the chauffeur mounted heavy isinglass and leather curtains on the car for the worst nights, the wind whistled through. Dad developed special arrangements to meet the problem. For the guests he provided great fur robes of black bear three inches thick. Although Dad took a chauffeur to park the car, he liked to drive. So he couldn't be tangled in a robe, like those of the guests. Instead, he had fur pants made of the same shaggy material. One night after a jolly dinner they got a late start, and although Dad burned up the road even faster than usual, they arrived barely in time for the curtain. After pushing their way past the none-too-pleased early comers, they had to take off their winter clothing at their seats. Dad had bought the very best tickets and in the fifth row he rose with majestic unconcern to take off his fur pants. He could barely endure the overheating of public places anyway—let alone with fur breeches. Diamond-studded women squealed and fainted on all sides.

An adventurous man, Dad always urged us to try whatever we felt ready for. The summer I was seven, I learned to shinny up the main halyard of his chartered yacht, the *Oonas*, to the yardarm, fifty-five feet above the deck—high enough to make the large boat look like a pumpkinseed when I looked down. Things got very sporting if a good-sized motorboat passed close enough to roll her. I had a thrilling feeling in my stomach as the mast swung back and forth. My proud father had me repeat the stunt for many of the guests on the boat. He found the horrified response of Mother's friends most entertaining. Mother's guests did their best to make her feel guilty about my exploits, but she could never change Dad's mind. He often said he'd rather see his children dead than afraid.

Raising children this way may make them interesting but doesn't make them easy. Now that I am a parent I know how our touchy dispositions and terrible tempers must have tormented Mother and Dad, not to mention the governesses. Sometimes we children played together nicely but often we would punch, scratch, bite, and pull hair with all our strength—in spite of having our choice of three room-length shelves of the finest toys money could buy. Mary and I were pretty evenly matched and would fight with tigerlike intensity. In one of our fights, Mary came at me like a cannonball. I was just approaching the age of giving up fighting, so I tore upstairs with Mary hot in pursuit, and got my door locked just in time. Mary sat down outside to wait, vowing not to move until I came out. Supper time came and still she sat. "Aren't you going down to eat?" I asked anxiously for I was famished. Mother called her. Dad called her. She was adamant. But I was my father's daughter. I opened the window as softly as I could, padded out over the porch roof, slid down the porch pillar to the first floor, and slipped in by the south entrance, which was far from Mary but close to the dining room. The family, much amused, must have sympathized because they played along. When I'd finished supper, I went back the way I had come. Only then did Dad give Mary the bad news. At first Mary felt betrayed, but the next morning we laughed together about our escapade. We children burned out our animosity on the field of battle. As adults we have been the closest and dearest of friends—perhaps because we are veterans of the same war.

In this incident, as in general, Mother and Dad were tolerant parents. Mother was a regular Solomon in the way she settled things. Once, when I was old enough to know lots better, I conducted the interesting scientific experiment on Mary of testing if she really did have a bone right in the middle of her chest. I started this test with a pin, but Mary most unscientifically wouldn't wait for the pin to hit bottom and let out what I considered a very sissified yell. Grownups came running from all directions. I kept a bold face about the honorableness of my scientific interest—until Mother quietly said, "Then why didn't you do it on yourself?" She deflated me completely. Both of my parents actually enjoyed any impertinence that hinted at the development of reasoning power. They encouraged us to say whatever was on our minds for neither could be offended by little foolish remarks and both liked to discuss our ideas with us. Dad and Mother took great care to stimulate our curiosity by showing us everything beautiful in nature. As Dad had more leisure than most men, he would spare no effort to teach us. Once when he found we were having trouble understanding how geysers spurt, he bought a glass beaker and tubing that he heated and bent into zigzags. He filled the bottle with water, stuck the tube in the bottle's cork, and heated the whole contraption on the stove. The result: a home-made geyser. Our cook could never tell what would happen in her kitchen.

The fall I was five and a half, my mother took me down to Mrs. Totten's private school for boys and girls. Mrs. Totten was kindly and firm, and school seemed fine until lunchtime. Then Jane, a big, smiling girl I liked very much, sat next to me and I shared my orange with her. Wanting a little more, she reached into my lunch sack. Trained by Mother and Dad never to throw picnic trash around, I had put the chewed pieces and peels back in the bag. "Oh, how nasty!" cried my ideal of womanhood. I felt terrible and hid under my desk. When Mrs. Totten tried to get me out, I spit. Nonplussed, she called Mother. I sobbed out my story. Jane exclaimed, "I never meant she was nasty—just those slippery peels." This consoled me and we got on uneventfully after that, but I suffered from painful shyness until I was an adult.

My parents noticed my shyness long before I went to school. If guests gushed over me when I was quite small, I would knit my brows until they made a straight, unbroken line across my forehead. Some saw and changed the subject, but the insensitive continued their sugary shrieks until I crawled under a table—and, as in school, spit if someone tried to coax me out. If I did these things because I hated such attention, my behavior only invited more stares and comments. I was such a nervous child that when Doris Schmidt came to work for us, I mistook her friendly smiles for jeers. Finally, after a few days, I asked Dad why she was laughing at me. Sincerely shocked, he explained that she was just trying to be friendly. Though I bellowed like a bull and fought like a tiger at home, I sat perfectly terrified in the long quiet rows of desks at the public school two years later, hardly making myself heard when called on: so gentle, so quiet, such downcast eyes. Few physical feats gave me pause, but other children frightened me so that I made friends very slowly.

My grandmother, sweet Mary Vance Maverick, said she always thought some of my shyness came from the way that a very severe British-trained governess—one of my first—stared at my every move. Grandma may have had a point since, before I was old enough to remember them, I had convulsions and digestive upsets. But I have my own theory to account for my shyness. When I was little, Dad was always very affectionate and would kiss us in a way I didn't like. When he gave me a big, wet kiss, I would turn away. He thought I did not like any of it but I would have liked hugging. So he did not pet me as much as Mary. Dad favored Mary for other reasons, too. She charmed him as I never did. Dad spanked us only occasionally and just with his hand. After the earliest youth, I didn't cry on these occasions—I was too angry. But Mary always wept, with a gentle little sob that gradually became a singsong, and then she called, "Daddy, comfort me!" He'd come then and take her in his arms and caress her. Though I remember being disgusted at such feminine weakness, the warmth of Dad's relationship with Mary made me feel second best and gave me an inferiority complex. As we grew,

Mary's prettiness, her ease in making friends, and her knack for getting dates reinforced my sense of awkwardness and ugliness, and, of course, made me that much more shy.

I also felt uncomfortable, sometimes, about the differences between myself and our neighbors. No one in my school had ever heard of socialism. In fact, as far as I could tell, the only Socialist in town outside of our family was an old German shoemaker, an honest, steadfast fellow who spoke with an accent. The presidential election of 1912 stirred much excitement in which school children participated by wearing campaign buttons. The other kids suspected I would be "Bull Moose," but when they looked at my Socialist button they just gave a vacant stare and passed on.

Religion was another problem. I was the only one in school who didn't go to church or Sunday school. Our not going seemed incredible to the other children and I began to wish that I could, so as not to be so different. Yet I knew Dad would laugh his head off if I said so. A complete skeptic, he joked about religion. Dad believed religion made people endure needless misery in the hope of a better life in heaven and that the wish for immortality fathered the thought. "My mother and father were always free thinkers," he said, "but when he died she began to believe in heaven. I don't blame her for wishing, but I can't believe it myself." Mother never joked about religion, which she said was a comfort and help to many people. Mother only wished more would follow the teachings of their own religion. She did not attend church herself. Instead, she used all the time she could spare away from her family to work for peace, women's rights, and the underdog. I did, finally, gather the courage to broach the subject of Sunday school to my parents. As I expected, Dad decried the idea of learning "so much that wasn't so." He said it was a free country, though, if I wanted to go. "Let her go and find out what it's like," was Mother's idea, and so off we went, Mary and I, to the Congregational Church.

I loved to visit my grandfather's Texas ranch because, surrounded by family and living in such informal circumstances, I felt less shy and intimidated. Every winter for four years through my tenth year, our family went to Texas for a month or two or three. I "discovered" Grandpa, and all his special qualities, the first winter on the ranch. A gentle and quiet man, Grandpa had a gift for delighting children. If my attention wandered from the job of eating dinner, he cut the meat in small pieces named frogs, and one longer strip named the alligator. The alligator kept eating up the frogs, at least Grandpa seemed to think he did, until at the last the alligator got eaten himself. If Mary and I fussed about something, he would ask, "Did you ever hear about the little boy named James?" "No," we'd exclaim and we'd run to his knee. "Well, his name was James, but his mamma called him Jimmy Jenine Gline Slossenjoshnger Jimmikins for short." And he'd go on from there. Not very far, though, because every time Grandpa mentioned the hero he took so long to say his name. We'd beg him to pronounce the name slowly so we could learn to say it. But he'd speed it up to protect his trade secret.

Small and dainty in her ways, Grandma sewed beautifully; she had attended a convent school in her youth, though her family was Episcopalian. Like my mother, she could cook for a few or a crowd, but never nonchalantly. In later years, the example of Grandma's perfect catering curtailed Mother's and, therefore, our social activities. Mother could never feel casual, or let us feel casual, about having a group of youngsters in any old time. Grandma's perfectionism surfaced in other ways, too. Her exquisitely controlled sneezes astonished me. Her "achoo!" was so delicate and finely modulated that I always wondered why she needed to do it at all. Not so with Mother: her sneeze cut the house like a knife.

Grandma's attitudes were somewhat less advanced than ours. Although she had found her husband considerate and honorable when she set up housekeeping at sixteen, and had reared two sons of her own, Grandma viewed all strange men with the greatest suspicion. She always urged us to be reserved and cautious. In our whole lives neither Mother nor Dad told me, Mary, or Georgia to do or avoid something because we were girls. Grandma Maverick, however, did suggest that we be "more ladylike," on more than one occasion. Coming from Grandma, whose age earned her a certain indulgence from us, we thought the expression sweet and quaint. If a nurse or governess used it, we considered her a poor, unenlightened slave to convention! Grandmother also took a dim view of my parents' liberal attitude toward the human body. On one of her visits to Illinois later, she was appalled to discover all of us taking a shower outdoors together. Grandma evidently protested to Mother and got nowhere, because she took it up quite earnestly with Mary and me. "Your brother Bill is a lovely boy," she said. "You shouldn't spoil him. You are getting too old to bathe like that together." But we were not moved. In fact, we considered Grandma quite dirty-minded, although we realized she couldn't help herself because that was the way people were brought up in her day.

Grandpa's eight-hundred-acre ranch had many buildings. My grandparents lived in the big house, a long, rambling structure facing the southeast breeze. Some strange Persian objects adorned the living room, which was constructed of beautiful natural stone. Over the huge fireplace sat the largest bellows I have ever seen—from an old forge. My grandparents displayed a pathetic little yellow gourd—hollowed out on one side to form a cup, with the neck forming a handle, in the central place of honor. My great-grandpa Maverick had to drink out of this gourd on his long march as a war prisoner to Mexico City. I had already absorbed the attitudes of my germ-conscious father. I shuddered at hearing that Sam Maverick often got so thirsty he scooped up a drink from any old mud puddle. Between the big house and the cook house was a cistern house, with a dull red tin roof and handsome diagonal green lattice. I loved to go there with a pitcher, and to hear the deep echoing noise of the water running over and back through the screening into the cistern. Besides two bedrooms and a sitting room, the cook house had an ample kitchen with a wood stove, faucet and sink, big pantry, and a "safe," a huge screened cupboard with legs sitting in little pans of water to foil ants. The great board table and two long benches stood outside on the screen porch, on a natural-rock floor that was a joy to behold and a terror to sweep.

Initially, we stayed in a little white frame house on stilts originally intended for the caretaker. Dad snorted loud and frequently about the way Texans built. "You'd think they never expected winter," he muttered, "although those northers are almost as cold as ours." While manfully striving to keep the stove full of cedar, and applying tarpaper inside in some places, he took other more desperate measures. He ordered a remarkable number of loads of manure, and piled the warm steaming mass all around the house to cut off the breezeway the stilts left under our floor. Our house was about a quarter mile from the big house and cook house, so nobody objected. I think they rather admired the gumption of the unconventional Yankee. To enjoy the beauty of her native hills, and give her children the freedom of the country and the joy of friendship with all the ranch animals, Mother did not mind these conditions, though primitive by our Winnetka standards.

Eventually, however, my parents decided to build a house of their own on the ranch—and what a house! Not every contractor would have followed Dad's specifications, but people who dealt with Dad did as he specified or faced an earthquake. The contractor's brother once told me that no one had ever built a house that way before or since in Texas. The design of the house resembled that of a boat. Each of the bedrooms had bunks built in right up against big windows. Under the bunks were drawers, and between them, a bureau with a big mirror—also built into the wall. Since the mirror was a window, the whole side of the room could be opened to the breeze and view. The wall on the opposite side was solid window, too, which permitted a fine cross breeze in hot weather. Each bedroom was just large enough to hold one chair and a washstand and give two people space to turn around in. The big living room had a magnificent fireplace and broad couch like the one Dad read stories to us on every night in Winnetka.

We attended a small, one-room schoolhouse during those months. I enjoyed it; if my own lessons were boring, I could listen to those of the others. And I found the school very easy going compared with the one in Winnetka. Only one bad thing happened to me there. I chanced to read in a science book that children of my age must sleep ten and a half hours a night to grow and develop properly. Being a serious little thing, especially about books, I worried dreadfully because I usually slept an hour or two less. Months later, lying in a hammock on the *Oonas* in Seagate Harbor, I listened to the ships' bells, getting more desperate with every half-hour. At 10:00 P.M., I burst into a storm of weeping. My not sleeping enough remained a preoccupation for years—all because of one page I read in a book at eight!

I recall one other incident vividly. We always celebrated Easter Monday with an egg hunt at our little schoolhouse. All the girls dressed in their Sunday best: pastel organdy and dotted swiss frocks and flower-decked hats. I don't know how it started, but the idyllic scene was marred, once, by some of the big boys tossing eggs at them. Maybe they just couldn't stand seeing the girls whose pigtails they had pulled looking so grownup and elegant. Suddenly our amazed eyes saw the teacher himself, Mr. Davis, join and pelt the girls. Some of the mothers had evidently been rushed that morning, for not all the eggs had boiled the due ten minutes. I'll never forget one streak of gooey yellow oozing slowly down a lavender organdy back—while the unfortunate girl sobbed bitterly and ducked round the house, pursued by the jeering males. Her real distress was too much for most of the boys. "Things have gone too far," said one of our cousins and his best friend. They started to egg the teacher and the idea caught on like wildfire. I can't remember how order was restored. This minute I can still see my cousin, "Brother Green," cowering under the schoolhouse, which stood up on stilts. First Mr. Davis boasted what he would do if he found him. Then suddenly he became very dignified and told the whole school that "Brother" and his friend were expelled. That didn't seem like fair play to us youngsters, nor, as it turned out, to our parents. They expelled the teacher instead. I think that had he just joined in the egging from sheer animal spirits, the Texans might have given him another chance— but they couldn't stand the airs of a man who would egg the girls and then lose his temper over being egged back.

At last every spring—and usually when things reached a climax of loveliness—we had to go back to "north civilization." How poignant to saddle up for the last ride with my cousin! Mary Green and I didn't say much on those rides, but our silence spoke worlds. Next morning, in a whirl of excitement, everybody gathered round to wish us good-bye—everybody except Mary Green. She was always missed that day—lit out over the hills in early morning, rather than say the horrid word. I felt bad too. But the delights of our train trip tempered my grief. We would get on the train just at the pretty time of evening. We generally had tightly clutched some basket with live mementos of the ranch, a pair of horn-frogs, or, once, four little pinkish yellow kittens. Great was the indulgence of our mother. Three kids and four cats in a compartment and a tendency to migraine—what a setup! Dad always slept in a berth outside, and who could blame him? At the very last, Grandma would press into Dad's hand a huge basket, covered with a soft white damask napkin, filled with golden fried chicken, home-baked biscuits and fresh butter, some fruit, and probably an angel food or special Maverick caramel cake. At a certain stage of nincompoopery I used to beg Mother to be like other people and let us eat in the diner. But what I wouldn't give for one of Grandma's baskets now.

II

Our household faced a major readjustment in the fall of 1913. Doris, the kind, jolly, hard-to-upset maid and nurse, who had become dear to all of us, left to marry her sweetheart, Carl. We knew that they had waited for years so that Doris could build a little store of money for them to start with, but we regretted losing her. Georgia, my baby sister, had just been born and Mother's recovery wasn't quick. We had spent the summer on the boat, barefoot and free, which had not left us any more tractable. A stream of governesses stayed with us briefly, happily shaking the dust off their feet when they saw what they were in for. Finally, and very fortunately in light of later events, Miss Russell, who soon became Sasha to us, arrived. A very conscientious, sensitive, and imaginative nurse, Sasha saw fine possibilities under our savage exteriors. She took us very intensely to her heart and sought to civilize us with love and almost no punishment. We reveled in her affection and I remember telling her once, "I like you as much as Dad and more than Mother."

During the next two years, I scarcely saw Mother. She believed firmly that all children need a little time to themselves—a little benign neglect, as she said years later. She felt that mettlesome, high-strung youngsters should not be constantly stimulated from the outside. If left to themselves, even to the point of getting a little bored, they would invent activities that corresponded to the exact needs of their development at the moment. Besides, in late 1914, Dad took Mother to a speech by Rosika Schwimmer, an internationally known pacifist and feminist. Schwimmer inspired Mother and soon led her into social activism. Schwimmer was a very intelligent and intense woman, and very sure of herself. She had more ideas in an evening than twenty people could carry out in a month. Her foreign birth and accent limited the effectiveness of her public activity for peace in America and that's where Mother came in. Mother drew the line when Rosika's demands went beyond the possible, but she did a great deal in those years and always felt Rosika wanted more. In 1915, Mother went to Washington to help found the Women's Peace Party, then attended the Congress of Women at the Hague, and afterwards met with heads of state, urging them to form a continuous conference of neutral nations to mediate the conflict. Both felt that Jane Addams compromised too much on peace and women's issues;

they thought the financial demands of running a large settlement
house like Hull House had made her too cautious. But they cooperated with her when they considered her actions appropriate. Mother
also participated in a feminist group led by Alice Paul, determined to
continue the struggle for the vote for women even into wartime.
When some suffragists said, "You shouldn't bother the President
during a war," Mother replied that there was no better time. After
all, Wilson claimed to be fighting for democracy.

When Mother returned from the Hague a foreboding coldness settled on the Winnetka house. Uncles on both sides visited and,
though they barred us from the parlor, the high voices reached us
upstairs. My parents avoided contact with each other. In that context, I recalled an unpleasant incident on the ranch that was becoming an ominous sign of things to come. I had gone into the main
closet of our house for a sweater, and my parents came into the room
from somewhere else. Their voices were loud and indignant. I was
embarrassed to come out of the closet in such circumstances. They
would think I had been eavesdropping. I waited for a while. But they
fought so long that I got impatient and finally sidled out apologet-
ically. When they didn't notice me, I realized how angry they were. I
kept hoping that the tension and trouble would pass or that I would
wake up and find that I had had a bad dream. But neither happened.
Mother's activism delayed the inevitable break. After an unsuccessful meeting with President Wilson, Rosika Schwimmer had per-
suaded Henry Ford to finance an expedition by ship to Europe to
mediate between the warring nations. Rosika wanted Mother to join
but she was unwilling to leave us in the house alone with Dad with a
divorce brewing. When Rosika explained the situation to Ford, he
said Mother should bring us along, too.

I was eleven, Mary nine, and Bill seven when we left. Mother
entrusted us to the care of a nurse, a lovely girl, one of two sisters
working in our home. But unfortunately for our discipline, she was
one of the fairest flowers of Norway; dozens of lively young students
and newspapermen on the boat could not leave her alone. After she
put us to bed and stepped out, we leapt back into our clothes and
went exploring. On our own, we would go into the meetings and
decide what animal the main speaker most closely resembled. Mother trusted Dorothy and was so involved in the administrative work of
the Ford ship, as one of Rosika's most devoted assistants, that she
didn't hear of our wanderings.

Mother didn't explain much about the trip, but I knew I hated war, and that one of the nicest people I'd ever known was Doris, our previous nurse, a German. Instinctively I disliked the smart alecks among the newspapermen; some of them, however, were much fairer than their papers. The blasts of cheap ridicule that emanated from the American papers only reinforced the determination of the delegation. We knew that in Europe, where the war's burdens pressed even neutrals, the papers and public welcomed the peace ship. One reporter, who worked for a particularly hostile American sheet, pushed me to write my impressions for her paper. I suppose that she judged from our not-too-constructive shipboard activities that anything I might say would be grist for her mill. Something about the way that she hounded me put me on my guard and when I asked Mother, she said I had no obligation to write the story. I felt greatly relieved though this postponed my entrance into journalism by a good decade. I enjoyed many of the other passengers, though, especially the young students, who had some idealism about the trip. The students treated us very well, even turned us into pets. My sister Mary, with her roguish grin and quick repartee, was especially popular.

One part of our journey on the continent bit deep into my soul. After a lot of negotiating, the Germans let our party go to the Hague through Germany on a "sealed" train at night—sea travel was no longer safe. I rode with Mother in a nice, quiet, dark compartment. To "seal" the train, the authorities tied down the cord of the window shade. I lifted the edges and looked out. Nothing could have prepared me for what I saw. The great long trains of Red Cross cars and the wounded men stunned me. Equally disconcerting was the inversion of my feminist ideals. In one town a round-cheeked, fluffy-haired policewoman directed traffic. I had read Charlotte Perkins Gilman's feminist magazine from the age of ten, and I really believed in woman's right to hold any kind of job. But I was saddened that this sweet-looking woman was a police officer because so many men were out killing other men.

III

One Sunday, after we returned home, the minister at the Congregational Church based his sermon on the text "faith shall move mountains." His words lodged in the depths of my heart, for I knew

of a mountain to be moved in my own home—my parents planned to
divorce. "I'll try faith," I thought. "Millions of people in all history
have believed. There may be something to it. I'll pray and pray, and
read the whole Bible." Quietly, when no one was about, I went to the
study—the third-floor room with a skylight where Grandfather
Lloyd had written his books. I found the family Bible, a huge thing
at least fifteen inches high and five inches thick with the rust-colored
leather binding beginning to powder. I lugged it downstairs and got
safely in my closet without meeting any curious eyes. Dad had recently ordered electric lights installed in the closets, and in the evening when I was supposed to be in bed, I would go in there and read
the Bible. Of course I knew Dad wouldn't forbid me to, but I also
knew he would laugh. And I just didn't want any talk about what I
was trying. I read and read, and came to many wonderful places. But
then I came to the begats: pages and pages, it seemed to me, of
names, one begetting the other, and on and on. Now, I had vowed to
read the Bible straight through, every word, not just the interesting
parts. I never thought of skipping the begats and going on. Doggedly
I returned, in the evening or early morning, and started another page
of begats. Yet somehow my recreant mind caused me to forget Bible
reading more and more often, until I got out of the habit. The net
result of my simple-minded determination to plow straight through
the Bible was to stop me completely, right at the begats.

My faith did not change my parents' minds, but church and Bible
school helped me through Sundays, which got grimmer as my parents became more estranged. To see friends arrayed in their best, to
giggle in the choir loft, to make up new irreverent words to the rous-
ing hymns gave me joy that I could no longer find at home. My
parents did not even stay in the house at the same time anymore. We
were not surprised when, finally, they told us there was no hope and
they would divorce. Very few people were divorced; in fact, we had
never heard of a divorce among our North Shore acquaintances. Our
sadness was compounded by shame.

In the old days when Dad said, "Let's go for a walk, I want to talk
to you," I was delighted. But now my soul winced: I knew I would
have to face more unpleasant facts. At the dinner table a few nights
before Dad left us, the poignancy of what he was about to lose came
over him and he burst into wracking, agonizing sobs. Mary, always
able to do the right thing, leapt up and put her arms around him, and

at length he could stop. I was paralyzed and I could not move or speak. Dad, the gay, the strong-willed, the always sure! I was frightened by how much he cared for us. Mother had not told us the legal grounds on which she was divorcing Dad; she merely said she could not go on because much as he loved us children, she did not believe that he was a good influence on us. Evidently they made an agreement that he would tell us the facts; and this he did, with great candor and pitiable sadness. He said that he was in love with another woman; that he thought the civilized thing to do would be to keep us in our big family home as before and for him and Mother to take turns staying with us, an equal length of time. But because of the grounds, the law gave Mother the right to have us most of the time. Instead of dividing it fairly, Dad said, she insisted on all except six weeks in the summer and a half Saturday every three weeks. He asked us whether we would rather have more time with one parent or another, or share evenly. At that period I am sure Mary would rather have had more time with him; and Bill and I probably more with Mother. Though I was very fond of Dad, I could hardly endure the way he kept talking about things, never letting us forget his intense suffering. But we could not bear to hurt anyone any more and so we all said we would rather share the time evenly, and signed a paper to that effect.

Oh, how bleak the lake shore seemed that March. And how hopeless we felt about the future. Actually, those days before the official break were our worst. We hurt to think that we'd never see our mother and father together again, but we felt better when they separated and could each talk normally with us. When they stayed together their turmoil and resentment filled the whole house. The very atmosphere became cold and mirthless. Whenever I hear people talk about staying together for the sake of the children, I shudder. Children are more sensitive than adults to the emotional climate they live in. Nothing could be worse for them than having their parents living together but constantly radiating disgust toward each other. I was miserable in the last days Mother and Dad lived together and I wrote in my diary, "I wish Mother and Dad would both die. They are suffering too much."

My faith in God did not survive the divorce. When I saw that the mountain wouldn't move, I decided that religion was just wishful thinking after all. I was greatly disappointed, but not really surprised. My faith was probably flawed all along. But my friends at the Congregational Church helped keep my mind off my problems so I continued to go. Fortunately for me a strong outside interest came into my life about this time: the Camp Fire Girls group took me in, even though they supported the war and our family did not. Among those dozen girls I met some magnificent characters. High in ideals, warm-hearted, full of fun, they brought happiness to drive out the family pain for a few hours each week. At this time I also discovered the philosophy of Marcus Aurelius, which became a lifesaver. "Which is hurting you, the fact that this unpleasant thing happened to you, or that you call it up over and over again in your mind?" Marcus asked of himself. And from his wrestling to conquer pain and annoyance and bad temper, I learned much. Perhaps Marcus Aurelius also helped me to get along with my siblings—to overlook some of the petty slights that would otherwise have caused a war. During this sad time none of us was nearly as inclined to fight as we had been. We felt very deeply we had trouble enough and we, at least, had to stay together.

The more painful the divorce struggle became, the more I determined that marriage need not be like that and mine would not be. Later Mother tried to explain, "Your father was very nervous during those years. I spent a lot of time trying to get him to relax." Dad gave me his own view a half a year before his death at seventy-one. I asked him what caused the separation originally between him and Mother—before any overt acts hardened the break. He said, "She was so inert. She wanted to rest all the time. And she wasn't satisfied just to be lazy herself, she wanted everybody else to be inert, too." Knowing how Mother in our grownup years was never idle, rarely even took time off from her peace work, art, sewing, housekeeping, or digging in the yard to read a good book, although she deeply loved them, I was astounded that this should be his abiding impression. Perhaps he misunderstood her attempt to get him, the whirlwind, to relax. Her efforts to work on Dad without telling him what the trouble was and her lack of frankness about small annoyances until they grew too deep caused explosions later. The cure for the disease, as far as I could analyze, was frankness from the beginning, and the ability to endure frankness, and a sense of humor, and the elimination of jealousy. Most of the pain in all the books I had read came from wanting to own someone. If you enjoy a person, enjoy him, I thought, but as for owning, you cannot really own what is not freely given anyway, so why fuss over a technicality?

As Mother said when we children fought and shouted, "She started it," it takes two. Dad provided plenty of causes for trouble. Dad didn't know Mother very well in some ways. He didn't understand that her modern attitudes on many things notwithstanding, she knew little of the facts of life. At fifty, she sincerely believed that masturbation would make people feebleminded and extracurricular sex demonstrated a lack of self-control that betokened severe nervous disorder. Her refusal to share us with him equally was not revenge, as he thought, but her desire to protect us from what she considered his dangerous temperament. While Dad could not seem to talk of much besides Mother's faults and her injustice to him, Mother never said anything against Dad to us, unless we pressed her hard with questions. She had lost the whole underpinning of her life for she had loved him utterly. Still she did not punish him by trying to destroy our love for him, which she knew he cherished. Yet Dad struggled with all of his eloquence, fire, and the ingenuity of love inverted to hate, to separate us from Mother physically and emotionally.

Dad, I found, had never really grown up. Although he knew the consequences of his infidelity, he was not willing to bear them. Dad was a remarkable man. His frank and genuine cordiality, his graceful originality of thought, his gallantry to women, his hale-fellow-well-met attitude toward men, rich and poor, attracted affection and friendship immediately. With his children he could be the most loving and lovable of fathers—with his wife, so thoughtful, so honest, so adoring. But the fact is, in spite of his high ideals of service to others, he was not naturally an unselfish man. Sometimes I thought he had a double nature, for he could be so cruel and unreasonable. Anger, which came upon him quickly and not infrequently, transformed him into a different person: cold, stubborn, almost unrecognizable. Then he lacked absolutely the power of putting himself in the place of another.

When I reflected on this later at Smith during another crisis brought on by Dad, I felt that had he only had to work for a living, he might have acquired some healthy self-discipline. Dad had had too many of the "devices and desires of his heart." His mother never disciplined him as a child and neither did the world, for he was protected by money. How terrific was his assault on Mother we never knew until we found some of his letters in her attic after her death.

IV

We children regretted that Mother wouldn't stay in the big house and use the chauffeur; Socialists, as we considered ourselves, we didn't like the idea of being as poor as other people one bit. No car! It was unthinkable. But we understood why Mother couldn't possibly live in a place where everything would remind her of the past. She would have returned to Texas, but Dad's court battle required her to stay in Illinois. So she rented a smaller house in Winnetka. We probably all benefited from the change. If I had gone on living at Dad's, I'd have been completely spoiled. We weren't allowed to so much as cut a piece of cake for ourselves there. Sasha, our governess, waited on us hand and foot, and though Mother didn't approve, she wasn't often around to intervene. I was glad, though, that we did not have to leave our school friends, who seemed then our one link with normal human happiness.

In the big household so dominated by Dad and the servants, I had almost lost track of Mother in the last years. Now in the small house she lived simply, as she preferred, and put thousands of dollars of her Texas money each year into peace work. We made our own beds, picked up our own things, and helped with the table and dishes on the maid's night out. Only in 1917, when I read a story on the distribution of income in America, did I realize how luxuriously we lived. After the big house, however, we had come down greatly. When we complained, Mother asked us which we thought was more important, to have a car and more people to wait on us, or to try to stop the killing of war. We knew that she was right.

Mother threw herself into the work, often spending whole days in town at the office. The house, though lonely to me, at least didn't have that cold feeling of the last year at the big house. When Mother did come home she told lots of interesting stories, and listened eagerly to the news of our day. We found many things to laugh about. But when Mother had a migraine headache, she couldn't eat, couldn't bear to hear us eat an apple or chew gum, and couldn't tolerate the leaning, pushing, and bumping of chairs that all children do.

What a miserable year for all of us! Dad struggled relentlessly against Mother. He constantly found fault with her care for our schooling, health, and general appearance. Suddenly, Dad, who had always gone barefoot in his off-white sailor suit, discovered the importance of proper grooming. He now demanded that we be impeccably brushed, combed, and manicured when he called for us every third Saturday. Mother insisted that he return us in exactly six hours. The threats that he wrote her, his fast driving, the possibility he might take us away, worried her. Every detail of our lives presented the possibility of combat. We were downhearted and often fussy. Mary, who had been so closely tied to Dad, was hard to manage. I didn't feel at ease in a high school of fifteen hundred with a preponderance of dashingly dressed and witty Wilmette girls. While they appeared in peek-a-boo blouses, lace camisoles, and long, tight black skirts slit up the back, Mother sent me in a middy blouse, blue serge skirt, and bloomers (which hung down slightly since I was growing out of the skirt). My ribbed-cotton stockings started brown but turned a sickly dung color after the first washing. A more worldly woman might have scouted around to see what was being worn to put her little girl in the swim. But Mother had the divorce and the peace and suffrage movements on her mind. Besides that, she had an almost fierce faith that I was all right and didn't need much guidance. Mother's confidence flattered me, but also left me feeling that she didn't realize how terrible it was to be so out of place.

High school intensified my problems with boys. I didn't dare talk to them. If I did go to a party, because I loved to dance, I would just be a wallflower. Mother told me I was pretty but I cried at night because I just knew I wasn't. Years later I saw a picture that proved I wasn't ugly, but at the time I could think of no other reason why boys, and people in general, always sought out Mary when they had a choice. When I was a junior, Mary was a freshman. As soon as she came to school boys invited her to go to the Junior Prom; she always had more dates than she could handle—a really popular girl who knew just how to talk to everybody. Great self-assurance. I'd have a crush on a different boy every term. I consciously chose one, saying to myself, "Who am I going to fall for now?" I would look around and idealize somebody but never speak to him. I didn't have the nerve even to say, "Hello." That's what I did every year, and if I could have said, "Hello," why I would have been thrilled. Well, I was a very unhappy girl in a lot of ways.

As the international crisis worsened, Mother focused more intensely on the peace movement. When all the proper people, including many of her best friends, began to call for joining the fight, Mother redoubled her efforts for peace. What a black day for all of us when the United States declared war! I particularly remember the paper reporting President Wilson's demand for conscription. "This is how you must read newspapers," said Mother. With bitter irony she read, " 'This is in no sense a conscription of the unwilling.' Well, when he says it is in no sense, he means it is, or he wouldn't bother to say it wasn't. And when our military men say 'We, of course, would never use submarines or poison gas,' that is because they are about to do it. Always read between the lines in a newspaper."

Naturally, at school the pressure began for subscribing to war savings stamps. "You can do whatever you like," Mother said. "I don't ask you to go against the current because of what I think. But here is why I am not buying them myself: war is not a cure for the troubles of the world; the quicker peace is made, the quicker the people will have a chance to do something about their troubles. So few people see this, that I want to put all the money I can spare into working for peace. War savings bonds are working for just the opposite." I had to agree with Mother. After the first week, I never bought any. Even on the Red Cross, Mother was an absolutist. "Instead of spending my money to patch boys up and send them out to fight again, I'd rather stop all the wounding and killing," she said. And I agreed with her on that, too.

Mother continued to entertain people who told us firsthand about the events changing the world. These visitors included Fania and Mikhail Borodin. Mikhail had escaped to America from exile under the Czar, and had studied engineering here, while working in the Socialist Party. When the Bolshevik Revolution came, he wished to return and offered his services. He soon got word that he should bring back as many skilled workers and engineers as possible. So he recruited exiles and others to take courses in the most needed branches of work, particularly machine repair, and then go to Russia. We liked his quiet humor, his slow, deep voice, and enjoyed Fania's exuberance. Although pleasingly plump, she once danced the Cossack *kazachok* for us. We youngsters copied her in squatting down and kicking our feet out forward—but only fell about the living room in heaps.

Mother gave us many lessons in those years about justice and its denial in American society. Mother was outraged when, in her work with the Women's International League for Peace and Freedom, she came face to face with Northern racism. When hosting the Prince of Dahomey, the committee tried to go out to lunch near their Chicago office. To her chagrin, Mother and her group had wandered around for some time, not welcome anywhere, at last finding only a cafeteria would seat them. "So discourteous! And right in the North! So inhuman! I was ashamed for America," she told us. Mother rejected elitism as completely as racism. Her discussion with a real estate agent about purchasing a lot ended abruptly when he mentioned what he considered an excellent selling point. Only those who could spend $10,000—quite a price then—would be allowed to build in that restricted area. Mother's reaction was immediate. "Why, I certainly hope to be able to build for less than $10,000. And I wouldn't like to be settled in a neighborhood full of snobs." So we crossed that section off the list of prospects, though our house did wind up costing more than $10,000.

Dad's efforts to break Mother's resistance continued, but our new surroundings gradually grew comfortable and familiar. My friends among the Camp Fire Girls filled in the datelessness; our activities— swimming, boating, crafts, athletic contests and singalongs—were a healthy, happy, robust challenge to body and mind. Mother started letting me choose my own clothes as long as I kept within the twenty dollars a month Dad provided, and I felt less out of place at school. I got on the high school paper with a weekly column of rhymes and quips. The paper gave me experience in writing, and in my last year, my first boyfriend. I shared a cozy office with the editor, a sophomore, the brightest, most composed, grownup boy I knew. At the last staff meeting before my graduation when the rest had left, he asked me to kiss him. I was furious because I was too shy to say yes. What kind of a man was he? He should have kissed me and not talked about it! I thought the girl was supposed to be very ladylike and reticent. She couldn't say "Yes, go ahead." But later Mary told me that a lot of them did. Nonetheless, that editor and I became close that summer, spending hours talking about everything under the sun.

====== V ======

Mother registered me for Smith when I entered high school. She didn't say I *had* to go, but knew I would have certain advantages since she was an alumna. Smith was as good as any other women's college. Mother did not insist on a women's college, but thought I might be relieved to be free of dating worries for a time while I grew up. "In a coed college," she said, "the boys usually get the important jobs in various activities. At a women's college, the girls can try everything according to their interests." Given my high school experience, her concerns seemed reasonable. I wanted to talk about the things changing my world: war, revolution, poverty. But the high school debating society excluded me because I was a girl.

In the fall of 1921 nobody from Winnetka was going to Smith except a sophomore named Marcy. On the train east I had dinner with her and two of her friends. As I leaned my right elbow on the table, I made a teaspoon jump up and dive into my suit pocket. "That must take practice," said one of Marcy's friends, chuckling. When I arrived at Smith, I multiplied the faux pas. We had soup every night at the dorm and I pulled the spoon toward me. The girls looked askance and then I noticed that they all pushed the spoon away daintily when filling it. Once again my clothes were all wrong. My stepmother, Madge, whom my father had recently married, had taken me out to get something special for my great venture away from home. She bought a soft, rich blue plush suit, and a rust-colored silk blouse—the kind of thing she needed for dress-up when she was studying nursing in Chicago. I loved the outfit but I never saw anyone wear that style at Smith and didn't dare wear it. I needed sweaters, skirts, and saddle-strap shoes. I had dresses.

More important, I knew nothing of the Smith style of talking and I soon became known as the freshest freshman in my house. Everyone expected freshmen to be quiet and deferential. But Mother always encouraged us to argue respectfully for principles in which we believed. Though still incredibly shy, I didn't have the social experience to know how *not* to be outspoken or what upset people or hurt their feelings. At Smith no one discussed national issues—things I always heard about at home. Smith girls talked a good deal about family backgrounds, weekends, clothes, professors, and classes. The divorce in my background didn't help me in these conversations, and neither did Dad's public row with Mother over custody while I was at Smith. I remember writing to Mother to ask her not to talk to reporters. Having the family's dirty laundry displayed in the press didn't appeal to me.

In general, my priorities differed so completely from those of the other girls. When a Smith girl got engaged, the rest of the house would squeal, "Ooh! Let's see the ring!" I wanted to see the boy. When, in 1924, I helped organize a mock presidential election, I realized just how few sympathized with my ideals. Bob LaFollette of the Progressive Party was not quite the radical I was, but he came closer than the candidates of the two regular parties and I supported him enthusiastically. He got fifty votes out of one thousand at Smith, with eight hundred going to Coolidge, the Republican, and the rest to the Democrat. I could only imagine how the Smith girls would have reacted had they heard about my father's political activities or known that he had recently been arrested for driving down Michigan Avenue with the Red flag flying from his Stevens-Duryea touring car. Perhaps it was just as well that most didn't follow the newspapers closely. One of the few who did often sniffed unfriendly things in my direction when I saw her. I did try to understand these girls, to see what they had to teach me, but I found little to imitate. In my courses at Smith, I put my beliefs to the test. I took my economics courses selecting only the most conservative professors. I wanted to see if they could convince me to abandon my Socialist beliefs. I really opened myself to their ideas, but I noticed that none of their theories fit the facts without making a large number of exceptions. I thought my socialism explained better what I saw around me. And so, I stuck to my guns.

At Smith, as in high school, I found good friends and stimulating activities in time. Carol Bedell, a scientist, wanted to be a doctor. She had a weak heart and hoped to find ways in medical school to deal with her own problems and those of others. We had long talks about the fundamentals. She thought that disease caused most of the world's suffering while I believed that economic injustice fostered human misery and was the major cause for disease. We rarely visited each other's rooms, but participated in many campus activities together including the orchestra, the *Weekly*, and the Press Board.

I was sorry to leave friends at Smith at graduation but excited about my plans for the next year. My mother's work to end the war and plan for a just peace afterward had turned my thoughts to Europe, and my trip on the Ford peace ship deepened my interest. My sister and I intended to sail for Europe in the fall and stay until the next summer. In spite of all our childhood battles, we had grown very close. We had no fixed plans: Mary would do some painting, I some music, and we both would study more French. Mainly though, we wanted to feel the variety of the world. My father had settled property on me, which along with generous allowances supported us nicely. Some family friends were alarmed at girls of twenty-one and nineteen going to Europe alone, but Mother's best friends were Europeans, and she trusted us.

After stops in beautiful cities from Lisbon to Trieste, we settled in Paris. Since we had to try the things in Paris most different from our life at home, we did a lot of cafe-sitting. The little saucers marked with the price of our orders would pile up beside us while we looked at everybody around and passing by. At first the cafe scene was exotic and interesting. Once Floyd Gibbons, the famous one-eyed correspondent, sat at a table nearby with a jolly crew. We watched as they bargained elaborately with a street rug seller, trying first one rug and then another on the concrete. Shortly after they bought it, they lost interest, leaving the rug behind at the cafe. I grew bored with all this cafe-sitting, especially since I didn't really enjoy drinking. Even a little drink affected me and made me feel like sleeping or dancing, neither of which could be done sitting at a table.

The British General Strike rescued me from the cafes. On May 3 the British Trade Union Congress declared a general strike, in support of striking miners against whom the government had invoked strong measures. The *New York World* cabled our Uncle John Kelley, who also lived in Paris, to cover the story. The paper's choice of Uncle John may have reflected their attitude toward the strike. He had previously covered the yacht races for the *World*. I said I wanted to go along and see this. Kelley tried to discourage me, but failing, made me promise not to tag along with him. So off we went.

After we landed, Kelley headed off at once to see newspapermen he knew at the *London Daily Herald*, including W. N. Ewer and Claude Cockburn. He told me most emphatically the people at the *Herald* had a national emergency on their hands and couldn't be bothered with youngsters. He advised me to walk around and keep my eyes open, so I roamed around London. Everybody was out on the street, waiting to see what would happen. People shed their formality: everybody talked to everybody. They paid no attention to the fact that I spoke with an American accent. I found no trace of the famous British reserve. While some doubted the wisdom of a general strike, all of the working people I spoke to believed the miners had had a raw deal and deserved support from labor.

I felt as if the strike lasted forever, but actually, in a few days, like a bolt out of the blue, came the announcement that the Trade Union Congress had called it off. I went to Poplar, the East End working-class district where I had spent most of my time, to see people's reactions. Everyone I talked to along the street seemed disgusted. "We were solid. It was really beginning to take effect. Why quit now?" People congregated in front of the union offices to see the typed notice on the outside bulletin board. "But that's just typed. It's not Smith's signature," people said, "We won't go back until we know they'll take everyone back."

Throughout the afternoon, many refused to believe the news. "The rumor may be another of their dodges. Stand firm until you hear from your unions." These were not broken men, eager to rush back to jobs. By evening, however, the evidence became too strong. Men and women gathered at the town hall to decide what to do. People, including women with babies in their arms, jammed the streets. When the mayor and union men told the people to stick together, the crowd cheered loudly. The parish priest congratulated the crowd for keeping the peace during the strike and urged them not to give any occasion to the police to break it now.

It may be true, as newspapers often report, that some riots are started by mobs bent on violence. But for myself, I've never seen a riot that the police didn't start. This was my first. While the priest spoke part of the crowd swayed like tall grass in the wind. Then I heard the noise of a motor and screams from the people. The policemen drove a truck through the crowd at twenty miles per hour. Incredibly, no one was hurt and the crowd agreed to send the priest to the police station to protest for them. The people intended to respond to the violence peacefully. But the police would not have it that way. The back doors of the van opened and some enormous police jumped out. The people made way and the priest, conspicuous in his maroon cassock, approached the officers to talk to them. One officer quickly moved to each side of the priest, and in a moment, without warning, cracked down on his balding head with their big night-sticks. Then they all ran into the crowd, swinging right and left, striking everyone in reach. In less time than I have taken to tell the story, I could see nothing but bloodied old men lying prostrate on the street. One young girl confronted the police, "You ought to be ashamed! Is that a man's work, knocking down old men?" A cynical sergeant stopped and said, "Take care miss. It would be a shame if the horses would come and you'd be disfigured for life, wouldn't it?"

When I asked the policemen why they had attacked, their answer was sickeningly familiar. "Rowdies on the edge of the crowd insulted and provoked us," they said. I hadn't seen the rowdies and neither had anyone else. "Aha!" I thought, "the good old American blanket excuse." Blame violence against working people on working people by accusing them of committing "crimes" no one reliable had seen. The next morning I read an account of the police quelling a "riot" in Poplar. I called the paper to tell them they were mistaken, but the editor said, "That's old news now—too small a matter to bring up again." So much for "objective" journalism. My experiences in the strike made a lasting impression and confirmed what I already suspected. At college, friends had sometimes asked me if I believed in class struggle. London had given my customary answer painful substance: "I don't believe in it, I see it."

When I returned to Paris after the general strike, cafe-sitting and sightseeing seemed more trivial and dull than ever. In grammar school, in my Camp Fire group, and even at Smith, I saw some denied the joys of childhood and adolescence. I knew some girls gave up school or sacrificed their private dreams to help support or care for their families. I thought them heroines for they made me acutely aware of how I had been pampered. I had wanted to work at a real job in high school, but Mother felt that I was too high-strung and needed relaxation in the summers. I resolved in Paris, far from family control, to share, albeit briefly and only partially, the experience of the working class.

To make the experience feel more real, I set a limit on what I could spend before I got a job. The women waiting in the hiring lines outside the factories spoke kindly to me. "You are not with your family?" they exclaimed. "Who will pay the rent? Factory wages won't do that." One angelic-looking girl advised, "You will have to find a serious boyfriend and, alas, too few are serious." I had no luck at various factories. Suddenly, when my money had just about run out, I got two jobs at once. A factory making Pullman cars (the Wagon-Lits) wanted me that afternoon, and one making typewriters (NAP) offered to let me start the next morning.

My allowance prevented me from feeling the frustration and insecurity familiar to ordinary workers living on a meager income. Though I decided to live on my salary, I always knew that I could go to the bank for money any time if my resolve weakened. My first job with the Wagon-Lits lasted one afternoon. I stood for the duration in front of three thirty-inch boards, bearing down on the polishing cloth with both hands, pressing round and round with a circular motion. Muscles ached under my collar bone that I never knew I had. And the job was so dull. My fellow workers did not have the luxury of quitting. The work at NAP was better. Though I stood all the time, I constantly changed motions. Lean down to the floor, pick up a rod, clamp the rod into the lathe machine, reach overhead to a big wooden lever to turn the power on, then turn the handle that pushes the drill into the end of the rod. Then unclamp the rod, put it on a pile, and pick up another from a different pile. How much better than leaning on the same three boards with the same circular motion for four hours! Theoretically, the company paid by the piece. If a worker's output did not meet a certain norm, he or she would be paid a minimum wage. My fellow workers, mostly young, explained that nobody ever exceeded the norm except the forelady and one other older worker. "But they talk about more to keep you trying."

I had been commuting on the subway from our hotel every morning, but soon I found a little local hotel with a tiny room for thirty francs a week—and no bedbugs. The Sorbonne cost twenty-five cents a day. Even so, the room ate up more than a third of my probable weekly pay. I couldn't have managed that rent alone for long. I figured out the cheapest balanced diet—bread, cheese, and tomatoes—for all meals. That way I just squeaked by.

Manual labor under factory conditions got old very fast. Drilling those endless rods, I decided that mindless repetition insulted the abilities of thinking, feeling human beings. But I thought that constant, high-speed intellectual decisions made under pressure every minute strained the nerves and physique. An ideal society wouldn't divide its people into classes in which each got only one activity or the other, but would give all a combination of both. My diet soon made me sick—all those tomatoes and cheese bits came back. When I heard that my mother was coming with my younger siblings, I quit. I lasted less than three weeks as a proletarian, but my experience reinforced my convictions. That so many eked out an existence that way so a few, like my family, could live in luxury was insupportable. But, in a strange way, my job also gave me confidence. For the first time I had found and held a job by which I could earn my keep, barely. I felt reassured—as if I had solid ground to stand on for the first time.

Mother decided to live in Geneva to take a closer look at the operations of the League of Nations. Living with my family with no definite work sounded deadly and I was becoming more and more anxious to get into journalism. It was almost a family tradition; moreover, the idea of having a job that would satisfy my own curiosity seemed perfect. The general strike had demonstrated to me once again what my parents had long thought: the mainstream press refused to report on the lives and problems of workers and the poor. Breaking into print took some doing. I had tried to expose the fallacious reports of the Poplar "riot" in a story I mailed to *The Nation*. But their editors didn't know me and the story reached them two weeks after the fact. Carl Haessler, a family friend, gave me credentials from the Federated Press, but that didn't get me into all the meetings for Federated Press was not a wire service—stories were handled by mail. The next time I was in London I decided to find out if the *London Daily Herald* had a correspondent in Geneva. By this time Kelley had gone back to America. All alone I entered the sacred precincts, so desirable and so forbidden to a mere young American twerp. The charming foreign editor, W. N. Ewer, received me most graciously. "Why didn't you come round?" he asked when he heard I had been in England during the general strike. He sounded indignant at Kelley for keeping me away and gladly credentialed me.

I still don't know how I walked alone into the great marble lobby of the League of Nations as a foreign correspondent for the *London Daily Herald*. I was so shy anyway that I hated to sit on the long seat of a streetcar facing the other side. I could only relax if sitting behind another seat in the transverse ones. The other women journalists— four or five in total—were all much older than I. The knots of reporters and delegates turned their heads as I passed, which disturbed me. I didn't realize for years that they were not looking critically at me; rather, the eye tends to follow a moving object. I read several newspapers—mercifully short in Europe—to get an idea what the issues were, and I enjoyed trying to get to the bottom of things. I learned little at the formal meetings, which consisted mostly of long, tedious speeches for the record translated from English to French or vice versa. The lively conversation of the experienced journalists gave me more of an idea of what was happening. If the older reporters sometimes patronized me, they also usually treated me well. Mine was a gentle apprenticeship.

===== **VI** =====

I couldn't go home without visiting Russia. I had applauded with my father when the workers and peasants overthrew the Czar. My father's friends and his leftist newspapers and magazines described the new system and I dreamed of seeing Russia myself. I had even made some preparations for such a trip in hopes that someday it would come my way. I took Sidney Fay's Russian history courses at Smith. Some language lessons from a Lithuanian graduate student supplemented my own work with a Russian grammar and dictionary.

Mother did not like the idea of my going alone at twenty-three. I must admit rumors about the Soviet Union and stories in the Western press, even occasionally the Socialist sheets, would not inspire the confidence of a mother. I recall some of the most lurid: the Bolsheviks "nationalized" women along with the country's other assets, and no lady's virtue was safe. Seven million children, orphaned by civil war and famine, wandered through the streets in packs robbing anyone who crossed their path. To fend them off, visitors to the Soviet Union carried pounds of candy that they could throw by the handful if accosted. While the children scrambled, the victim could slip away. A secretary at one of the embassies carried an extra trunk that held nothing but chocolates. Whiskered, free-loving Bolsheviks crept about with a bomb in each hand and pocket, and a dagger in their teeth. Could the Revolution really have gone so wrong? I had to find out. Luckily, about this time, a woman from the Quaker famine relief mission in Russia visited Mother and told her that conditions were poor, but I would be safe!

Dad viewed the trip skeptically. Dad's politics in general had swung dramatically to the right after the working class rejected his bid for the Senate. He could not forgive the workers for voting against any Socialist. The American Socialist and Communist parties disappointed him. The Communists grew increasingly doctrinaire and he couldn't bear Party discipline, which he considered regimentation. He believed that Socialists and other activists came to him only when they needed money; he wondered if he had any real friends in the Movement. He raised a considerable sum to bail out Wobbly leader Big Bill Haywood, only to have Haywood jump bail and head for the U.S.S.R. The money didn't bother him as much as the fact that Haywood, who had been arrested with twenty-six men, left the others to face the court without their leader. Dad considered him a deserter, and was deeply disillusioned. The reports of repression in the Soviet Union seemed more plausible to Dad as he became estranged from the American left. Finally, he washed his hands of it all. "Marx was right," he said. "The emancipation of the working class will be the work of the workers themselves, and I'm going to leave it to them." I felt Dad's disillusionment but didn't share it. For all the bad reports, many admitted that the Soviets had undertaken exciting, creative, and humane measures to improve the whole nation. I told Dad I couldn't reject the Revolution without seeing the Soviets in action.

I took a train to Moscow, which meant I had to change at the border since Russian tracks were wider than those of Western Europe. My introduction to the Soviet people came on the very frontier. The Russian porters, big and cheerful, wore natural linen shirts with collar and side placket embroidered in red and black. Unlike their European counterparts, they refused tips. I must have fallen for some of the Western propaganda for when I saw that my berth was comparable to that of the Western train, I was surprised. The train came quite near Moscow before I noticed the city. Low, two-story wooden or stucco houses of all colors were the most common buildings. Red brick factories and the spectacular golden domes of the churches stood prominent against this backdrop. The biggest dome, with a ton of real gold, blazed in the morning sun. A tower that looked like a wire wastepaper basket rose above everything else, however. A fellow passenger told me it was the radio of the Trade Unions.

My enthusiasm flagged a bit after I got off the train. Nobody met me in Moscow and, though I hadn't really expected anyone, I felt lonesome. I got into one of the *drozhkies* lined up outside the station and gave the address that I had carefully practiced. The wooden wheels rattled and bumped on the uneven cobblestones. The driver's badly worn clothes were a dull brown. Everybody seemed to be wearing either brown, khaki, or gray. The wind blew dust at me from among the cobbles. Though so far north, Moscow was as hot as Chicago! Up close, all the buildings looked rundown rather than quaint or picturesque. The whole scene depressed me.

I settled into a quiet, clean hostel run by some Quaker ladies in the city. This restful place initially offered none of the adventure I had been taught to expect around every corner in Russia. So I ventured out shortly after arriving to learn from my own experience about this revolutionary city. My education began at my first stop, the post office. In my hopelessly shy state, I mumbled very softly, "Please give me some stamps." The clerk glanced out from behind the desk only a moment and then went on reading her paper. A husky Russian strode past me and in a near-Chaliapin bass exclaimed, "Give stamps," in the familiar form used by workers and peasants. The clerk put down her paper and served him, and when I did likewise she waited on me. I decided she just thought if I really wanted something I'd make my wishes known, as the Russians did.

Another early encounter occurred in a little restaurant, a stony cellar with four tables. A big, fierce-looking man with bristling black moustache sat at the next table. He leaned over toward me. "What now?" I thought. "Citizeness, will you lend me your knife to cut my soup?" At first I thought I had misunderstood because of my very faulty Russian. Then I looked down—sure enough, a big slab of meat covered the bottom of my bowl, too. In Russia, people needed more than a spoon to eat borscht. I knew that the Soviets thought "citizen" or "citizeness," salutations with antecedents in the French Revolution, the way for a Russian to address most of his countrymen. "Miss," "Mrs.," and "Mister" recalled noble titles now abhorred. "Comrade" was reserved for fellow workers. I was touched to be called "citizeness" by this Russian, who must have seen by my clothing that I was an outsider.

When I rode the streetcars and buses, I noticed that everybody in Moscow, a city of two million, seemed to know everybody else. People who got on at widely separated points soon started talking as easily as two old friends exchanging the latest chapters in a continuing story. When my Russian improved, I realized that they did not say hello, or greet each other by name, for, in fact, they didn't know each other. They had just seen or thought of something they wanted to comment on, and they counted on a lively response. The fact that they had not met their neighbor on the bus before in no way inhibited them from self-expression. That secure friendliness all around me was a powerful antidote to my shyness. Not much "alienation of modern man" there. I wondered, at first, if on long rides they talked about their souls as Russians always seemed to do in novels. The answer, I found, was sometimes.

The poverty around me weighed heavily. I looked up Albert Rhys Williams, a writer, whose enthusiastic reports about Russia had been my staple fare before the trip. "How is it possible," I asked him, "that in ten years things are still so poor here?" He replied, "They haven't had ten years." In any case, he said that I couldn't get the feel of the place in the city and I should go with him to the village where his wife was making a movie. I did and what I saw and heard changed my perspective. Williams reminded me that, in addition to the losses of World War I, Russia had suffered a Civil War in which the armies of seven different nations had fought on eleven separate fronts within the country. Famine and typhus followed the bloodshed and many skilled workers and managers abandoned the country. "It's a wonder anything works at all," he concluded. "If it does, it's a tribute to what cooperation can accomplish when it doesn't have to pay tribute to capital."

The village justified his position. The well-fed peasants enjoyed robust health. I couldn't translate their conversation, but noted their tone. They spoke with great vigor and cheer—none seemed restive or unhappy. The visit frustrated me though. I wanted to understand these Russians without a translator. The peasants tantalized me and I resolved to learn the language quickly. On my way back to the city, one man unwittingly strengthened my good impression. I walked the train platform, in my different clothes and shoes and big round tortoise-shell glasses, obviously a foreigner. A middle-aged man walked up and spoke to me in German. "Freedom is what we don't have," he said. He was well educated, one of the "former people" who had enjoyed many good things under the Czar that he lost after the Revolution. I was delighted that, in spite of his complaint, he felt free to voice his criticism to a perfect stranger in a public place. The Western press had given a very different impression.

The Quakers held meetings at the hostel every Sunday. Followers of Leo Tolstoy, who shared their belief in nonviolence, sometimes came to the meetings where I met them. I remember Vladimir Chertkov, Tolstoy's secretary, with his large head and intense eyes. Another, Antonin, a smaller, thinner man, had been jailed for his anarchist-pacifist beliefs, and would be again. The widow of Tolstoy's son Andrei, Olga Konstantinovna, came with her daughter, Sofia Andreevna Tolstaia Esenina, who was almost twenty-eight. Within a week of our meeting, Sonia, as she was called, invited me to rent an extra room in their apartment. They probably had a spare room only because they were related to such a distinguished writer. I leapt at the chance. To practice the language in a Russian family— and such a family! To accommodate me, Mrs. T. moved into the maid's room and the maid slept on the bench in the kitchen. Marfusha, a tiny, great-hearted peasant from *Yasnaya Polyana*, the old estate, had a slight hump in her back and a gnomelike face that always smiled. She had been with the family for years and loved them dearly, though I think she found that I took some getting used to. Once she saw me cleaning my fingernails and asked what I was doing. When I told her, she dismissed me saying, "Well, I don't have time for such vanities."

Sonia was a highly intelligent person with a rich sense of humor. Her mother told me once that she needed to have a young person in the house who knew nothing of her tragedy. Before I came, she said, Sonia had been married to Serge Esenin, a Soviet peasant poet whose work celebrated village life. Sonia married Esenin after he and Isadora Duncan, his first wife, separated. She loved and admired him, though he drank terribly. No one knew exactly why he finally killed himself, but his suicide shattered Sonia. Mrs. T. said she would sometimes lie in bed with her face to the wall for hours on end. When I met her, Sonia had lots of friends, writers, actors, artists. In the evening half a dozen would gather in her ten-by-twelve-foot room. The liveliness next door was seductive. Everyone participated in the conversation. No little knots of separatists formed. The discussions rose to a crescendo like a symphony, each adding something, then suddenly fell to nothing after someone expressed a stunning thought. I was all the more eager to learn the language.

Though Sonia criticized some of the policies of the Bolsheviks, she acknowledged that the Revolution had offered opportunities to people who had a right to them. Her favorite time was the hardest materially: when war communism was in effect. People had no money, but would barter and share. If a neighbor found some potatoes, she would share with all around her, as would the Tolstoys if a peasant friend brought them bread. "There was a wonderful spirit. Now it is getting to be each for himself again. It doesn't feel so good." Sonia acknowledged the good the Communists did for women and children, workers and peasants. She admitted that the Bolsheviks supported the arts, even if they denied recognition to some talented people whose work strayed from the Party line.

What she saw of the West impressed her—but often not favorably. Once Sonia said she would like to meet some of my American friends, so I invited the wives of some correspondents for tea. They spent the time talking about supplies they could or couldn't get. After they had gone Sonia asked me if most women in America were so absorbed with material things. I said I thought the women's preoccupation understandable. They couldn't get so many things in Russia that they were used to. But I admitted that Americans devoted a lot of effort to acquiring material things. "Oh!" Sonia exclaimed, "I think if I were surrounded by those people steadily, I would become a Bolshevik in a week."

Sonia worked in two museums, the Writers' Museum and the special Tolstoy Museum. I didn't know how she could hold her jobs since she didn't get up until one or two. When I asked, she replied, "They know I'll do my work." Sure enough, when Sonia had to prepare many special exhibits for Tolstoy's centenary, she worked day and night, often sleeping on the museum tables, instead of coming home. Like most Russians, she was not methodical. The exhibit itself was totally Russian. The authorities had decided that the museum needed a fresh pastel wash for the great event. But on the big day the job was only half done. However, the pictures and exhibits were breathtaking. The museum displayed five handwritten drafts of *War and Peace*. Apparently, Tolstoy was inspired to improve every clean copy he saw. The wife who bore him thirteen children produced readable copy from each of his revised drafts. Sonia said that Tolstoy's living habits took a toll on his wife also. When he adopted the simple life, he insisted that peasant food be served at his end of the table. His followers gathered around him at that end and criticized his wife for serving the usual bourgeois food to the other guests. Tolstoy did not simplify her life much.

I had planned to stay a month, but I had seen just enough to know I needed more time. I returned to Geneva to tell Mother I wanted to live in Moscow for a year, to say good-bye to Mary, Georgia, and Bill, and to pick up my winter clothes. "So, you left your violin there!" Mother exclaimed. "You were pretty sure I'd let you go, weren't you?" Of course I was. In Geneva, I picked up a few things for the Tolstoys. When I had asked them what I could bring them from "outside," their requests were very modest. "Bananas," exclaimed Sonia lovingly. "We haven't had any for years." Her mother wanted a few lemons, which were sometimes hard to get. Marfusha asked for fine sharp pins and needles for the local product was coarse.

I returned to Russia with new resolution. Perhaps the revolutionary ideas had already infected me. I was tired of pretending to be an observer of life. "Ye Gads!" I said to myself. "You can't even observe intelligently until you've been through a little action." I wanted to whet my steel against the real forces of the world—near enough so I could feel the shock, and enjoy the battle. That is the only way I would know if there was steel in me—or just sawdust or jelly. I applied myself seriously to learning Russian and writing. I did not take any lessons, but spent many happy hours each day with a newspaper and my dictionary and, when stumped, asked Sonia. Though amused by my struggles, she actually enjoyed explaining her mother tongue. My ear was not as finely tuned as hers. Over and over she tried, for instance, to get me to hear and say the difference between "Z i a," "z ya," and "z soft sign i a." They all sounded alike to me. But I made reasonable progress. On the other front, things went a bit more slowly at first. The British Trade Union Congress published the *London Daily Herald*, which accredited me. But the Congress had just broken off its ties with the Soviet trade unions and didn't care to print much news of Russia. My stories rarely got into the *Herald*. Since I sent carbons to Federated Press, I knew they saw the light of day somewhere.

Yet I soon felt the frustrations common to all young writers. I got a letter from my agent saying he couldn't place a feature article I had written on business in Russia. Editors wanted somebody with an established reputation for that sort of thing. But I couldn't begin my career with an established reputation and, a fellow correspondent who had that reputation had said mine was a good article. Somebody, I felt, ought to have been telling American businessmen about the greatest commercial vacuum in the world's history. Still I could see what the agent meant. An unknown could only expect papers to take amusing or picturesque pieces, or those they could verify on internal evidence.

In the meantime, I happily went about the business of discovering Russia. In the process I saw, and sometimes met, many interesting people. Once, I sat four rows behind Stalin and Bukharin in a small theater. They had come to judge a contest of essays on the play. The audience noticed them at the first intermission and clapped sporadically as they hurriedly escaped. In the second intermission, when the management announced why they had come, the audience applauded a lot and most everybody stared at them and smiled. On the way out people all filed past them—no security people stood guard. Most were friendly, though I saw one old man come down and stand about five feet behind them, staring at the backs of their heads as though they were the most dreadful thing he had ever contemplated. A friend had been in this same theater when Rykov was present a month before. She told me that Stalin and Bukharin got nothing like the hand he did—Rykov's was a deafening thunder. But that may also have depended on the audience. Rykov came on a first night when Party members dominated the crowd. However, Stalin and Bukharin's audience lurked around grinning until the attendant asked them to please move on. I lacked the brass to go up to the lions and get acquainted as a correspondent.

In November, a party of American and Russian trade union organizers came to Moscow on the Trans-Siberian train from China. They had been working at the invitation of Mme Sun Yat-sen, the widow of the founder of the Chinese Republic. When Chiang Kai-shek came to power, he did not relish strong unions. So he banned them, executed some leaders, and expelled the foreign organizers. In protest, Mme Sun, his sister-in-law, left with them. I was fortunate enough to meet the group in Moscow. I also met Anna Louise Strong of Seattle, a big, buxom woman with ever rosy cheeks. Nothing seemed to phase her permanently, although she could stage a spectacular explosion when thwarted by red tape. While she knew that Russia had problems, she believed the Soviets did their best for their people. Because the American press printed only the bad parts about life in Russia, and so much that had no foundation at all, she almost never included anything negative in her own stories. The good things she wrote about really happened, no doubt about that. But by leaving out the bad entirely, she failed to convince some of her readers. Her reports were a good antidote, though, to the one-sided picture being given by most of the American press.

A lovely red-headed American girl, Rayna Prohme, had been working with Chinese textile workers, and Vincent (Jimmy) Shee-han, a freelance writer, had been traveling with her. Rayna said to me cordially, "You must come and see me when I get settled—I have a lot to tell." But a few days later I heard that she had taken sick. The doctors discovered a brain tumor and she died within a few days. Fania Borodin, who had returned with Rayna from China, invited me to join in the funeral procession from an outlying district to the main crematorium, where a service would be held. "Come at 10:00 A.M. sharp," she said. "You don't want to miss us." I obeyed—then we waited, and waited, and waited. A little after 11:00 we set out, marching too slowly to keep warm in the cutting November wind and sleet. The small band droned the sad red funeral march over and over, some of the horns off key. We got to the B Boulevard at 12:30, and I had promised to be at the Quakers' at 1:00 for a Thanksgiving Day dinner. So I left the procession and took the tram to the Quakers'. When I told them where I had been, they got very excited. "An American girl? From China? Here?" They turned down the oven, which was beginning to smell most tempting, and all rushed out to join the procession I had just left. I was too chilled to join them. That's how it happened that I did not meet my husband until two years later. Harvey's group got started late and did not join the march until the A Boulevard! We missed by a few blocks.

The funeral gave me a taste of how callous Americans could be abroad. Bill White returned from the proceedings quite upset. He had been trying to help Sheehan, who was in love with Rayna and completely desolated. With it all over, Jimmy seemed to be a little relaxed on the way home in the streetcar. Suddenly two American women, evidently just tourists, sitting behind them in the streetcar began cackling. "Did you go down to the fire chamber too? Wasn't that something? When the fire hit she sat up as if she were alive!" When I heard what had happened, I was ashamed of the women's heartlessness.

Shortly after the funeral, the Soviets celebrated the Tenth Anniver-sary of the Revolution, which I covered for the *Herald*. It was the first street celebration I saw in Russia. Early on the great day, groups of workers gathered in all the streets leading to Red Square. Russians, with no foreknowledge of a radical future, had named the square in ancient times. "Red" can mean handsome in Russian. In fact, the Russian word for beautiful can also be rendered "especially red." The authorities did not permit traffic to disrupt the columns of marchers converging toward the huge square. As in all old fortress cities, the boulevards of Moscow radiated out from the center. People filled each one, waiting, stopping, starting, and stopping again, finally meeting in Red Square. Here and there an accordian played and the marchers danced. Some people wore festive peasant clothes. Every group carried banners, naming their workplace and cheering "Long live" this or that. Occasionally a militiaman tried to pin me down to some group, but I showed my press pass and hurried ahead. I stood with the other correspondents on a raised platform near the government leaders in the square, but I kept my eyes on the people in the streets. First came the military parade, including some ugly big guns on trucks. Then the cavalry staged a remarkable demonstration: they galloped at full speed, picking off impossibly small targets with their sabers. Finally, the people, workers and peasants, from so many different enterprises, entered the square. They kept their holiday spirit in spite of the many hours they waited in the streets.

Watching all day tired me, but I had to go to the press department to send my story to the *Herald*. I was slow writing, as usual, but finally presented it to the censor in triumph. When he passed the story, I thought I was home free. But when I went to wire it, the operator asked if I had a special permit to get press rates. Nobody had mentioned that before. I went back to ask the censor to help me, but he said he couldn't take the responsibility. I told him this was my only chance after months of blackout to get some of Russia's story before a trade union audience in Britain. The answer was still *nyet*. I probably cried. I remember for sure that the stupidity and waste of the opportunity hurt me to the core. I could have sent the story straight rate at a cost of fifty dollars. By that time, angry, I refused to spend money out of my own pocket. In any case, I didn't have a lot of extra money then. Once again, my story didn't see print in the *Herald*.

On December 28, Sonia took me to my first Russian cultural meeting. The Soviets held a memorial for her husband Esenin on the anniversary of his death. Sonia got tickets for me and some friends, though she did not sit with us. She stood backstage holding the hand of Anton Chekhov's widow, Olga Knipper, the renowned actress. Knipper had starred on the stage all her life, but the thought of making a speech terrified her. I didn't expect much of a memorial meeting to a dead poet, but I couldn't hurt Sonia's feelings by not going. Well! How wrong I was! The atmosphere of the whole square outside the hall was electric: as soon as we got off the streetcar, men and women came up to us with a desperate query, "Have you got an extra ticket?" For the two blocks to the theater, eager people offering their money for a ticket besieged us. The same thing happened in the packed lobby. One tall, dark, young Red Army officer had taken the Trans-Siberian train from Vladivostok, a twelve-day ride, to attend this meeting. And now, he had no ticket! Henry Wadsworth Longfellow Dana, an American in our group, finally wangled him a place in his box as a translator.

Lively Russian audiences never merely sat and listened to speakers. At first I thought they were throwing spitballs at them, but my hosts explained that members of the audience wrote notes to the speaker containing questions and observations and tossed them toward the stage. Whoever the notes fell near would toss them on. Listeners in the highest gallery could have their thoughts considered. Every so often the speaker glanced through the notes. Sometimes a dark look would come over his face. Russians also felt free to tell a speaker to sit down when they had heard enough. The representative of the government received an extra lot of these notes during his speech. Finally, when, true to the Party line, he called Esenin a proletarian poet, many in the audience cried, "It's a lie!" The audience booed and stamped on the floor until the official retreated. They knew Esenin had gloried in the peasants and the simple old life of the villages; he wrote sadly of the locomotives, black monsters devouring the beautiful countryside. When poets and other speakers came on, the audience regained enthusiasm. Sometimes the hall vibrated with excitement. One thing was obvious to me: in that year the people did not fear to criticize the authorities.

I got to know all kinds of people, just by asking my way. These people, in turn, taught me much about Russia. One acquaintance was Nizov, an older man who looked as if he had suffered hardship. A tinsmith, he now worked in an artel, a cooperative formed usually by handicraft workers who made things not produced in Soviet factories. I gathered that though Nizov did not find the materials he needed to make a living easily, he understood why and still supported the Revolution. Sometimes he would come to talk about life here and in America, but most often he took me to museums. The small "Without-God-nik" museum was full of exhibits that pointed up all the inconsistencies the authorities could find in the orthodox religion. A huge pile of pieces of "wood from Jesus' cross," and an equally enormous pile of nails from it had been collected from thousands of Russian churches. Clerics had taught that touching them would cure all kinds of diseases. Museum posters illustrated the scientific way to treat disease. Nizov also took me to the Museum of the Revolution. Vivid displays of popular struggles reached further back in history than I had expected of Bolshevik-designed exhibits. The Bolsheviks gave credit where credit was due. They did not suggest that all ideas of revolution began with them. We came out early and I expected to do something more, but Nizov said: "You have seen many things that you will want to think about, so we will not do the art museum today. I will take you home and say good-bye."

After Nizov came a few times, Sonia warned me that he was not my type. I never thought he was, nor had he, I am sure. He never made a pass at me, or even hinted at one. Sonia noted that he was simple, not intellectual or polished. I had to agree, but I knew he was a very sensitive man. One day he arrived after the mail had brought very good news about my father. Nizov said a few things and I thought I answered all right. I don't think my friends at home would have noticed, but he suddenly announced, "I see you have something on your mind; I will come back some other day."

Truly, I did more thinking in Russia than ever before in my life. When I lived according to habit, I didn't think. Now that everything seemed upside down, I thought constantly. Once I noticed a boy about eleven staring at me and laughing hard. "Why?" I asked and he smiled in a very friendly manner and said, "*Ochki*." I didn't know that meant glasses till I got home. Those big round dark rims drew his attention. When I knew more language I got into many conversations, which usually started like this: "My, you look funny! Where did you fall from?" When people stared or seemed to whisper about me, I felt embarrassed. But in Russia they came right up with a friendly smile and said what was on their mind, and I didn't mind. I didn't spend my time wondering and worrying about what they thought of me. When I answered "America," a raft of questions followed. Did we really have skyscrapers and lots of cars? I lost count of the number of times a Russian invited me home to dinner to tell all about America. The Russians were also curious about me personally: how could my family let me go so far away at my age? Why wasn't I married? How could I stand such an uncultured country after living in America?

I came to understand that "cultured" had a special meaning in public discussions: cultured people were careful about sanitation and did not spit on the floor. On the main hall of the public library I saw a cartoon exhortation saying, "The books belong to us all. Do not use them to step on to reach a high shelf. Do not leave them out in the rain." Another poster decried the ultimate outrage: "Do not use books for pot lids" was inscribed below a gruesome picture with some of the spaghetti crawling out under the book like worms. All the drawings were funny, sort of a reduction to the absurd, not likely to be forgotten. And all were part of the push to be cultured. Citizens, take off your outer boots, be cultured. Citizens, leave your coats in the garderobe, be cultured.

When the ordinary Russians said *kulturnyj*, they did not mean loving poetry and music and theater—they took that for granted. They meant technical matters—like neatness and being on time. I had to admit there *was* room for improvement in those things. But sometimes the Russians' "uncultured" ways seemed best. If Russians could be very late, they were not annoyed when I was late. If I didn't come at all, they cheerfully assumed I had something else I wanted to do. They expected me to make similar allowances for them. I knew they'd be pleased to see me, but understanding if something else came up. The Russians' strong sense of human solidarity warmed me and my shyness evaporated. Once, sitting in a crowded bus, I leaned over to tie my shoelaces. I felt a gentle arm across my shoulders and a woman exclaimed anxiously, "What's with you, darling?" She thought I had fallen over in pain. Then we had a long conversation about everything in the world, and I got another invitation to dinner.

The buses and streetcars cost almost nothing, were always crowded, and were often instructive. Certain people were allowed to avoid the push and get on the front end: pregnant women, war wounded, the handicapped. Once I saw a rosy-cheeked woman, the picture of health, get on at the front. Though she didn't seem to fit any of the categories for preferential boarding, no one challenged her. Fortunately, she didn't get off soon. And after a few stops I worked my way up and asked her why she got on in front. She bubbled with enthusiasm. "I am just a cleaning woman at our factory, but our fellow workers thought enough of me to elect me their representative to the Moscow Soviet [council]. In that work I have a lot of things to do around town, so I was given a permit to enter in front. They didn't want me to waste time." I asked her if she was a Communist. "Not yet," she said. "You have to prove you are good enough before they take you. But I've applied."

This young woman was a true product of the Revolution. Old Russian customs often degraded women. The government reassigned the village land every ten years in proportion to the number of souls per family. But the authorities didn't count women as souls for this purpose. So when a woman bore a daughter, her husband would sometimes beat her. She had produced one more to feed but no more land. The men had a sick proverb: "Beat your wife, then listen. If she is still breathing, she is still deceiving you, and needs more beating."

Lenin and his wife Krupskaya wanted to change all that. "Every cook must learn how to run the state," he said. At the time I was there, the Soviets were visibly working to elevate women, to broaden their options, to offer them a life in which they could be healthy, happy, and free. The Bolsheviks adopted a policy called "*vydvizhenstvo*," "moving forward." The Party urged every factory and office to push their best women into positions of greater responsibility. The Soviets asked factories to provide safe and constructive day care so women would not have to worry about their babies while they worked. Articles in the press and on factory bulletin boards repeated the message. I didn't hear resentment from male workers on this affirmative action policy. I'm not sure why, but perhaps the smallness of the pay differential between jobs had something to do with it.

The Bolsheviks used every possible medium to get the message out and often did so with a fair amount of humor. One movie, *The City of Light*, told the story of a young woman who feared her husband was unfaithful. The heroine, a pretty peasant, had married a handsome factory worker. The movie showed much of the factory, but the skating rink at the Workers Club formed the backdrop for the prettiest scene. The poor, unsophisticated little peasant, who couldn't skate, saw her husband having a great time with one of the beautiful, sporty women from his factory. When the sporty woman came to the heroine's home with a lavender note for her husband, the heroine became nervous. She couldn't read, but the old lady across the hall, who also couldn't read, said lavender *always* meant a love note. The little peasant was furious and ran away. But when she nearly froze in the snow, she decided to come back and simply ignore her husband. She studied reading and writing on the sly; she got a job in the factory, bobbed her hair, and flirted with other men. Now her husband became convinced *she* was unfaithful. When, at last, she could read, she took out the lavender note with great trepidation. The love note began with a tender, "Comrade" and continued, "Don't you think you ought to start your wife in the class for illiterates?" Of course, husband and wife reconciled at a public meeting—where else?

The Bolshevik divorce laws often freed women from alcoholic or abusive men. The Soviets tried to let all Russian women know they had the right to leave violent spouses and drunkards. The first scene in one play, acted in a village outside Moscow, was set in the countryside before the Revolution. A peasant woman, a mother who had just delivered a daughter, wept in the kitchen. In the next scene the daughter, Katya, now a woman, was also married. Katya's husband, Ivan, had been celebrating Easter for days. He came home very drunk and beat her until he passed out. Though she could barely walk, she went to her father, begging him to take her back. But her father wouldn't have her. "All men who love their wives beat them," he said. "Your husband feeds you well and I can't feed another. Go back and do your duty." But Katya heard rumors that the revolutionary laws said women had as much right to land as men. Women could divorce easily by going to an office. The children would stay with the mother who had borne them. When a Communist woman came from the city to talk to the women of the village, Katya sought her out. The Communist quickly showed Katya how to get a divorce, her children, and all of the land except a small parcel on which Ivan would have to support himself.

Outraged at this turn of events, Ivan threatened to beat Katya again. But now, alerted, the village Soviet warned him that times had changed, and he would be punished severely if he did. Ivan decided to remarry, but none of the women would have him. They sympathized with Katya, and had no desire to suffer at his hands as she had. Ivan became depressed and lonely. A friend on the Soviet suggested that if Ivan "tried to be comradely with his wife," he might like it and she might return. In the last scene, years later, Katya got dressed for a meeting; Ivan stayed home to care for the children. Katya, now on the Soviet, was trying to raise interest in schools, prenatal care for mothers, and classes for illiterates. In the last line of the play, Ivan said, "Give it to them! I like to see my wife waking people up. Some of them haven't a glimmering that a woman is a person. The blockheads!"

The Soviets were as concerned about children as their mothers. They strove to reach high ideals: to educate mothers on health and diet before and after their babies' birth, to be certain that no Russian children would go hungry, and to offer all an education. If the Soviets didn't realize all their goals, the effort itself seemed noble. They developed a Socialist science of pedagogy to raise the quality of education. The Soviets ran experiments on the influence of the collective on character, and on quantity and quality of work accomplished. For example, they found kids could put out more muscular force in front of the crowd than by themselves. But children did work that required higher intellectual judgments (such as building arguments against a certain thesis) best alone.

The Party believed that unless humanity was to go to the dogs, children had to learn to work together. They gave kids little things to do collectively before the age of three. They would set the final goal for older children, but let the kids figure out their own means of accomplishing it. They believed that children disciplined in the old way had no idea how to get together and do anything. At that time, the only discipline the educational experts in Moscow wanted was that which came from a common purpose and socially useful work.

Soviet teachers could be very creative. One nursery had very big, but lightweight blocks. One three-year-old alone could not handle them. "We don't attempt to preach the virtues of cooperation to them," the teacher explained. "They just find out it's the only way to move the blocks, and get in the habit of cooperating from an early age." At another school I discussed punishment with them. "We never give added work as a punishment," the teacher said. "Children are not stupid: if work is punishment, they will want to avoid it. If they are very disruptive, we take away their work, do not allow them to do the regular little tasks they are supposed to do. And of course, they feel the shame of it." I was really impressed and later, back at the central office, I said so to an official. To my surprise, she bristled, "What school was that? That punishment is too cruel for a little child—to cut him off from the honor of collective work entirely!"

First-rate actors staffed the children's theater, a lively branch of the Department of Education. Besides entertaining a lot of children, and stimulating them to new insights, the theater taught the teachers. I finally got sight of the "infamous" orphans I had heard rumors about before I got to Russia. "We have had all kinds of audiences and find great differences in what moves them. We have groups from the factory workers, from the peasants, from the shelters for the wandering children, some little criminals, and so on. What would you think would be the worst audience?" I didn't know, but from what I had heard, I thought the wandering children. "The children of the nice neighborhoods, when attending with their parents, behaved worst. The orphans are angels compared to them." I couldn't resist asking more about the wandering children. The teachers admitted that in the worst periods of the war, many children had been homeless. The vast majority had since been convinced to move to government homes where they received shelter and education. A few had grown used to their lives and resisted, but I never saw any rampaging in the streets.

The Russians tried to use children to reach the parents. Though undeniable progress had been made, the illiteracy rate remained high. Teachers encouraged the children to help their parents and grandparents learn to read. Indeed, the Party appreciated the importance of popular education. I had avoided the Park of Culture and Rest for it seemed self-consciously worthy in the boring sense, but in the spring I decided to take a look. Suddenly, I saw a man carrying a sign that said, "There will be an interesting discussion here." I tried to get his attention but he kept on walking, and several people followed him. I joined and so did others. "But how do you know there will be an interesting discussion?" I finally asked. "Because you will make it so," he replied. When he had enough followers, he stuck his pole into the grass, asking "Now, citizens, what would you like to discuss?" Some of the people said, "Let's discuss the marriage question." But one old fellow derided that idea: "What for? Talk it up, talk it down, it's always a mess." The man with the sign guided their choice some and they finally decided to discuss upgrading production. But, in those days, the government often sought the people out, taught when and wherever an opportunity presented itself, and tried to teach them what they wanted to know.

Sometimes the things that interested the Russians amazed me. I went to a lecture, "The Hygiene of Mental Health" packed full of tough workers. Some of them looked slow, but they wrinkled up their brows as if they would understand or bust. The Bolsheviks told them they had inherited the earth, and nothing was too big for them to take on. Heavy and unaccustomed responsibilities had fallen on many of them, but they strained and stretched to have their powers grow to match. This may explain the interest of Russian workers in such lectures. They weren't pretentious intellectual exercises, but gave concrete advice to the workers on how best to get on with their own and the country's business. From every platform, every paper, they heard of the backwardness and inefficiency of Russia. But they also heard that life could be better for the people when all worked harder or became more cultured. Many workers knew that as production had gotten better organized, wages had risen.

Hence their hope and determination. A scientific film was to precede the lecture on this occasion, but the audience—always active in Russia—shouted it down. The movie explained the functions of nerve cells and showed rabbit reactions to various stimuli and so forth. "We paid our money to hear about the best way to work. Bring on the lecture!" they shouted. The people in charge of the meeting replied: "We are running the evening to please you," stopped the projector in mid-movie, turned on the lights, and produced the lecturer, amid great applause. I thought an American audience would prefer even that movie to a lecture on mental hygiene!

The lives of many of the workingmen had improved dramatically since the Revolution. I visited the workers' quarters at a model textile factory. The house lodged 470 people in 103 rooms. Workers had access to big public kitchens on each floor and a hot water supplier that looked like a giant samovar. The toilets were very clean. A big central bathhouse that administered a very steamy Turkish variety was available to all workers for free. Since the factory employed eight or nine thousand workers, rooms were fairly small, but clean and well kept.

I asked whether the workers thought life better now than before the Revolution, and a wonderful discussion ensued. One woman—

very drunk and at the same time very religious—said she lived like a dog, before and now; but now she felt the fist more. She seemed very nervous, in fact, half-crazy. All the young kids stood around smiling at her with good-natured skepticism, and then one of the young men began to tell me why he thought life had improved. He said now the workers had some control over their own life. They were not just cogs in a machine, but could influence their conditions of work. The government provided for the workers—jobs, unemployment insurance, education, medical care—even clubs. Before, there was one children's nursery, now nine. Before, if the man of the family died, his widow and children had to leave the factory home within two weeks. Now they could stay. One man would think of one thing, one of another. I had no doubt how the young people felt.

This woman was not the only person to complain to me of Bolshevik policies on religion, and I understood some of her frustration. One of Mrs. Tolstoy's friends had been in jail several times for organizing religious teaching for groups of young people. The Soviets could not prevent religious teaching of family in the home. But since they wanted to give science a chance, they prohibited formal religious teaching of children under eighteen. Nekrasova, tall, slender, and determined, with piercing blue eyes, had been arrested for breaking this law. She said she was going to keep right on doing what she was doing. "I know what I believe and they know what I believe. They can come and get me any time: I do not walk in the dark." The Bolsheviks released her because she had so many friends who were outraged that such a woman could be put in jail. But theirs was an uneasy truce.

At Easter the Bolsheviks made a special attempt to wean the people away. The Russian church traditionally made more of Easter than of Christmas. I looked forward to the celebration, not to mention seeing how the authorities would carry on their "without God" campaign. The main church services were Saturday night, the last night of Lent. The Soviets hoped to compete with a series of new films. For the occasion they strung up huge white cloths in the trees every so often along the big A and B boulevards so they could project free movies. They hoped that the young, at least, might get absorbed and not bother to go on to church. But it was snowing and blowing ferociously, and people commented that obviously the Almighty disapproved of the films. The would-be screens bulged in the gusts, then sagged limp, making a weird picture. The novelty held quite an audience, at least for a while, but then they went to church. And what was the ideal bait the godless had set out? Old American slapstick comedies, one after another, on and on without pause or respite. I went to church, too.

As I walked on toward the big church at Arbat Square, I saw Roman candles shooting up all around. "This time the atheist propagandists have gone too far," I said to myself: "This must be really counterproductive, invading the very churchyard." But as I got closer, I realized the priest was shooting off the fireworks, and leading a joyful procession around the church chanting, "Christ is risen!" The congregation sang, as all reentered the church, and as soon as I could I followed, greatly helped by the people who were pushing behind me. The place was as crowded as a New York subway in the rush hour. I doubt I would have had the nerve to push so tightly against strangers if I'd had a choice. But the crowd behind me would step on my heels if I didn't move forward. I heard a lot of tinkling and noticed that everyone passed coins up to the altar. The people in front passed back lighted candles. How the candles got to the people who paid, I don't know, but I heard only one cry of protest: "Look out for my beard!" cried a big burly man in the heavy, stiff felt boots of the peasant. There were no seats in the church. The congregation was infinitely patient and very pleased with the long service, speaking and chanting with rich voices in parts.

After the service people went to parties that lasted until dawn. I went to the one given by my translator. The one room in which she now lived and entertained had been a bathroom in her father's house before the Revolution. I met her husband, a doctor drawing unemployment insurance to stay in Moscow, though he had been offered a job in the countryside, where doctors were desperately needed. Life in the countryside was far harder than in Moscow and this doctor didn't want to face the difficulty. Ironically, just at this time, friends told me of an article by a Polish Socialist that said Cossacks were riding down the unemployed in the streets of Moscow.

Life was more difficult in the countryside than in Moscow, but it could also be very merry. Shortly before Easter I had a lovely trip, along with some Quakers, to *Yasnaya Polyana*, Leo Tolstoy's estate. Although Alexandra Lvovna, his thirteenth child, was a countess, the Soviets didn't discriminate against her yet. She still ran things on the estate.

Only one train stopped anywhere near *Yasnaya Polyana*, and it arrived at 2:00 A.M.. A cheerful peasant met us with a sledge cozily lined with hay and ankle-length coachman's coats with a layer of sheepskin inside. It was early March during what Russians call a frost: thirty below zero. As we slid over the moon-bright rolling fields, we heard nothing but the swish of the snow and the dropping of the horses hooves. Once we passed a village laid out geometrically with a double row of houses with square, peaked roofs—the sides in the moonlight showed silver and those in the shadow, blue. We sped past handsome birches and firs, enchanted by the uncluttered, auto-less landscape.

Arriving at 3:00 A.M., we thought to go quietly to our bedrooms, but Alexandra Lvovna greeted us herself at the door and insisted we sit down for tea, hot biscuits, and native honey. She played her guitar and sang. A young man, who had also waited up for us, tried to teach us a beautiful song, "*Slyshish, slyshish, zvuki, zvuki*." The first lines went: "Dost thou hear the sounds of a heavenly polka? Let's go, my darling, to dance the polka." The young man lived as an "exile minus six"; that is, he could stay any place but the six main cities. Since theater and art centered in those six cities, the punishment was a cruel one for a Russian.

Alexandra Lvovna had her share of trouble with the authorities, too. She cooperated with the Soviets to make the place a model village to honor Tolstoy. And the village Soviet, which invited us to all their meetings, was very relaxed and cordial. In Moscow I had to go through the tense process of getting a written permit. Even so, Alexandra had to struggle to keep the school, of which she was principal, truly Tolstoyan. The authorities wanted to organize a troop of Young Pioneers (scouts) in the school, but Alexandra Lvovna felt their military drills an insult to Tolstoy's philosophy. "If they insist next year," she said, "I'll have to leave." Sadly enough, that's just what happened, but I still cherish the memory of how it was then.

I found *Yasnaya Polyana* delightful, but nothing in Russia impressed me more than my visit with Krupskaya, Lenin's widow. She was a lovely woman—fine and broad-minded and utterly unpretentious. Krupskaya had none of the overconfidence of some of the younger Communists whose faith had been coarsened by reduction to unqualified formulas. Her belief in people and the Revolution seemed a higher achievement than theirs. Anyone could believe if he or she swallowed things whole and without question. To look the world in the face, to see it as it was, and still have faith took more courage. Krupskaya also had a wonderful tolerance and facility in working with people. She was fairly old. There was already a little of the grandmotherly in her way of talking. But she worked all day long as the head of the Department of Education, never thinking of her own life.

I learned my father was going to be in Europe. I was going to meet him in Berlin and return home at last. Though I had ventured into the countryside a couple of times, I had spent nearly all of my time in the city. I saw peasants at the markets and on streetcars and talked with them briefly. Still, I wanted to return to the countryside now that I spoke the language reasonably well. Sonia sent me to the village of Tetiushi on the Volga to meet a man she knew, Misha. Tetiushi was a small village, so I found Misha easily. He was big, handsome, and surprisingly blond, his hair cut in a sort of page-boy bob. Most of the time we sat on the high bank of the river and talked about what the village had been through. "The Soviets were fine at first," he said. "They gave us the land, and drove out the bad landlords. Actually, we had a decent landlord here and for a while she stayed and helped us manage. But the time came when they would no longer permit it, and she went abroad. Communists have done some good things," he said. "They helped us with seeds, though not enough, and they helped educate our youngsters. They were fine as long as they stayed in Moscow. But why do they have to come down here and tell us how to run our lives?" Misha was a philosophical anarchist and loved to talk about his view of the world. No doubt that he was really a peasant, though. I remember sitting on the green grassy bank, watching with American sanitary horror as he absent-mindedly fingered dried horse dung to punctuate his remarks.

What was I feeling about Russia and the Soviets as I left in the fall of 1928? Soviet did not have to be a bugaboo word. The American press to the contrary, much of what the Bolsheviks did was fundamentally democratic. People chose representatives on district or city councils not by locality, but by work place. They had more chance to know the representatives personally than our candidates chosen by political parties over large areas. I knew the Communist Party members in the plant or office got together and chose a slate. But they were under pressure to choose worthwhile people so that the promises to the workers could be fulfilled. The Communists I knew were not in it for money or prestige: if they wanted a lot of fancy loot they would have to hide it, or be denounced as bourgeois. Human selfishness existed everywhere, but at least the Soviet Union rewarded it with social condemnation.

I noticed over and over again, in talking to people on the streetcars and buses, that most of them spoke with pride about this or that accomplishment since the Revolution. When I asked, "Are you a Communist?" they would usually answer, "No. I like to have a little home life, time for myself. I don't want to have to go to meetings every night." "But," I would say, "you said *we* did this. I thought the Communists did it." They replied, "Right, we all did it." At that time, among city people, the majority seemed to be well disposed toward the government. Though Russians suffered from a lot of bureaucracy and red tape, the Bolsheviks didn't invent that. Ridiculous tie-ups caused by the processing of many needless but required papers were common—but I had similar problems elsewhere. The Russian identity card reminded me of work permits of many European countries. And the Soviets had made great progress in educating their people. Before the Revolution, most were illiterate and marveled at people who could read and write. Education had never been offered to ordinary people: it was a privilege reserved for the rich. So when they had the opportunity, the people took to school with zest. People always crowded the subsidized bookstores buying books at fifty cents.

I found absolutely no basis in fact for many of the rumors I had been fed. Children were not being taken from their parents. The family was not breaking down. Rather, women and children enjoyed health and safety they had never known before the Revolution. There were nowhere enough nurseries and play schools for the demand and all had long waiting lists: women welcomed the cooperative work experience and the children seemed happy in school. As to charges of looseness in sexual morals, the Bolsheviks were protecting the rights of women and children. They permitted no lascivious ads in any medium, which stressed instead tasks to tackle for bettering life. True, you could get married by registering at an office, for a small fee, and get divorced as easily; but the Bolsheviks did not interfere in intimate life.

The Soviets considered religion a real obstacle to modernization because they didn't want people to be patient with conditions they should not tolerate: "the opium of the people," as Lenin said. They knew prohibition would not work, but they conducted a steady, relentless propaganda against it, which outraged many people. I didn't think that people should be jailed for teaching children religion and didn't agree with much of Soviet policy on religion. But I also felt that the Soviets taught one of the positive tenets of religion more actively from the nursery up than did people in many "Christian" countries. The Soviets strove to raise children who would work together for the cause of humanity.

I did not realize how much I was enjoying the lack of clutter in Russia until I got home again. The streets were not full of little wrappers and papers (Russians didn't have the paper to wrap small items) and there was no advertising of material things to grab at my attention. My mind was free for human relationships, books, theater—the important things. Perhaps what I enjoyed most was the feeling of friendship I sensed all around. One thing I will never forget is a cold night in November early on my visit, not a real frost since the temperature was only twenty degrees below zero. A gale blew right in our faces as we walked the long three blocks from the streetcar to a Workers Club. I heard jolly noises outside, but as we opened the door, people began shoving me out. "*Byelyi, byelyi*," they cried, pointing to their noses. They were saying, "White, white." My Russian wasn't good yet and the translator was back behind me. I didn't understand right away, but I did when a man came out with me and began washing my face with snow. The tip of my nose had frozen. The workers knew it must not be allowed to warm up in that condition or bad things would happen. What a reception for a stranger! But it was pure Russian, pure kindness. The frankness and warmth of the Russians gave me a sense of security I had never known before, and as my self-confidence grew, I did things I'd never have believed possible. I left one thing behind very happily: my cursed shyness.

VII

After visiting with Dad in Europe, I returned to the United States to join Mother for a winter on the ranch. She loved to get away from the too-long Northern winters and so did I. The ranch, I also thought, would be an ideal place for a project I had thought of in

Russia. So many false stories had been published in America that our people were not aware of the kind of place I had found there. I felt a burning desire to let Americans know the truth and understand what the best of the revolutionaries were trying to do. As far as I could see, the most I could do in the mainstream press was what Walter Duranty, the Moscow correspondent for the *New York Times*, called the "sandwich method." He knew that the American press had been publishing only the worst about the U.S.S.R. "If you want to work in anything good," he said, "you must precede it with something negative and critical and follow it with something similar."

The sandwich method didn't appeal to me and I had already decided to try for a book, one which I hoped would reach a wide audience. I thought that few would read a serious book about Russia. Anita Loos, who had just wowed the country with her *Gentlemen Prefer Blondes*, gave me an idea. I decided to use a naïve and not terribly bright flapper as the narrator of a humorous novel. Her reactions to the unfamiliar there might illustrate my point in a lively way.

Polly Hayden was the beautiful and spoiled nineteen-year-old daughter of an American millionaire. Her father, a self-made man, was dedicated to the pursuit of wealth, pleasure, and social status. Admired by his friends for his knack of getting something for nothing, Mr. Hayden was, nevertheless, furious when his daughter ran away from the most respectable finishing school in the country to elope with his own bootlegger, Joe Tinkenduffer. Hayden decided that Polly's desire for excitement, rather than any great love for Tinkenduffer, motivated her elopement. He resolved to send her to Europe with her steady, sensible cousin Sally. With enough freedom to satisfy her desire for adventure, but not so much that she could get into any real trouble, Polly might settle down and return ready for a socially acceptable marriage. In Paris, tired of the cafe scene, Polly resolved to go to Russia where, she had heard, adventure was an inescapable part of life. For the same reasons that he had sent her to Paris, her father agreed to support her in Russia.

Polly's adventures in Russia gave me a chance to describe the advances made since the Revolution. Polly found out, as I had, how silly many rumors about the U.S.S.R. were. Throughout the novel, I contrasted Polly's frivolity, ignorance, smug racial conceit, and selfishness with the vitality, earnestness of purpose, altruism, and internationalism I saw in many Russians then. In the end Igor, the idealistic, hard-working, handsome young Communist Polly had fallen for, spurned her. Igor had always given Polly the benefit of the doubt, assuming that her bizarre and sometimes inexplicable comments were a consequence of her genteel and sheltered upbringing. Only when he found that Polly intended to live off her father's income after their marriage, neither working nor raising children, did Igor realize how deep was her egotism, how distorted her values:

> Don't you see that every self-respecting human being who enjoys the fruits of somebody else's work must give something pleasant or useful in return? To live without work is the most immoral thing you could do. Phooey, I spit on a woman who wants neither to have children nor to work. You are the same as a prostitute for all you have to offer to the world is sex.

I, too, felt that a woman who was not raising a family should work.

After I got the manuscript mostly done, I went to New York to find a publisher. New York had the best publishers and literary agents, and offered an exciting alternative to the ranch, where I was beginning to feel understimulated. I took a tiny room in the Kenmore Hotel for single people, to work on improvements on the manuscript and to get back in touch. Having been abroad for three years, I felt duty-bound to read the whole *New York Times*—even the financial pages—to catch up. Reading the *Times* often took half of the day, but as Elizabeth Dilling duly noted in her book, *The Red Network*, I also had time for some political work. When a delegation of Soviet flyers came to New York, I served on the reception committee. And when the Soviets launched Amtorg, their American trading organization, I visited the office to ask where I could purchase some of those jolly embroidered leather Tartar slippers. The Soviets were planning a handicrafts exhibition and asked me if I could write an article about it. Enthusiastic about the idea, I asked an editor at the *Times* if he could use such a piece. Though he was doubtful, I did it anyway.

I had been impressed with the work of the *kustars*, as the artisans were called, when visiting Russia. By 1912, I learned, some three million Russians had produced handicrafts for sale or domestic use. The war slowed production tremendously, killing many of the best artisans. Revolution brought production practically to a standstill. In the first great surge of revolutionary zeal, mass production was the rallying cry. Only modern machinery, the Soviets believed, could free the people of drudgery. Like all the policies of the Revolution, this had a slogan to express it: "handicraft is the scourge of the people." The government discouraged the *kustars* in more concrete ways, too; the Soviets denied them the necessary paint, tools, and sales outlets. Necessity and the Russian appreciation of beauty eventually rescued the *kustars*. Factories operated at 15 percent of prewar levels; many, including the *kustars*, therefore, couldn't find work. Artists among the revolutionaries protested that Russia's peasant craftsmen were a valuable, inimitable part of her heritage that no industry could supplant in any case. In 1920, with a new slogan—"we turn back our faces to the *kustar*"—the Revolution reasserted the value of the craftsmen and supported their work. It was not the only instance in which I knew the Bolsheviks had freely acknowledged and rectified a mistake, and that had pleased me also.

I enjoyed writing about the work of the anonymous craftsmen who had created such marvels in the dead of the long Russian winter when agricultural work was impossible. Though few craftsmen had worked collectively—probably no more than 5 percent before the Revolution—each piece they made drew on tribal or local traditions that were centuries old. These nameless artists built, one upon the work of another, each generation continuing the evolution of design, color, and form. The poorest peasants employed their entire family in the work. A little boy of six might nail together straight pieces; a girl of seven smooth figures with sandpaper; a child of twelve, I knew, could already carve a very respectable frog or rabbit. Children laid the base colors of paint while adults traced the designs. In the article I recorded the wonderful, evocative descriptions of the work I had heard in the U.S.S.R. The family gathered around a roughhewn table, with a dim lamp flickering on gilded icons in the shrine, or "little God-corner," while the great square clay stove that filled a third of the room radiated heat. They would often sing folk tunes, falling quite naturally into the complicated harmonies that Russians seemed to know at birth. Every trade in Russia had its own ditty, and all shared the half-sad, half-merry ballad of the struggling artisan: "Poverty leaps, poverty dances, poverty sings us a song."

I presented my completed article to the editor who had discouraged me previously. He not only accepted it for the *Magazine* but invited me to do another. I chose to write about Soviet education. I talked about positive changes Soviets had made in education—

readers of the *Times* already knew the negative. My headline read: "Eagerly Young Russia Goes to School; Student Life is one of Hardships, but Books once Forbidden are Wells of Knowledge." The *Times* published the articles in March and April, which turned out to be good timing.

My manuscript was not faring well. My attempt to explore the comic angles and write for nonintellectuals was a grave error of judgment. Basing the humor on a situation so totally unfamiliar to the average reader did not come off. At least, the readers for the publishing houses I submitted my book to didn't think so. My friend, Louis Fischer, and my agent told me I should write a book like the articles I had done for the *Times* and abandon my novel, "that silly thing," as Fischer put it. There is a Russian adjective that described my effort, "nowherish." I might have continued, but the summer proved to be a busy and momentous one for me.

I had avoided socializing too much in New York—trying to concentrate on my book and finish. In midsummer, I bethought me of my college friend, Marian Davis, and decided to see her. I remembered her husband sometimes wrote for Federated Press and I thought they might have his address. I called up and got it, and then the nice voice said: "May I ask to whom I'm speaking?" I answered and he exclaimed: "Oh, you're the one who's been sending us those good human interest stories. Carl Haessler told me I should look you up." As a matter of fact Carl had told me that I should look up the New York editors but I had been trying to keep my nose to the grindstone. Well, Harvey O'Connor, the voice on the phone, invited me to lunch the next day, and that was the beginning of a long story.

When we met Harvey said, "You've been writing some good stuff. Why don't you come work for us?" Harvey had checked things out with Carl, who said I could come to work if I promised not to do it in a dilettantish way, which seemed a fair condition. Carl knew my family, realized that I never held down a job for any length of time, and was brought up to get anything I wanted. He didn't need a reporter who had had her own way so long that she couldn't be expected to go out on a rainy day or cover things under hard conditions. Actually since they didn't have the money to hire another full-time staffer, I could be a help to them because I didn't need a salary.

For myself, I had wanted to get the right job and to do it well when my novel was finished. I wanted to investigate and report about the debilitating conditions in which America's poor lived as I had written about what I had seen in Russia. Many Americans like myself had been insulated from these realities all of their lives. One of my class-mates at Smith said she didn't like to read *The Nation* because it always had so much bad news. "Don't you think it's bad news when the average income in 1925 for a family of four is $1,200 a year?" I asked. "Money isn't everything," she replied. True, this wealthy girl was no showoff, loved good reading and art, not fancy clothes. But she never realized that her ability to travel, to telephone friends, to eat well, to give gifts, depended on money. I wanted to help people see the waste of human possibilities that grinding poverty creates, and make them want to do something about it. And I very quickly figured that Harvey would respect me more if I was working dili-gently on the job. The circle was complete: I wanted to do it, Harvey wanted it done, and I soon decided I wanted Harvey.

Harvey had invited me to dinner the evening after we first spoke on the phone. We drank some beer and ate a good meal for eighty-five cents at the Teutonia, a couple of blocks from the office. Then we walked, talking the whole time about the labor movement. This went on every evening for two weeks. His wide knowledge, his way of describing things, his humor, his devotion to his ideas and lack of factional prejudice pleased me greatly. My experience with men in high school, in college, and in Russia had convinced me that I didn't want to marry a man of my own social class. Those that I met did not share my vision of marriage or my goals in life and I didn't think it likely that any would. Then I thought, given the sometimes bitter factionalism of the Movement, that I'd have to marry someone very doctrinaire who belonged in one camp and insulted the ideas of all others. Harvey's great good sense and magnanimous understanding delighted and astonished me. Some of the snobbery of my class was obviously still with me for I never expected to find this combination of qualities in a man of Harvey's background.

I began to love him a lot, but he never spoke a personal word. "He must like me," I said to myself, "or he wouldn't want to spend every evening with me. But he's so businesslike!" It was discouraging. Fi-nally one evening I spoke out. There was still no personal talk, no touch of the hand, but I was emboldened by the fact that Harvey seemed to want to spend every possible moment with me. As we walked over the Williamsburg Bridge, I took all my courage in my hands and said, "I think you're the kind of man I could stand to marry." He looked pleased but surprised. "You have a very different background. My life might amuse you for a while but you would be gone in a year. What's the use of going through all the red tape of getting married, then having to get a divorce?"

Harvey considered marriage a bourgeois trap and I didn't care so much for the ceremony. I wanted nothing to come between us, not even a ring. A big wedding with all the trimmings for an untried couple seemed particularly impertinent. Give them a quiet year, I thought, to see if they'd make it, and then, if they did, celebrate with a big housewarming. Harvey and I were not an "untried couple" for long, and, though I shared his view of marriage, my parents did not. "In my family," I told him, "you get married." My mother would be desperately distressed if she heard I lived with a man unmarried. Dad sometimes thought "free love" a nice idea, but not for his daughters. He wanted steady family lives for us. Dad was afraid that without the commitment of marriage, we'd be left with children and without protection. They were both always pretty conservative on such issues. Private and public values belonged to separate, unrelated sets. Whether people should be left poor and hungry was not in the same category as how and whether women should choose and change marriage partners.

I told Harvey I had spent years trying to figure out what qualities might have kept my parents from breaking up when I was twelve, and was determined to make a go of marriage. With his calm temper, fairness, sense of humor, and indifference to small things, ours could really last. Being friends who adore each other's work for a common cause would tide us over any rough spots. Harvey finally agreed, though he was fond of bursting into song:

My mammy told me long long ago
She said, "Son, don't you marry any gal you know
She'll spend all your money, hock all your clothes.
Son, don't you marry any gal you knows."

Initially, Harvey was uncomfortable with my wealth. Once, after the subject had come up in a phone conversation, I wrote him:

Some day I'm going to have quite an argument with you on the text, "In general, I think people ought to marry people of the same social station." What chance would I ever have to know anything if I did that? *NO!* I was raised a bourzhooey [bourgeois], unfortunately, but at least

I know better than to marry a bourzhooey—and I have some hopes of outgrowing my own evil effects of being such.

Sometimes the problem could not be put to rest as lightly. I recall once being very upset by the quiet, distant quality of Harvey's voice on the phone after an argument about money. I don't remember the details of the disagreement, but I wrote immediately:

Don't worry about little things, even on rainy days. I'll never argue again if it annoys you (not about that, I mean!). Only I wish you could feel how little money means to me and I don't even feel I am giving it when I see something that ought to be done with it. Ye Gods! I don't go around expecting the I.L.D. to look up to me or be particularly grateful—much less expect to call any of their tunes. When I toss away money I've shed it, like water off a duck's back, and I don't think of it again.

But if you *would* think of it again, all right. I can see it might be a canker in your bosom, etc., etc., and the last thing I'd ever want to do would be to insist on something that would hurt you. I wish such little things wouldn't hurt you. But, I know it's hard for a proud person to be helped, no matter how joyfully the other would do it. "It is more blessed to give than receive."

As I said I wouldn't think of offering it for your daily life—but for an extraordinary measure, by which my life is made secure and happy as never before, it seems ridiculous that you should take all the grubbing, when stuff that means nothing to me is rotting in the bank. Viewed in the large, it's an economic maladjustment like tariff barriers—just the kind of thing I'd like to abolish on the earth, and resulting from just the same bourgeois distinctions—between what is mine and thine. What ought to be ours is an equal chance to go ahead with what we want to do, without paying interest on the past. If it was some terrible fault of yours that brought this on, and it would teach you to have to pay, I could see some use to it. But in this case I can't see any use to it at all.

Well now I'll stop. I've said my say so I won't need to say any more. I don't expect you to be detached enough to look at this money business the way I do— naturally, in the ordinary texture of human affairs, money is used to buy something, with all kinds of overtones of sapped independence, etc. But just try to imagine what I feel about it, so you will understand what I mean. It's very hard not to see you and talk to you right now.

Frankness got us through our differences, and Harvey's special qualities helped. Harvey was great-souled and had no male chauvinism and I learned to be sensitive to his feelings. I also soon showed him that I was serious about my job, my beliefs, and him. I accepted my salary at Federated Press, so as not to stand out from the others, but always discreetly kicked it back, expecting no applause or particular influence. I worked as long as everyone else and very quickly took my share of hard assignments. After Harvey found that I was not a flibbertigibbet, that character meant more to me than money, and that I would not leave him in a year or two, he withdrew his bantering, teasing opposition to marriage.

Harvey had moved out of a cold-water flat on the East Side to a studio apartment in Chelsea. I kept the room at the Kenmore for the family's sake. At Harvey's we could cook, although he had no kitchen. We threw a piece of plywood across the tub and made do with a two-burner electric plate. That was no problem, but day-to-day living did force us to make one adjustment. When I tried to get Harvey to go to bed earlier, he put his foot down. "My mother used to try to tell me when to go to bed and I'm not going to have you doing it." I replied that I could never sleep late. "My internal clock wakes me up no matter what." We agreed to retire when we wanted: each one, same room, same bed, but freedom of choice. We settled in and waited until June, when Harvey's divorce would be final.

In the meantime, though people said I was doing a good job of reporting for Federated Press, writing still came slowly to me and many's the time our mimeo queen had to nag me to finish. Some days for practice Harvey handed me a batch of minor reports from our stringers around the country and told me to make shorts out of them—four- or five-line paragraphs that could be used to fill in the bottom of pages. We had no money for telegrams so all of our stories were mimeographed and mailed. Still we often scooped the wire services, which did not deign to cover much labor news. We operated on a very short shoestring and couldn't afford to waste space at the bottom of a page—hence the need for a supply of shorts. This was the hardest thing I had to do. My interest in everything and desire to save everything has given me trouble all my life. And it killed me to cut out the hard-thought words of our brave friends, some of them painstakingly scrawled on poor paper. "But otherwise it won't get in at all," Harvey said. "You have to get the vital gist—and don't be all day about it!"

Hold the Fort

After Blanche and I landed in New York, I went to see Art Shields for tips on jobs. He said that the *Newark Ledger* needed reporters, as usual. The *Ledger* had three shifts: one coming, one on the job, and the third going. Any old port in a storm! Over to Newark I went and sure enough I landed on the copy desk at the going rate. The *Ledger* left much to be desired. A former Marine sergeant, who was brutal and drunk most of the time and who had served in Nicaragua, became my boss. He welcomed me by throwing the woman's page copy at me. He wanted to show his contempt for me and the subject matter. I lasted six weeks, until a job opened for me in New York. When I announced my departure, the Marine dangled an offer of a substantial raise, but I very happily told him to shove it.

My editing experience began to pay off. Carl Haessler offered me the job of Eastern Bureau manager of Federated Press. Carl took a long chance on me but he thought the results good in the end. The Federated Press office, located at 799 Broadway, below Fourteenth Street, had two desks, typewriters, and a mimeograph machine. The building was a nest of radical, liberal, and progressive organizations, the owner being a woman who preferred such tenants so long as they paid their rent. Our daily routine started at 8:00 A.M. with the early mail. We would receive a sheaf of stories from people all over the East and Atlantic South. Our correspondents, generally the editors of member labor papers, passed us carbons of their stories. When a hot labor struggle broke out and we could afford it, we sent a correspondent. If we couldn't swing it, we depended on a union organizer on the spot for the news. We also scanned and clipped the New York dailies for run-of-the-mill stuff. By 11:00 A.M. I would hit the street scouting for the lead story of the day in some union or radical office, and then I'd get back to our place to write it up. By midafternoon the day's quota would be ready for mimeographing. Our schedule taught me to get to the point quickly in clear, direct language. No agonizing over fine points. Our daily output went to about fifty clients. Once or twice a week we sent an edited version to a larger list of a hundred or so. The mechanical part of the job was quite a chore, but usually we rushed the stuff to the mailboxes by 5:00 P.M., some by air, most by surface mail.

At first, I ran the office alone but after a while Haessler permitted the bureau a stenographer-bookkeeper. I got an extra hand and the Chicago bureau shed the responsibility for our bookkeeping. Haessler still paid our field correspondents, most of whom worked as stringers. At best, they got fifty dollars a month, a modest sum but worth a lot more than now. Our clients, our main source of money, met their assessments responsibly, for Federated Press was the only independent labor news service and had a high-quality staff. Though much of labor and the left relied on us and, I suspect, thought we were doing a good job, we couldn't satisfy everyone. One correspondent friend wrote me from Moscow in 1930 with an analysis calculated to keep me from overconfidence, even if I didn't agree with him. "I am beginning to think," he wrote, "that Federated Press is rapidly becoming an open mouthpiece of the enemies of revolutionary workers and the fact that it may have a certain amount of 'liberalism' and 'independence' and utilizes quite left phrases in some of its news will make it a worse enemy than an open enemy." Can't win 'em all!

In spite of our critics, I thought the Federated Press the perfect place for me, a radical and journalist. We covered the news that the commercial press ignored and/or feared. As our advertising said—all the news not fit to print. When Mary Capretti, mother of four, wife of a miner, was roughed up on the picket line, we printed her admonition, "We got to win this strike, the children are hungry." We followed the struggle for old-age, unemployment, and medical insurance closely, giving their proponents a vehicle to express their views. We pointed out racism, when we recognized it (which, unfortunately, was not always), publicizing violence against blacks and explaining how the workings of the economy particularly victimized them. We supported workers struggling for unionism and better lives, North and South. We exposed the workings of American capital abroad, especially in what is now called the Third World, and defended the only Socialist country in the world, then, the U.S.S.R., when she was attacked in the other papers. We noted the actions and victories of the whole range of labor-left groups from the A.F. of L. to the Communist Party. People came to expect these things of us and many, who had no hope of communicating with poor and working-class Americans, looked to us to do so. General César Augusto Sandino chose to send fraternal greetings to the American workers in 1928 through us at Federated Press:

> We know that the majority of the North American people is not responsible for the ferocious crimes that the marines commit every day in our country. We know well the situation of the working class in your country, who also are the victims of oppression of the exploiters, the same interests that are now fighting to enslave the people of Latin America.

The news that, in April of 1928, the Daughters of the American Revolution proclaimed us a dangerous organization shocked no one on the staff.

Though I spent most of my time in New York, I got a chance to see some other labor hot spots for myself. One vacation Art Shields, Esther Lowell, and I cranked up an old car and went South. Art and Esther had already visited the heart of Dixie to investigate the significance for workers on both sides of the Mason-Dixon line of the South's rapid industrialization. Southern competition, we all knew, was a serious problem confronting millions of non-Southern workers in textiles, coal mining, furniture building, and other important industries. We learned, at each stop, that industrialization also often meant the degradation of the Southern worker: long hours, poor conditions, low pay, few civil liberties. We stopped at Hendersonville, North Carolina, where the cotton mill workers were on strike—one of the first such strikes in the South. The Full Fashioned Hosiery Workers, a progressive section of the United Textile Workers, were in charge with Tiny Hoffman, a 250-pounder as organizer. We attended a meeting on a Sunday, held out in the open for a hall big enough for the crowd didn't exist (even if the union could have afforded one). The workers wore their Sunday best—denim overalls. They were called lintheads, for the lint in the mill settled in their hair. We stopped at Durham for another union meeting, confronting racism since black people were forced to sit in the rear. In allowing blacks to attend the meetings at all, the Southern unionists outdid most of their neighbors, and we publicized all of their attempts to reach across the bitter and bloody color line. But I could see with painful clarity that a long road lay ahead. I was much amused, however, when the chairman, nodding toward Esther, said he was glad to have "a nawthern agitatah in female fawm" at the meeting. We also examined the situation at Gastonia, one of the biggest mill towns in the South. Hours were so long, wages so low, conditions so poor, that I wrote a story predicting that if ever a big strike broke out in the South, Gastonia would be the location. Little did I know that my wife would be one of the most important labor correspondents covering it.

Aside from Federated Press, I kept occupied while in New York with other enterprises. Roger Baldwin of the American Civil Liberties Union ran a worldwide committee on political prisoners. I kept tabs on excesses in Venezuela and I became all too well acquainted with the tortures of General Juan Vicente Gomez, the "Tyrant of the Andes." I wrote press releases when underground Venezuelans reported the events occurring in their country. I handled some publicity for Roger's Anti-Imperialist League, which spread the word about United States, British, and French oppression long before the colonies gained independence and a voice in the United Nations. I also worked for social security and unemployment legislation. I knew from my own childhood the devastating consequences for working-class homes of sickness, disability, or death of the wage earner. Abraham Epstein established a small organization devoted to making these "Socialist" programs, as their detractors called them, a national reality. We collaborated on press releases for general distribution and stories for Federated Press, but the first bill was not introduced in Congress until after I left New York, and only the Great Depression jarred Congress loose; the especial shame was that the A.F. of L. fought the idea from the start. I helped out with the League for Mutual Aid headed by Adelaide Schulkind, which gave modest sums to indigent writers, labor organizers, and others engaged in worthy enterprises who were up against it. The idea was that they would repay when they connected with a payroll, and many did so. I helped Robert Dunn on the Labor Research Association to write economic analyses of poverty, unemployment, and similar outrages.

New York was an experience in itself. Blanche and I lived on the sixth floor of a six-story walkup—at least we had plenty of sun and air. Since rents declined with the height, we paid only twenty-one dollars a month. We hauled coal and ice up and took down garbage by dumbwaiter. Our cold-water flat had three rooms: a tiny bedroom looking out on a narrow court, a windowless kitchen in the middle, and a living room facing south. A contraption called a bathtub in the kitchen could also be used as a laundry basin. As the tub stood on high legs, we had to use a chair to climb in. A pot-bellied stove supplied our heat. We shared a two-seater toilet room on the hall outside the apartments with our next door neighbor, Hollace Randall. Once the landlord tried to raise rents by two dollars a month. We nearly had a revolution.

We didn't share the apartment for long for Blanche and I had grown apart, she having little interest in my concerns and I even less in hers, if any. Her life with me was dull as I was quite taken up with my challenging and time-consuming job at Federated Press. When I worked with the Oil Workers Union in the forties, I frequently saw similar estrangement between man and wife. When the husband became a union representative or district director with enlarged interests, the "little woman" remained at home housekeeping and wondering what the old man was up to. Blanche made a bad tactical error when she up and left. Though she regretted it later, I felt enormously relieved. I soon abandoned the apartment for even smaller and simpler quarters elsewhere. I looked forward to complete freedom to pursue my journalism and other activities.

Blanche and I were in no hurry to finalize our split, though we lived separate lives. I had no intention of remarrying and she was not certain she wanted a divorce. Little did I know, I wasn't to be on my own for long. One morning a cheerful woman called on the telephone to ask me for an address. When she announced herself as Jessie Lloyd, I realized that she had corresponded for us in Moscow and that Carl Haessler had told me to treat her courteously. So I asked her to lunch. As Jessie was writing a book and needed diversion very badly, she accepted. She appeared at the Teutonia with her hair all ablaze in the noon sunlight. I was quite fetched as we tossed down a beer and I made a note of her telephone number at Kenmore Hall, a segregated place in which men and women lived on alternate floors. Jessie didn't invite me up for her room was littered with papers, she said. So the next day I asked her to accompany me on a walk on the toll-free Williamsburg Bridge. Since that also went well, our outings continued. On other occasions we ventured on the Staten Island Ferry, which cost a nickel. A rather curious courtship—spent mostly walking and talking—I about labor and radicalism in the United States and Jessie about her experiences in the U.S.S.R. and elsewhere. Later on our daughter, Kathleen, would characterize me as a "cheapskate" for my style of courting and Jessie would complain that I never got personal enough to broach the subject of marriage. It seemed acceptable enough to me!

Since I had not filed for divorce, remarriage would have been bigamy. And I wasn't interested in marriage in any case. I had had enough of an "ideal" wife and hankered not at all after the bonds of further matrimony. Blanche had unwittingly convinced me that the old radicals I knew in Seattle were right about marriage. Women restricted your movement without adding a great deal to your life. I needed freedom to do the political work I considered important and wanted to stay far away from the bourgeois trappings of family and home. Jessie's experiences, interests, and aspirations suggested that she would not be the kind of quiet, dependent, stay-at-home woman so often divorced by men in the movement. But there were other problems in her case. I could not help but be aware of her class background and, as a good Socialist, I had nothing but contempt for wealth. My feelings on the subject didn't square well with marrying one of the heiresses of the *Chicago Tribune* fortune. In addition, I suspected that Jessie would stay around for a while, leaving when I or the job got too dull. Though Haessler was delighted to have Jessie aboard, I knew he was unsure about her staying power and he had known her far longer than I. If the marriage weren't going to be permanent, why bother? Jessie's parents were the answer to that question.

So, in spite of my doubts, I yielded to the lady, wondering why her family, considered somewhat radical, should be so formal. Divorce in New York was messy, requiring perjury about adultery. I had a couple of friends who consented to produce the necessary proof. When we went down to see a Wall Street lawyer, he exploded in righteous

Harvey's World War I seaman's certificate.

Photograph by Jessie of her mother Lola Maverick Lloyd, sister Mary, and son Stephen in spring 1943 on the Texas ranch.

Harvey and Stephen, Christmas 1942.

Jessie's father, William Bross Lloyd, in 1915, shortly before her parents' divorce.

Jessie (in white) at about age seven, climbing the mast of her father's yacht, the *Oonas*.

Jessie, Florence Holbrook, Rosika Schwimmer, Jessie's brother Bill, her mother (Lola Maverick Lloyd), and sister Mary (from left) on the Ford Peace Ship.

Harvey in the late sixties.

Jessie in Chicago in the early forties.

Jessie in Vermont in the late sixties taking a picture of (sitting, from left) a family friend, Susie Jones, and Jessie's niece Robin Lloyd, and (standing, from left) Haze Jones, Harvey, and two other friends.

Harvey's mother's family in Tacoma after his father's death. The woman in plaid in the center is Harvey's grandmother. His mother is sitting to her immediate right.

Harvey during a recess in his interrogation by H.U.A.C.

The O'Connor family in 1951: Jessie, Stephen, Kathleen, and Harvey.

Jessie and Stephen dancing in Little Compton in the late fifties.

Harvey and Jessie dancing at a Little Compton house party in the sixties.

wrath. You would have thought he had never heard how people got the job done. (A year or so later I was amused to read that he was the principal in a breach of promise suit.) Fortunately, neither Jessie nor her parents insisted on a large, elaborate ceremony. We couldn't get married in New York for a year after the decree was granted, so we went over to Newark only to find a three-day waiting period there. Too long for us! We took the B & O to Baltimore, haven for the lovelorn, winding our way down a dismal street by the railroad station littered with "Marriages Performed" signs. We chose the Reverend Way, who operated out of a basement apartment. When he found we brought no witnesses, he bawled out to the rear room, "Come in Maria and be a witness." So for five dollars or so, barring railroad fares, we were hitched at last.

Our marriage was a greater success than I would have imagined possible. We learned a tremendous amount from one another. We could talk openly about things going on in our lives from the most trivial to the most profound. It wasn't that we had no problems, but that we could work on them. I think a letter I wrote to Jessie while she was in Gastonia shortly before we married gives a sense of the openness and closeness of our relationship:

Angel,

The afternoon and the evening, too, have been to you. While I don't fall for any of this psychic guff, I do know that my memories of you, whether in Gramercy, at 426 or up in Vermont are so warm and direct that it is almost as if you were with me instead of working like the devil for dear old FP down in North Carolina. Against a physical malaise of the past day has been the glow that comes of thinking of you and thinking of a future living and working with you for common ends. How long we will be together only fate knows, but I am certain that life has great things in store for us so long as we are—and what more than be asked on this uncertain strand? Already, in a way, I feel the warmth and color of Mexico in my veins and the promise of companionship with you down there—even if for only a short time. Pittsburgh is grayer— and redder too—and from this distance looks serious and even forbidding. That's because it's a huge problem that will try the best there is in us, a sort of supreme test in these formative years of ours, which will probably determine my course for all the future and be an experience in yours of even more importance than Russia.

The difficulties in my own way in really living are tremendous, to me, at any rate. First there's the annoyance of legal entanglements

which despite their pettiness nevertheless have a way of gumming up
the works between us. I hope we can surmount the secrecy and separation they involve without too much harm. Most fundamental, I feel,
are the physical handicaps under which I labor and which keep my
efficiency down to 50% of par. To have one's body tugging down on the
mind is a feeling that you don't experience much—not at any rate the
constant downward pull that at times reduces life to a vexatious problem of existence. Just a month or two below the border isn't going to
help much, either; probably I'll even have to become a faddist to overcome these difficulties. Just what to do about this is beyond me. Then
there's mental confusion and a feeling of inadequacy in the face of
problems that I can see. Some sort of regimen, a re-ordering of the
mind, and a pretty fundamental one at that, is all that can remedy that.

I hope you can stand this dismal recital: we shouldn't build on any
cock-eyed basis but rather on a calm perception of difficulties. I know
I'm not infatuated and I hope you're not. If we are to build at all it
should be on firmer stuff than that. I thoroughly dislike cant and senti-
mentalism and lack of clear perception: it is all an insult to the intelligence. I should hate to build any hopes with you, only to find them
tumble because you hadn't been candid with both of us, or had been
too enthusiastic, or had deliberately hood-winked yourself to enjoy a
transitory happiness. (I have a pretty firm conviction that you're made
of stern stuff, and yet I can't get away from the fear that life has been
too easy with you—too many problems solved easily or automatically.)

It is not easily that I drag myself to put all this on paper. Maybe it's
an error all around similar to others which have been prevented in the
nick of time. For thinking of you is unalloyed pleasure and being with
you is as much happiness as I have ever known.

Try to keep your stories as cleancut as your wires; you rely too much
on the editor carving. Don't pay much attention to the details of testimony or attempt inclusive accounts. Play up the highlights, use color
and aim at the main effect of each yarn. Now that you've forgotten all
about me being on the receiving end, fancy you've got a captious critic.
Eventually you'll have to get around to writing fast clean copy under
tension against deadlines. Might as well begin now; in Pittsburgh it
will be imperative. A resume of what's gone on before should be written for Tuesday and Friday: this is *most* important for nearly half our
editors don't see your daily copy. These yarns can be interpretative
with significant sidelights. Don't tie yourself down too much to courtroom routine; if a good story is elsewhere, you can pick up courtroom
stuff in the afternoon from other correspondents. What is the NTW
actually doing for example in Gastonia, and elsewhere: How are mill

owners reacting to trial, and to national spotlight? And that David Clark yarn; Jimison has lots of dirt on him. Sketch of Nell Battle Lewis would interest our editors, and the fight for labor legislation, etc. Also a yarn on the labor jury; on the personnel of the defense counsel, etc. The point is that we shouldn't give our editors too much trial *details* which they can't assimilate.

Pix very good. I shall scatter them to places where they will do the most good. The camera is clear and sharp, a splendid instrument and one which would set Art's covetous nature on edge. Aim for contrast, for things to *stand out* of the background—white on black or black on white. Action when possible. Kids and gals close up. Faces as close up as the camera will permit. And send up more, for we can use them to good advantage. The picture service idea takes form and substance and may be started within a month.

You've won praise in all sorts of quarters, right, left and center, for the glowing copy—and it's the sort that comes spontaneously from appreciative hearts of those who don't know you from Little Eva, God bless her heart. I do wish you'd keep FP in mind in your plans, for it's going to be the toughest sort of struggle to put it on a better basis, both from financial and news points. I don't want you to be exclusively an FP news hound, and yet I hope that you will find it possible when big stories break to be able to go out on them when they're in striking distance from New York. Having a roving reporter hitting the high spots has been on our schedule for a year, but just a dream until you, an angel, appeared out of the blue sky.

How I wish you could be here for just a little while! I need some of your warmth and glow and comfort and stimulation. You are *balm* to me; not just a retreat from the world, for you are that too, but an incitation to the world, too. But it's good for both of us not to be too soft. Go to it, but for the love of me, write me a letter once in a while so that I will know that you love me with a radiance at least 1/10 as luminous as that with which you have graced me in early days.

Harvey

I

Jessie and I married in June of 1930 and we stayed on the job all fall until Christmas. We had decided, as the letter suggests, to leave New York and move to Pittsburgh. Why Pittsburgh? Because we knew of Pittsburgh's reputation and we wanted to crack it. Granted, no place could be considered easy for radicals in 1930–31, not even New York. When the Unemployed Councils called all workers "Negro and White—Men and Women—Young and Old" to demonstrate and strike in favor of work for all, free rent for the unemployed, free food and clothing for their children and unemployment insurance, the New York police behaved as brutally as the most abandoned Cossacks, as Jessie says. In New York, though, the large liberal community joined leftists to condemn police riots and other excesses. When Police Commissioner Grover Whalen tried to start a Red Scare with the assertion that the Communist Party had ninety-seven hundred card-carrying members in the city, liberals challenged him to produce a list. Prominent New York attorneys, including Henry T. Hunt, asserted that Whalen could lay himself open to prosecution if he brought about the dismissal of any worker on groundless charges. If Whalen had proof that New Yorkers had committed crimes, the attorneys argued, he had a legal obligation to charge and try them. Whalen quickly reduced his figures—New York had "many" Communists. Such a scenario would have been impossible in Pittsburgh.

The behavior of the coal and iron police made it difficult to even speak of democracy in the area. One man, a prosperous insurance agent in a big firm, told me, "I'm yellow. I've spent ten years building up my business, but they could shut me down in twenty-four hours if they knew I gave to the miners or joined the ACLU." At Federated Press, we referred to the area as the "Pittsburgh War Front," because of the bitterness of the struggle. I believed that the men and women fighting for basic humanity desperately needed and had a right to get their story told. And I, who had come of age in Seattle's General Strike, was ready to be back in action. I was getting tired and worn down by the ease and routine of my job in New York—the leading edge of struggle was the place for me.

But the fall had been busy and Jessie and I were both tired. Before we opened the office in Pittsburgh, we decided to take time off on a long-delayed honeymoon. Jessie received an allowance of $166 a month, quite a sum during the Great Depression, and more than enough to finance a trip to Latin America. I had followed the fight of General Sandino in Nicaragua and had already written stories about the collapse of world sugar prices, which resulted in the unemployment of two hundred thousand workers in Cuba alone. In the broadest sense, we, at Federated Press, were all aware of the colonial relationship between the United States and much of the Spanish-speaking portion of the hemisphere. We often visited and interviewed Latin American refugees at the offices of the Anti-Imperialist League. In fact, in several of my stories, I specifically referred to Cuba's dictator, Gerardo Machado, as the puppet of National City Bank. I wanted to see if Cuba was as close to revolt as I heard and hoped, and I also wanted to check out the progress of revolution in Mexico. Since Jessie was anxious to visit her father in Jamaica, we were both pleased to go south. We took a Ward Liner to Havana, a dismal ship, but we reached our destination without incident. At least in weather, Havana in January was a joy compared with New York. As soon as we settled into our little penthouse apartment, I went looking for trouble, and did I find it!

At the leftist Workers Center of Havana, the headquarters of the Havana City Confederation of Labor, which controlled nearly all the important Cuban unions, I saw blood spattered on the walls from a recent shootout by Dictator Machado's troops. I had credentials from Federated Press and decided to interview Juan Arevalo, the secretary of the tame Cuban Federation of Labor, a right-wing organization (controlled by Machado) that was always trying to curry favor with the A.F. of L. Imagine my consternation when next day the outfit's daily came out with a two-column headline that I, a representative of Federated Press and an emissary of the president of the A.F. of L., had brought greetings from the American labor movement to this bunch of labor thugs. A neat example of reporting in a Latin American fascist newspaper! I forced them to print a retraction the following day.

Behind the plummeting sugar prices and overproduction, I found starvation and destitution among the sugar plantation workers. Before the crash, assured six months' work, they were, by 1930, lucky to get three or four months. During the busy season, twelve-hour days yielded Cuban sugar plantation workers forty cents, down from sixty cents in 1928, and a top figure of four dollars in the booming days of 1919 before the panic. Small growers, who rented their own farms and hired no laborers, were being ruined by the American sugar companies. Of the $1,250,000,000 of United States capital invested in Cuba, at least three-fifths was in sugar. American companies intensified the chronic unemployment on the island by importing black laborers—under slave conditions—from Haiti and

Santo Domingo. The companies kept these people in semimilitary compounds, guarded by troops and denied every civil liberty. In 1925, the Machado dictatorship broke up the sugar workers' union by force of arms, assassinating Enrique Varona, the president, and other officials. Though the plantation workers had been without any defense (save underground committees unable to function as a union), spontaneous strikes had broken out.

By the time we arrived, the position of the dictator was, indeed, becoming untenable. Reports of Cuban unrest appearing in the United States papers had made the tourist season a flat failure. The big hotels were less than half occupied and famous tourist hangouts had only a thin fringe of customers. Nearly every important person and organization not directly subsidized by the government had taken, or took while we were there, an open stand against Machado. One story I wrote for Federated Press, under the title "Lackeys Desert as Dictator Machado Weakens," gives the mood of Cuba during our visit:

> Unrelenting struggle by class-conscious workers, rebellious students, and foes of terrorism has seriously checked the bloody progress of Cuba's dictator, Gen. Machado. Their attitude of no compromise may result in his abdication in the near future.
>
> The dictator has cried for truce by offering to release the hundreds of workers, students, doctors, chemists, lawyers and other opponents held in penitentiary and fortress. The Cuban supreme court, regarded as a supple tool of the terror, has sensed Machado's growing weakness. It has decided by unanimous vote that his suppression of nearly all the Havana newspapers and magazines early in the year was unconstitutional. It has further held that recent elections were not free and has ordered new elections. This decision has forced Machado to restore constitutional guarantees in certain districts in preparation for the new elections for senate and chamber. The craven autocrat, cowering in his heavily guarded presidential palace, did not dare attend the opening of his new packed Congress in the new $20,000,000 capitol for fear of attempts on his life.
>
> Workers and students ignored Machado's offer of amnesty. The novel tactics that have struck terror into the butcher's own camp continue. The weapon used is dynamite in small quantities "for its moral effect." Hundreds of "bombillas" and petardos—small bombs—have exploded in Havana and the provincial cities in the past two months. Little damage has been done to property and few have been injured. But the result has been uproar, terror in government circles, crackling

cable wires, and a neverending search for "enemies of the government" on the part of Machado's 2,000 police and 12,000 soldiers. Every house in Cuba has been ordered searched for guns, ammunition and dynamite.

Infuriated by any expression of free opinion, Machado has extended the net of his arrests to members of the Conservative Party, which supported him in the last election. The brother of former Pres. Menocal is one of the latest residents of Cabanas fortress. Workers, students and others held in Havana prisons were recently hustled off to the penitentiary on the distant Isle of Pines. Arrests of his own soldiers has been a new factor, perturbing to the dictatorship but bespeaking unrest in the army.

Prominent Cubans see a change in attitude on the part of the U.S. State Department in Machado's recent retreat. His proffered amnesty, the supreme court's rebuff to him on suppression of the press, and the restoration of constitutional guarantees for new elections all point to the contention that the Secretary of State believes Machado is making a mess of it as American viceroy in Cuba. Either the dictator must make a cleaner job of ruling the island for American capital, or he must make way for a more efficient ruler. The present situation, with the threatened breakdown in government, is becoming intolerable for American business and investors. A revolution might fail to respect American interests in sugar, banking, power and light and the huge trade in American exports to the island.

Once again, always the optimist, I thought revolution just around the corner and, once again, I was a bit premature. Though conditions continued to deteriorate, Machado did not fall until 1933, and even then the government that replaced him was not much of an improvement.

After a short stay in Jamaica, we decided to spend the whole spring in Mexico. The more I saw and heard of America's southern colonies, the more I wanted to know Mexico. A revolutionary nation, whose people had attempted to write their experience into the very constitution, Mexico fascinated me. The Mexican constitution instituted universal, free, secular, and public education; redefined the rights of private property, making them contingent on the needs of society, and gave labor the right to organize, unionize, and strike. On paper, the Mexicans were far ahead of the United States. The workday was eight hours, the state set a minimum wage, and no discrimination on the basis of nationality or sex was allowed. As soon as we arrived at Progreso, the port of Yucatán, we met bona fide, class-conscious proletarians: the stevedores charged us an outrageous sum to carry suitcases a short trip down a wormy dock! We used Mexico City as a base of action; before the days of *Gran Turismo* it was a different and pleasanter place. I settled into learning Spanish and shorthand and both of us nosed around Mexico, filing stories now and then for Federated Press.

I soon saw the limits of the Mexican Revolution. The labor bill of rights, written into the constitution in principle, had never been enacted into the Mexican federal code. The general idea received a great deal of lip service, but no law defined specific provisions, modes of enforcement, or penalties for violation. Among the representatives of both workers and peasants, the fear was growing that the government had sold out the Revolution. I was glad to see the energetic and vigorous response of the peasants and workers. Against a conservative proposed labor code under discussion in the Chamber of Deputies, responsible leaders of organized labor in Mexico urged a general strike, if necessary, and even hinted at armed revolution when they addressed sometimes large protest meetings of workers. They didn't flinch in making their points; I still remember one large rally of the dispossessed. "This proposed law would hand over the Mexican proletariat to the exploitation of Yankee capitalism. Either the deputies wrote it in bad faith or they carry their brains in their feet," declared Ricardo Trevino, speaker for the Crom, which, with the A.F. of L., was affiliated with the Pan American Federation of Labor. "Both," the crowd yelled back and Trevino nodded. "We are going before Congress to fight for our rights, but if we are defeated there, we will go on fighting in our trenches," said Trevino to thunderous applause. Ernesto Velasco, of the Electrical Workers Union, attacked the vagueness of the wording on the eight-hour day, the recognition of company unions, and the practical abolition of the right to strike: "laws like this are what bring on social revolution." Salvador Romero, of the Railroad Workers, seconded these sentiments, against "this attack on unionism, we must go forward and do constructive work—at the cost of a new revolution if it be necessary." The speakers openly challenged the government while recognizing the complexity of Mexico's problems. Said Trevino:

> For a permanent law defining the rights of labor, the government has come forward with a code which sweeps away all the rights gained by

the blood and tears of the revolution and written into the constitution. Naturally labor cannot accept it. We realize the country is in a crisis. We have offered to make even more sacrifices, if capital will make sacrifices in proportion. But this must be through a temporary agreement, to last as long as the crisis, not by a permanent law.

Willingness to go to the limit in fighting the proposed law was echoed by other speakers. "If Mexico is to destroy the workers to attract foreign capital, I say that we need other investments—the capital of the workers, the only capital they have—in new flows of blood which we will pour out before we let conditions go back to worse than before the Revolution," said Chairman Mario Rojas Avendano, of the graphic arts union.

The workers also had strong support from organized peasants at this rally. A representative of Mexico's peasantry joined in criticizing the government. The government had abandoned the ideals of Emiliano Zapata, the agrarian revolutionary, and failed to break up the big haciendas for the peasants, said R. Lope Fuentes, of the National Peasant League. He described Mexico as a great estate divided between the old and the new landlords: "The new law would exclude all peasants and agricultural workers from fair labor provisions. It is a crab law—walking backwards to 1908." (In 1908, Mexicans lived under the absolute dictatorship of Porfiro Diaz, a man remembered by all workers and peasants as a slave driver.) I remembered many rallies like this—militant, clear-sighted, and steadfast—long after leaving Mexico. Everywhere oppressed people fought back, even when ultimate victory seemed beyond their grasp.

II

On our way back to New York we stopped in San Antonio to spend some time with the Mavericks. I then headed on alone while Jessie went to her mother's home in Winnetka. I bought a jalopy for forty dollars, loaded it with our household goods, and headed for the mountains of Pennsylvania with my old friend, Hays Jones. Highway Thirty, the main route to Pittsburgh, had only two lanes, but countless hills. Up one hill—and then more and more—with the old car puffing, steaming, and stalling. I knew immediately that Pittsburgh was the real stuff. Its appendages reached to Beaver Falls, about thirty miles out, working up to a grand industrial inferno-climax along the river to the heart of a town, gray and black, grim, huge, and hard-boiled. Even the police dressed the part in dark gray, almost military, uniforms. What an introduction, but we made it and eventually rented a second-floor apartment in a working-class neighborhood on a steep hill overlooking the city.

I had just arrived when the news from Harlan County caused a shake-up in our plans. A letter I wrote to Jessie hit the highlights:

> Verne [Smith] told me an amazing story of Harlan County, Kentucky, where the U.M.W., in response to appeals, organized the mines. Then the boys wanted action and went on strike. The U.M.W. threw 'em out and the Wobblies came in. The companies organized squads of gunmen who began closing in on all mine camps, searching every house methodically for guns and literature.
>
> These bimbos wear armor plate over chest and back and mail around arms, thighs and bellies. They move in squads of six to ten cars, two of which have machine guns mounted. One car has an airplane gun—the rest of the deputies carry sub-machine guns. Fortunately, one gang got ambushed and ten deputies were killed, and one miner. In other cases the miners blow off the deps' heads with shotguns as other parts are armored.
>
> After the big ambush the deps swept through the county and now thirty miners are held for first degree murder. Trial to start Aug. 15. Check this with I.W.W. defense committee, Chicago. If this story appeals to you and trial really starts, can you resist going to Harlan? The county seat is fairly safe if you conceal real objective and go as a capitalist reporter. A West Virginia reporter was shot in the legs and the dirty work takes place out in the mining camps. . . .

My facts were not entirely straight. For one thing it was none other than Boris Israel, *our* Federated Press correspondent in Harlan, who had been forced into the car loaded with deputies, taken to the county line, told to run, and peppered with birdshot. (What a name for a reporter hoping to work in Harlan County!)

Jessie was somewhat less than enthusiastic about the idea initially, but she came around. Her family connections made her the logical person to go for us. Presumably, a woman of her social and class background would be treated more carefully than the run-of-the-mill labor reporter. I still warned her about the consequences, because she was newer to the racket than I and because, just before she left, we got some news that was about half-funny and half-frightening:

Please understand that this may mean jail, Jail, JAIL, and if you don't want to go to jail you'd better stay away. A Union Theological Sherwood Eddy goody-goody boy was tossed into the can just like that because he had in his brief case, among other revolutionary documents, *a CPUSA pamphlet on Gastonia by a certain Lloyd* . . . if you get tossed in, I have no assurance that you'll be gotten out right away.

Jessie went—with some sort of disguise for protection, and we, behind the lines, tried to help by urging all of our Federated Press clients to feature her stories, particularly if she were threatened. The theory was that, hopefully, the more public a figure she was, the less likely she'd be attacked. Our strategy didn't, as she explains, work as well as we had hoped. But as soon as she was threatened, we swung into action—I wrote immediately to keep her appraised, to reassure her, and to urge caution:

You're holding out swell. The wires hummed on the day we all heard of the threat. The governor promised a "diligent inquiry," *Editor and Publisher* was duly informed and FLP tells me there were five AP wires on the subject in one day.

Please don't feel so cocky about your safety. Don't go around alone. They'll probably pull off some kidnapping stunt, if nothing else, and the experience might be decidedly unpleasant. If anything happens, we're all primed to sic Dreiser, Dos Passos, Vorse and as many others as possible into Harlan. They may go anyway. . . .

You're doing a swell job down there and everyone around here is lost in admiration of your pluck and nonchalance in stepping into such a hot spot—and getting away with it for the time being anyway.

And we certainly were! I had complained facetiously to Jessie, just before she left, that the first thing people asked upon seeing me was "how's your wife?" I had said, "dammit, that's the trouble of being married to a gal like you. I'm merely your husband." Jessie's first-class journalism in Harlan didn't change that—thank goodness—though I was glad to have her back in Pittsburgh.

We opened a Federated Press bureau and sent out stories to the main office twice a week. Pittsburgh, indeed, the whole of western Pennsylvania during the depths of the Depression, was a gruesome sight. The Depression hit steel harder than any other industry, and, perhaps, Pittsburgh harder than any other city. Steel production fell, in 1932, to its lowest mark in the twentieth century. Blast furnace activity in the week of March 31, 1933, was the lowest ever recorded. Rail production hadn't hit such a low since 1865. Iron ore shipments on the Great Lakes did not exceed their 1880–1885 levels. The mills throbbed no more under the pounding of steel ingots and billets roaring through the rolls. Production under the best of all economic systems virtually halted. The view of Pittsburgh Jessie and I had from our hilltop home was an historical first. We could actually see the town. Natives told me that before, when the mills worked, smog and smoke hid the city.

I traveled the area from one steel town to another, though I must admit, I did little in the way of union reporting. The failure of the Great Steel Strike (1919–1920), in which the workers had been viciously attacked by J. P. Morgan's minions and sold out by their own union, had left proud memories, but little organization. Some men I talked to still remembered that to break that great effort the industry had prepared as if for actual war. They said that the Corporation—U.S. Steel—was too big to lick then, but they would wait for a propitious day. For the one week of September 21, 1931, I turned the following grim catalogue over to Federated Press:

Two miners were found burned to death by an explosion in the Brothers Valley mine at Berlin. They were Paul Cruik and Frank Slifco.

A structural iron foreman, Harold Mathisen, was killed on the 20th floor of the new Mellon Gulf Oil Bldg. when he was hit by an elevator drain. Union building trades workers quit the job for the day.

Out of work, unable to provide for his wife and three children, John Lutheran, 54, Clairton, hanged himself near his home.

Stephen F. Cuneo, 62, and his wife, 57, took heart depressant to end life as starvation faced them in their home in Bellevue. She died but he may recover to face the uncertainties of life in a world which has no place for old workers.

Basil Kofwaski, Midland, drank lye to end a jobless life. He will recover.

Robert C. Hager, from Aliquippa, the Jones & Laughlin steel town, turned on the gas to end existence for himself and family, including five children. Unsuccessful, he was jailed.

Mrs. Marion Witherspoon, 64, is in the McKeesport hospital expected to die from swallowing poison. Her husband Charles, 72, is unable to find work.

John Novak, 38, father of four children, unable to find work, jumped from the second story of his home, suffering probable fracture of the spine. He is in McKeesport Hospital, expected to die.

Several employees of the Seven Baker Bros. Co. plant were asphyxiated by leaking ammonia fumes. Soft mud on the Monongahala river bank saved the life of Oliver Kayler, laborer, when he fell 30 feet from the new McKeesport bridge.

Her husband out of work, seven children living out of ten born, Mrs. Ed Nicholson bore twins. "I had only prepared for one baby, and scantily at that," she said.

The response of the steel magnates? In Braddock, Rankin, and Homestead, Carnegie Steel, out of the goodness of its heart, would hand out food baskets to employees filled with stale, sometimes moldy bread, sour old bacon, and flour laced with maggots. These workers had to be kept alive until the Depression was over and they could be used again.

No one needed a union more than these people. As long as organizing depended on Mike Tighe's Amalgamated Association of Iron, Steel and Tin Workers, however, the unionization of the area seemed a pipe dream. One might have expected to find a lean, bitter, wary strategist in the person of Tighe, the man who dictated the labor betrayal of the Great Steel Strike. Actually, Tighe was a complacent old man of benevolent mien, short, pudgy, and self-satisfied—known as "Grandmother" Tighe to serious unionists. I interviewed him in 1934, but what he said to me then, he had told others for years. His views were tragically consistent for the whole time I lived in Pittsburgh. I could scarcely remember that Tighe, a member of the Amalgamated since 1876, was once the Union Terror of the Wheeling iron district. An aggressive, hard-hitting young puddler, Tighe rose to the attention of the Amalgamated leaders in the 1890s and became assistant secretary-treasurer of the union in 1899, ascending step by step to the presidency in 1918. In 1934, Tighe ushered me affably to a chair in the front parlor of his home in suburban Pittsburgh. He was voluble. In a high, piping voice he explained his philosophy and detailed the tragic history of his union. "There is no hope for a large majority of the workers in the steel industry," he said. But he hated to dwell on the present. Fondly he recalled the old iron mills of his boyhood when work abounded for good men at good wages.

But the majority of the workers now, I asked him, do they get good wages? His face puckered, he shook his head. No, they don't. And the Amalgamated? The Amalgamated, he declared proudly, was one of the oldest trade unions in the country—sixty years old. He scampered back to the good old days in the Wheeling district when the iron puddlers and heaters and rollers fought for their rights as up-standing workingmen, called no man their superior, knuckled down to no trust. His eyes kindled, his manner was animated. And then he thought of the steel mills and his voice changed. No, the men weren't strong enough to cope with the money powers of Wall Street. The Homestead Strike was lost, and so was the strike of 1901, and of 1904, and of 1910. He catalogued them all and sighed, "You cannot fight a two billion dollar diversified corporation."

He became philosophical. "Only those directly connected with the movement can readily understand the problems that a man holding my position must face," he explained. The workers, in a sense, were to blame. The Amalgamated had always been ready to organize them, but they had not heeded the call. They were too shortsighted. "My dear old friend and collaborator, Samuel Gompers, said: 'The movement cannot proceed faster than the intelligence of the workers.'"

Tighe closed the interview. "Yes," he said, on the way to the door, "the responsibilities of being the president of a labor organization are not easily understood by the general public. On the one side there are foolish, cruel and stupid employers who will not give justice to their employees. That breeds an unintelligent, irresponsible element in the industry that is susceptible to Red preachings. It is our duty to guide this great movement between the rocks of prejudice and igno-rance on the part of employers and of designing men who are using honest American workingmen as tools of Moscow." With such lead-ership, the likelihood that the Amalgamated would grow beyond the horseshoe factory in Buffalo that constituted one of its major locals was not great. In the early thirties many workers believed Mike agreed not to organize if Carnegie Steel and the rest would give the Amalgamated a little hall in Pittsburgh for the union officers. They had only a few thousand members. And during this horrible period when the mills were shut down, the union was pretty well shut down too. Maybe Mike Tighe went into hibernation. He certainly had nothing to do.

The Communists did the only real organizing in Pittsburgh before FDR. Their Unemployed Councils raised the loudest and most con-sistent voices against oppression, though the Socialist organization, called the Workers Alliance, did good work. These groups demonstrated for relief, food, clothing, and fuel. One group of the Unemployed Councils met every Saturday in the Hill district near downtown Pittsburgh—and the police came every Saturday to beat them up. Still, week after week, they came back, bloodied but determined to be heard. Jessie and I observed and reported the outrages for the Pittsburgh Civil Liberties Committee, of which I was a board member, and the Federated Press. We complained to the chief of police and the mayor, to little avail. The Unemployed Councils didn't secure their immediate goals: recognition of the dignity of human labor, the right to shelter and sustenance, but I do believe that they kept the fires burning and helped stave off complete surrender until the fighting days returned.

Though I concentrated my interest and activity on left and labor issues, I also cooperated with Pittsburgh's few and frightened liberals. The Hungry Club met once a week. Composed largely of lawyers, small businessmen, and social workers, the Club was one of the main forums for liberals. Listening to speakers who criticized the status quo was the main staple of the group, pretty mild stuff, to be sure. One had to have guts in Pittsburgh to even go that far. Among the liberals, Jewish people were the most active. Relegated to their own ghetto, middle class but separate, they dug up money for the hunger marchers and Pittsburgh's settlement house—no other ethnic group responded as they did to help people.

And in the early thirties, valuable and necessary work was available for all to do. When hunger marchers from the Middle West to Washington passed to the south of us on Highway Forty, we gathered tires, food, cash for gasoline, and clothing for them. I see, even now, that pitiful procession—weary, hungry men, women, and children in ancient jalopies and trucks going to petition their government to save them from starvation. One such hunger march in the dead of winter was stopped on the highway outside of Washington—President Hoover did not want to be bothered by the sight of them. Another, that of the veterans of World War I seeking a bonus, camped along a river in the eastern part of the city until troops under the command of Generals MacArthur and Eisenhower burned them out. These notables won the Battle of Anacostia Flats against the bedraggled hosts of ragged veterans!

III

As I got the feel of the place in researching stories and helping in various struggles, I came up against one of the overwhelming facts of life Pittsburghers lived with: Andrew Mellon. Anecdotes of Andy Mellon and his family were a regular feature of conversation: had I heard how the county had to chop off a piece of the Court House to widen Grant Street, which would facilitate the development of the Mellon's heavy real estate investments in the area? Did I know how the Mellons allowed the Bank of Pittsburgh to fail tying up the savings of tens of thousands through the bitterest winter in the city's memory? And on and on. Among the common folk of the city, the Mellon name did not excite the glow of civic pride. The family's sixty-year history of money lending aroused deep distrust and animosity. Some people feared the local de Medicis, and were circumspect about what they would say for attribution, but that didn't mean they wouldn't talk.

They told me that Andy Mellon owned the town—more specifically, Union Trust, Mellon National Bank, Gulf Oil, Aluminum Company of America, Koppers Coke, Pittsburgh Coal, and many lesser outfits. Andrew's brother, Richard K. Mellon, had expressed the family's social philosophy only too aptly when he testified before a Senate committee, "You can't run a coal mine without machine guns." Andy himself had held offices at cabinet and ambassadorial ranks. Yet, the *New York Times* had never printed Andrew Mellon's name before 1921, when he was mentioned for appointment as the Secretary of the Treasury under Harding. Mellon, a shy, wispy tycoon, the biggest billionaire in western Pennsylvania, the fat cat there of the Republican Party, a major architect of national fiscal policy, was surrounded by mystery. His celebrated plan for shifting the burden of taxes from the rich to the middle and working class made him "the Greatest Secretary of the Treasury since Alexander Hamilton," in the commercial press, which had little interest in his private finances. As the Great Depression wore on, Mellon became a liability to President Hoover, who shifted him to the Court of St. James. He lasted until Roosevelt's time, and then disappeared into the mists of history. All the while he paid and supported the Coal and Iron Police of Pennsylvania who roamed the steel and coal towns keeping law and order. Their horses, trained in riot control, were adept at using the sidewalks instead of the streets. They, along with the private police forces of other companies, supplemented the ordinary constabulary. None recognized any limits to brutality directed against workers. A seething cauldron of humanity kept under control by legitimated force and violence was at the core of the Mellon story—no wonder no one had told it before.

I was starting to feel that workaday journalism no longer presented much of a challenge to me and I felt destiny had called me to do a book about the Mellons: no one else had tackled the subject and the Mellons' story seemed too vast for an article or two. I was ready to try my hand at a more demanding kind of writing than cranking out articles for the Federated Press. News reporting had introduced me to the research and organizational skills necessary for a biography. Though the kind of writing I had done would not help me construct psychological interpretations of Mellon's behavior, I believed the less said about his psyche, the better.

Most of the material for the book came from congressional inquiries into Mellon's labor and business practices, dubious even by the minimal standards of contemporary federal law. Beyond what I heard informally, I found out little in Pittsburgh. The newspapers feared the family too much to violate the Mellons' protected privacy. Andy's father, Judge Thomas Mellon, a salty, thrifty, old-line Presbyterian character, had written a biography for his family's private use. A few copies, however, fell into public hands and I used it to advantage. Old Thomas was at least honest in his parsimony and acquisitiveness, though this did not seem to be a family trait. Finally, I had access to the fatuous biography of Mellon written when he was being touted for the Presidency, of all things. What a wretched piece of work—though authentic.

The results of my research sometimes surprised even me. Few knew by what means the Mellons had drawn such prodigious nourishment from a whole nation's needs. No other Croesus levied a toll on so many articles and services. The householder of Pittsburgh, Milwaukee, and the Twin Cities bought Mellon coal; in Philadelphia or New England he bought Mellon coke; in Boston or Brooklyn his wife cooked by Mellon gas. By the thirties, most intelligent housewives probably realized the relationship between the high price of aluminum wares and the Mellon monopoly. Yet cooking utensils were merely one phase of the tightest metal monopoly known to history. All industry bent the knee to the Aluminum Company of America; electric companies needed aluminum wire for long-distance transmission; builders required aluminum for lightweight beams or embellishments; auto and airplane manufacturers needed aluminum for parts. And this list, of course, did not include those who depended on Mellon for steel, plate glass, or paint. This summary does not comprehend Mellon's vast investments in a maze of related and unrelated companies across the nation.

Pittsburghers had underestimated Mellon, for he owned a large part of the continent—which became something of a problem for me. I finished the book in a year and sent it off to David Lloyd, Jessie's cousin and a most able, affable literary agent. He had great success with the manuscript. The chief readers for Macmillan, Harper's, and other leading houses thought it was a great book. When the manuscript went to the legal beagles, they, one and all, turned thumbs down. Though they knew I had not libeled Mellon, the house might spend tens or hundreds of thousands of dollars to defend a suit brought by the Mellons, to whom legal costs would be chickenfeed. It looked hopeless in 1932.

Anna Louise Strong came to the rescue with a diversion just when I thought I was doomed never to be a biographer of Mellon, or anybody else. Anna Louise had become associate editor of the Moscow *Daily News*, an English-language paper published for some thirty thousand American engineers and technicians who had fled their native country to find employment in the Soviet Union. The opportunity to observe the Soviet system firsthand was a real inducement and we decided to go. I was to be technical editor—a position unknown in U.S. journalism but comparable to make-up editor. All copy passed through my hands for layout and ultimate production.

The staff of the *Daily News* came from all parts of the English-speaking world, from Britain to Australia. Some were natives, but others were Russians recently returned. The result? An awesome combination of all the dialects known to English, and often, a wooden style unworthy of either Russian or English. Our clientele must have been amazed at this mixture of British, American, and Russian English. The cultural hodgepodge sometimes amazed me too. The Britishers were a stubborn lot whose ideas about journalism reflected those of the *Times* of London, in which the ads covered page one and the news began somewhere around page eight.

One principle sustained our whole staff—disdain for the typewriter. Each "editor" on the *Daily News* had a stenographer. The hubbub when all dictated to their stenos was indescribable. The stenos would then steal away to a typing room to produce copy for the "editors" for revision. My desk was the final stop. Since I used my own typewriter, and kept some hard-working graduate of the Foreign Languages School out of a job, I was considered something of a backslider. After this mess was assembled for an eight-page standard-size paper, I took the last dummies to the print shop several blocks away. I never got used to the Russian system of *propuski*, passes needed to enter any building. Once, running rather late, and unable to find my *propusk* immediately, I dashed upstairs. The clamor built behind me as various dignitaries of the doors screamed at me and began to follow. They knew me perfectly well, but the ritual rigmarole had to be observed.

We spent most of our time in the offices of the *Daily News*, the second floor of an old mansion in what had probably been a ballroom. We unbuttoned our sheepskin parkas when the temperature climbed to a stifling sixty degrees. Only Anna Louise and Mikhail Borodin, the editor, had private offices. Jessie was Borodin's favorite translator—after Stalin had made a speech, he would bring the copy to her and say, "Now Dzyayssie, I want a good translation, but not *too* good." One of the few members of the staff fluent in both languages, Jessie was invaluable to him. The Bronxites, who thought they spoke English, represented the other extreme.

Living for Jessie and me was spartan. Though we had access to the store for foreign workers, quite a cut above the stores for the natives, I lost thirty pounds during the winter. We didn't complain for the Russians endured much worse. As a matter of fact, we felt rather guilty. People in the shop actually mailed loaves of bread to relatives in the Ukraine, the Socialist breadbasket of the Soviet Union. Pathetic remnants of vegetables and wormy apples fit only for the garbage can stocked the shops. Even shopping in our store was quite a chore. Various comestibles rested on several counters. You queued up at one counter, finally got in an order, then went to the cashier, got a receipt, went back to the counter, picked up the order, and then moved over to the next counter to resume the same weary routine. We found we couldn't both work and shop so we hired an English woman to shop for us. Russians didn't have this option. The only efficient stores were the liquor stores, all brightly lit and filled with Soviet liquors. Vice always found a way, even in the Soviet Union.

Jessie was unhappy. It was not like the old days in 1927 when life was free and easy, the restaurants good, the company tops, the work interesting. Now times were hard, the food miserable, the company at the *Moscow News* rather on the dull side, the work of translating Russian stories of Socialist triumphs in new paper mills and state farms hardly earthshattering. With me it was different—an old dog in the slot doing what comes naturally. I did have problems with Soviet journalism. Charting the Party line could be tricky. Once, a riot occurred in Geneva when the police shot people down during a peace rally. Tass had reported the incident rather fully so I thought, naturally, the *Daily News* should also. My headline for the day was "Fifty Shot in Rally in the Peace Capitol," or something like that. The night editor took one look at my work and said, "Comrade O'Connor, you have no sense of poleetical seegnificance," and substituted "Incident at Geneva," for my headline. As on the *Daily Worker*, two under editors kept an eye on the chief editor, Borodin. We had no idea at the time that Borodin was in trouble and, of course, could not know that in a few years he would be dead in a Siberian labor camp, or for that matter that Anna Louise would be expelled from the Soviet Union as an American (or Yugoslav) spy.

I was relieved when a cablegram arrived from David Lloyd, my agent in New York, who had finally placed the Mellon manuscript. We were on a one-year contract to the *Daily News* and would need Borodin's consent to break the contract if we were to return. Jessie and I marched into Borodin's office with the cablegram. He looked at us sternly and said, in effect, "*Nyet.*" After that he chuckled and remarked that we were very poor specimens of life under the Soviets and would have to go to Yalta in the Crimea for a couple of weeks. It was a welcome gift. I had just been elected an *udarnik* by the staff— roughly, a hard-working, devoted Socialist—so I guess Jessie and I were entitled to a little fattening up. I remember on the trip down how forlorn the station looked at Kiev. We got off for some refreshments, but nothing was available. We found ourselves at the center of the great campaign to collectivize the peasants and rout the *kulaks*. There just wasn't any food for love or money. At one point, somewhat later at a rest home, I picked up a copy of the *Communist Manifesto* and read it on a bench overlooking the sea. Little children in rags came up and begged—"*Khleb pozhalujsta*"—bread, please. They were children of the *kulaks*. What a heartbreaking contrast between the ideals of the Communist pioneers and the stark reality!

How did I deal with these disconcerting and, sometimes, frankly depressing facts of Soviet life? For one thing, I had no idea how the peasants were suffering. Stalin had not committed his most gruesome excesses and much of what he had done was kept from public view. Reports of Soviet "terror" and injustices in the Western press almost always turned out to be half-truths and fabrications, and I came to reject them reflexively. I did know the Soviet Union had serious problems, but so did my own country and, in those days, at least the Soviets *espoused* a much greater ideal. Remember, I had seen children starving in Pittsburgh; I had seen their parents jobless and humiliated; I had seen those who dared to dissent from this state of affairs clubbed bloody by the police on a weekly basis. And the most basic, most minimal reforms were regularly rejected as un-American. My writing in defense of the Revolution often set the Soviet experience in the context of a troubled world. I wrote many Federated Press stories like this one:

TALES ABOUT RUSSIA AMAZE WORKERS THERE

To the foreign worker in the Soviet Union, the gossip, rumor and unintelligent observations broadcast by the Will Durants and the Isaac Don Levines concerning conditions in the workers' and peasants' republic create no little amazement, especially when contrasted with the facts concerning the financial paralysis and industrial crisis in the United States and the bloody terror in Germany.

Against the Isaac Don Levine complaint that the Soviet Union lacks natural resources to become a first-class industrial nation is the indisputable fact, pointed out by the Berlin Institute of Industrial Statistics, that Russia in 1932 stood second only to the United States in industrial production. The opening of new factories, mines and mills is now such a commonplace in Soviet papers that often the news is tucked away in a 3-line filler at the bottom of the page. From every corner of the immense land come reports by scientific expeditions of the discovery of new mineral resources. And why not, in a nation three times larger than the United States, a nation whose soil has merely been scratched by geologists?

Levine's latest fabrication—that Russia's alleged shortage of coal has caused the importation of "large quantities" from Spitsbergen—is an illustration of the use of half-truths. The whole truth is that the Arctic

Coal Trust recently acquired two small mines in Spitsbergen, closed since war times, in order to assure Murmansk, the Arctic railroad port, a convenient coal supply. Murmansk's coal will now come 500 miles by water from Spitsbergen instead of 2,000 miles by rail from central Russia, a tremendous saving in transportation costs.

In any event, to foreign workers here, it seems an odd complaint to come from America, where coal production is at disaster levels, that Russian industrial expansion in the past few years has outgrown her immediate capacity to furnish enough coal. Unemployed American coal miners may well envy the "plight" of the Soviet Union, where new coal mines can't be opened rapidly enough to supply industrial needs.

The lurid "red terror" tales also cause no little amazement here among foreign workers, who read in the American papers of police attacks, with clubs and gas, on the American unemployed. At least the so-called "red terror" is not used against workers and poor peasants. It is directed exclusively against Soviet enemies— against those who attempt to sabotage production in the factories, and against the richer peasants who are opposing the socialization of Soviet agriculture by every means from passive resistance to sowing weeds in the collective farm fields and poisoning cattle.

Recent news of the financial panic in America, the deepening of world crisis, the war in the Far East, the terror in Germany and the imminence of war in western Europe make the Soviet citizen feel that the years of sacrifice spent in building a Socialist state were richly worthwhile. In the international field he sees the growing prestige of the Soviet Union, with France desperately seeking an alliance with Moscow against the Hitler menace and with the Roosevelt regime reported ready to grant recognition, in an effort to strengthen the American position in the Pacific against Japan.

I remained deeply committed to the Bolshevik Revolution throughout the thirties. It was the only reasonable position in the face of the facts as I knew them.

When we returned to Pittsburgh, I was quickly caught up in the final stages of work on the book. I entitled the manuscript *Mellon's Millions*, which I thought rather catchy. The John Day Company rushed the manuscript into production and it proved to be quite a success. As for libel, Walsh said his was a small concern and he was willing to take the chance that the big houses had refused. I must say we were surprised at the reception the book got. The *New York Times Book Review* gave it page one in a most laudatory review and the daily edition followed up with another. My book benefited from the changing times. When I first submitted the book in 1932, Hoover was finishing his Depression reign, and my thesis was taboo. By 1933, Roosevelt had been elected, the New Deal was in full swing, and my own attitude toward the Mellons reflected widespread national disgust with the inept malefactors of great wealth. The first of its kind in this new era, the Mellon book was followed by many others, such as Matthew Josephson's *The Robber Barons* and Ferdinand Lundberg's *America's Sixty Families*. I enjoyed the acclaim my book got from one end of the country to the other, especially since adverse reviews were few and far between. It ran through two or three printings, and a one-dollar hard-cover reprint by Blue Ribbon.

At first people couldn't buy the book in Pittsburgh. After all, as I had proved, Mellon owned the town. Department and book stores kept the book under the counter to be produced surreptitiously upon request, but not to be displayed. Some enterprising fellow got the idea of renting a vacant storefront downtown in the so-called Golden Triangle—and there were plenty of vacant stores in 1933. He filled the windows and counters with *Mellon's Millions* and did a land office business.

IV

After the excitement was over we began taking a look at the Pittsburgh area again. How things had changed in one short year! Hope had spread across the land with the New Deal. Mills were beginning to open. The New Deal gave industry the steel code and workers Section 7A of the National Industrial Recovery Act. This provision guaranteed workers the right to organize—a right denied since the Homestead Strike of 1892—and electrified the valleys. All over steel country union locals sprang up spontaneously. Not by virtue of Mike Tighe's Amalgamated, which couldn't have cared less. Every mill town—Duquesne, Homestead, Braddock—had its local and each carried a name that celebrated the new regime: the Blue Eagle, the New Deal, even the FDR locals. Most of these workers had no experience in union organization, but they knew they had the need and FDR said they had the right.

The workers still had an uphill battle, as they were soon to find. Roosevelt's act was quite emphatic on the *right* to organize, but silent on enforcement. In other words, no teeth. The steel and coal companies complied with N.R.A. so far as price-fixing under the guise of the steel code but confronted with collective bargaining—they said no deal, New or otherwise. The most the companies offered were employee-management committees, as they called them. These pathetic, readily manipulated company-run "unions" were as much as the steel men would give workers. The companies refused to recognize or deal with independent unions that the workers organized themselves. The existence of the Amalgamated Association of Iron, Steel and Tin Workers complicated matters still further. Mike Tighe was delighted to have dues flowing into his office from the unions springing up throughout the industry, and since his was the only A.F. of L. union that included steel workers, it was the logical one for the new locals to join. But Tighe had no more interest in leading a hard, harrowing fight for recognition now than he ever had. He gave the new locals Class B status—the right to pay dues but not to vote. He knew the rank and file wanted to strike if necessary: "They are a lot of deluded fools, inexperienced and raw. If their plans were carried out, this organization would lose its great investment in money and good will and would have no standing with the public. The Amalgamated has a splendid name, it is honored and respected everywhere. We can't trust such an institution to inexperienced hands." In the years that followed Mike was as good as his word. For once he acted decisively and when workers dared to reject his no-organizing, no-strike, no-energy unionism, he revoked their charters, sometimes effectively disbanding whole districts!

Happily for the American labor movement, the workers were better than their weak-kneed leaders. They rejected the sham company unions consistently and often at great personal cost. The companies brought enormous pressure to bear on them to participate in the management-run organizations. The capitalists hoped to make these bastard outfits seem viable and legitimate. Time after time the workers, native and ethnic, said no. "Company unions are good for the company, no good for workingmen," said one. "I don't vote. I don't want to be a Judas." A gray-haired man stepped up to me briskly in the Duquesne union hall and recounted his experience with the company union. "The boss came around and said, 'Right this way, boys.' But I told him I'm a small man, I can't use two chairs. And I can't use two unions. One's enough, and I got that already. 'Well,' he says, 'you're making an awful big mistake.'"

Indeed, in the very first week of October 1933, the masters of steel faced a labor revolt. The workers closed every important captive mine down. For the first time in fifty-three years not a pound of coke was made in the Connellsville beehive ovens. Hundreds of coal miners and half of Clairton mill hands circled the gates of Clairton steel in an endless, round-the-clock march. In Weirton, West Virginia, twelve thousand men struck in the name, but without the blessing, of the Amalgamated. Thousands more declared war on Ambridge, the seat of U.S. Steel's American Bridge Company. This first strike wave did not secure unionism; the riot sticks, tear gas, shotguns, and submachine guns outdid the workers. The struggle for the union would take years, but this time the workers refused to turn back. So hard, but what a change from the hopelessness of the twenties!

In the context of this organizing campaign, I found myself under arrest for the first and only time. Jessie was covering the Ambridge strike for the Federated Press. She lit out one morning for Ambridge, as usual, while I went downtown to deliver a tame lecture on labor at the Y.W.C.A. That afternoon, to my surprise, a flock of cops showed up at the house asking for Jessie. Time wore on until evening and more cops showed up—Pittsburgh and Ambridge. When the Ambridge chief saw a map of Russia on the wall, his worst suspicions were confirmed. "We'd get him for that in Ambridge," he exclaimed. About nine o'clock they wearied of waiting—probably wanted to have dinner—so they took me down to spend the night at the Allegheny County jail in lieu of Jessie! Next morning, rather weary and disheveled, I appeared in court and the judge waved the case aside. The story hit the front page in the Pittsburgh papers and the wire services carried it across the country. "Mellon Author Jailed in Mellon's Town." Most folks thought sure that Mellon was behind the arrest. Actually, Mellon wasn't that dumb, only the cops were. But it certainly helped sales at that downtown storefront. Thus ended one of the most humiliating incidents in my life—being arrested because the cops were looking for my wife.

By 1934, I was substituting for Laurence Todd, our Washington correspondent, so I was in and out of the city a good bit. I monitored the hearings in the workings of the N.R.A. steel code, which controlled production and prices, and theoretically set standards for minimum wages and maximum hours. In fact, the companies used it for price-fixing while they refused to reform labor practices and tried to crush any possibility for unionism. FDR found himself in a bind. He was no radical, but he had promised the workers the right to fair conditions and to unions, and they had acted on his word. Though the N.R.A. director, General Hugh Johnson, was all for the steel companies, FDR knew he needed a compromise that would give the workers something. As a reporter, I tried to keep workers informed and, hopefully, pressure the government to act.

The steel workers were down but far from out. Back in Pittsburgh, Mike Tighe tried to assemble a peaceful convention of the Amalgamated, but faced swarms of delegates he had never met before and who thought little of his brand of unionism. The rank and file were a spirited but inexperienced bunch, and Tighe wasn't about to help them out with strategy or procedure. If the Amalgamated turned into a democratic union, that would be the end of him! Jessie and I, along with others, stood by with our typewriters, listened to the rank and filers and helped draft and put through their resolutions, and encouraged as much as we could. All the resolutions carried, the rank and file went home elated, and nothing came of it. When the locals began to act on their own, Tighe expelled them. But here, finally, Tighe made the fatal mistake. By then even the liberals and New Dealers could see that expulsions could not solve the problem. In the long term, the policy discredited Tighe and the Amalgamated.

In the meantime, I also acted as a liaison between the rank and file in Pittsburgh and the labor strategists working to put teeth in the steel code to protect the steel workers. Our main contacts were Heber Blankenhorn, Harold Ruttenberg, and Stephen Rauschenbush (who, along with me, became known as the Four Horsemen). Blankenhorn was Senator Wagner's assistant in getting the Wagner Labor Relations Act passed. He had had an ongoing interest in the steel workers, having written the Interchurch World Commission report on the steel strike of 1919, which sharply criticized the owners and for which he was branded a Communist. From habit, having served in military intelligence in both world wars, Blankenhorn worked behind the scenes, so few will ever know the decisive influence he had on labor legislation.

A controversy arose because of the activities of the Four Horsemen. Did we deliberately advise the rank and filers against striking and thus prevent the rise of a militant rank-and-file union in steel? None of us would have ventured to tell the rank and filers to strike or not to strike. We Washington people had no inside knowledge of how well organized the rank and filers were, but I never heard anyone counsel against a strike. We knew that many if not most of the steel locals had organized only recently and had inexperienced leadership. We believed that a large-scale rank-and-file strike would be risky. It might be successful or it might peter out after a series of isolated and bloody skirmishes from lack of a centralized leadership. The fact is, however, that John L. Lewis of the U.M.W.A. and Myron Taylor of U.S. Steel settled the argument. At meetings in the Waldorf-Astoria in New York these two decided the fate of the newly born movement in steel. The result was the Steel Workers Organizing Committee (S.W.O.C.), headed by Phil Murray, Lewis's right-hand man in the Miners, and financed by the miners' union and other members of Lewis's Committee for Industrial Organization. That was the beginning of top-down unionism in steel instead of from the bottom up, as with the United Auto Workers. Still, Lewis and Murray faced a dilemma. U.S. Steel had said to them—you are welcome to organize our employees, if you can do it. But it wasn't likely that a bunch of miners could do it. Only the steel workers could, and the industry had purged all potential native organizers over the generations.

Once again, the people in Duquesne, Homestead, and Braddock, who understood organization and weren't afraid to do it, were the Communists. They came from the multitude of ethnic literary and drama societies that had already built a strong bond of unity and solidarity among their members and were often led by Communists. Murray turned to these people, who had already demonstrated an ability to organize and lead, to get S.W.O.C. going. They had seen action in strikes in Ambridge and elsewhere, where the opposition of the companies and their police had overwhelmed them. But the leaders had gained experience. Lewis had no compunction about hiring Communists as organizers since he had no alternative. He probably didn't have a great deal to lose since the bosses believed that all of the leaders and organizers of unions were Communists, anyway. The hard-headed corporate officials just assumed that their employees should want to join the Communist Party. Communists would be the natural political allies of a courageous worker, bosses felt, as they tried to put themselves in their employees' shoes. Communism, therefore, was the real enemy. They assigned the best operatives to Communist meetings, to check the movements of Communist leaders, to examine their habits of life, to record their residences and their friends.

One afternoon a mysterious person, who refused to identify himself, called on the phone. He asked me to meet him in the lobby of a downtown movie house. Jessie was apprehensive, but I reassured her that he would have trouble taking a good shot at me in the dark. I went downtown and made the acquaintance of Jack Spivak, the star labor spy man. We went to a restaurant and he told me that in New York he had worked his way into a labor spy factory and had obtained connections with Carnegie Steel's labor spy operation. He had been accepted on the eighth floor of the Carnegie Steel building as one of the boys. Into these offices poured reports from all the company's labor spies in western Pennsylvania. As he had the run of the floor and the files he looked to see what they had on me. I was favored with Carnegie cross-referenced file cards and reports. I was, of course, called a Communist although the report added, "Apparently the Communist leaders themselves do not know he is the directing hand of Communism in the Pittsburgh district." The closing note was distinctly blue: "When we reflect . . . he can get in to see most any Government official of prominence, including the President, we cannot keep from thinking that probably Professor Wirt of Gary, Indiana, was not altogether wrong in his charges against the so-called 'Brain Trust.'" I was a Washington correspondent at the time!

The Communists relied on solid and courageous rank-and-file leaders who showed superb qualities in the rough and tumble of organizing. Most important, all of the organizers counted on the willingness of the steel workers to battle it out. Their anger and determination grew steadily. I particularly remember a worker in Braddock, articulate and worth quoting at length:

> When will there be an end to this goddamned system? Anything would be better than this. Work two days a week, loaf around five days, wife sick, one of my girls needs a good doctor, and me with no money, a bunch of rent bills, butcher bills, grocery bills.
>
> What the hell is it that's holding all of us back? Isn't there any way out of this? I heard a fellow say the other day, "Why, it'd be better to blow the whole goddamned mill to pieces than keep on this way, starving and wanting." That's crazy, of course, and still, what good is the mill, anyway? It only works a few months a year. Nobody wants a workingman any more. What are we supposed to do, go jump in the river with our kids? Guess that'd solve a lot of problems for the bigwigs.
>
> A lot of them say it'd be better to die fighting than die by inches this way. Better to die on the picket line than to drag on this way. I wouldn't

mind that myself. Trouble is we don't have confidence in ourselves. If we did start real hell, old Mike Tighe and Bill Green would be on the other side of the picket line and Roosevelt would call out the army. But God, there's got to be a break in this some day. It can't go on this way forever. And when that day comes, what we won't do!

He was not atypical. I knew when I heard workers talk like that, unions couldn't be far off. And they weren't. Of course, as soon as S.W.O.C. became a viable union, Lewis and Murray ruthlessly dumped the Communists without so much as a "Thank you." They wanted S.W.O.C. to be another business union, and they won. In a few years, it was rechristened the United Steel Workers.

I couldn't be satisfied with watching and doing liaison work for this exciting union movement in steel. I decided to write a book surveying the industry, its labor and social policies, and the abysmal conditions in company towns. The book, which Jessie helped research and revise, appeared as *Steel-Dictator* in 1935. I concentrated on the rise of J. P. Morgan's U.S. Steel. Theoretically a public corporation, it was presided over by as greedy a group of pirates as ever scuttled a ship. They were clever pirates. In 1920, led by U.S. Steel, the industry had convinced the Supreme Court to make a mockery of antitrust laws. The Court looked for an old-time monopoly, with blend of Rockefeller and Carnegie practices, which ruined competitors, dynamited mills, purchased legislatures. Instead the Court discovered a suave corporation whose competitors testified to a perfect and permanent harmony in the industry and whose consumers, carefully selected, swore they appreciated stabilized prices. As Dr. Frank A. Fetter put it, monopoly became a gentleman crook who outwitted the police by his manners and his disguise. The police were looking for a thug armed with a blackjack and found a gentleman who used sleight of hand. Bizarrely enough, by such genteel maneuvering U.S. Steel earned the nickname "the Corporation with a Soul."

The thirties demonstrated the absurdity of the title. The steel magnates subscribed, on paper, to the "American Plan." As the president of the Philadelphia and Reading put it, "The rights of the laboring man will be protected and cared for by Christian men to whom God has given control of the property rights of the country." In fact, ruthless drive was the key to profits for the industry's owners. Morgan saw human beings, from lowly laborer to executive, as possessors of certain abilities to be exploited to the last ounce. When exhausted, the man was tossed on the scrap heap with discarded machinery. That the steel monopoly recognized no rights but its own was obvious in the scandalous linkage of arms makers and steel men and preparedness advocates before World War I. (Still more depressing, by 1934 the same sequence of events unfolded in preparation for what would be called World War II). War improved steel prices, and so steel sacrificed young lives. What did the nation get out of all this? Virtually nothing. The prosperity of the glittering twenties covered up a host of steel's weaknesses—its bureaucracy, its reactionary attitude toward new processes and new markets, its obsolescent plant and grossly overvalued coal and ore reserves. The Great Debacle had laid bare the effects of monopoly more effectively than could any economist—though I hoped in my book to describe and publicize it.

Steel-Dictator was not the smash hit of the Mellon book, but reviewers treated it favorably. Hopefully, I won some sympathy and support for the men still struggling for unions and basic human rights. I also had an opportunity to warn about the dangers ahead. Given the activities of the Steel bosses, I thought that they might try to lead the country "through fear and force to Fascism." And I made my pitch for the best form of industrial organization, socialism:

> The vast possibilities of America's machinery for producing plenty point instead toward social ownership of steel and other industries. The dogmas of private ownership are turning into fictions. The nominal owners of the Steel Corporation control nothing and contribute nothing. The Steel Corporation has become a racket for the nourishment of bankers, brokers, gamblers, lawyers and executives. It is no longer able to furnish work or wages sufficient to keep its employees off the relief rolls. The conclusion is plain that private ownership of the Corporation has outlived any usefulness which the classical economists once postulated. In exacting their pound of flesh, the financiers are dooming the Corporation, as a social enterprise, to decay. From their policies come black poverty, intensified by the red flash of war.
>
> The workers in the steel industry and the plain people of America, as they begin to understand that they can expect little nourishment from private ownership, turn to consider the alternative—social ownership. Under socialism the steel mills can be used to make steel instead of profits. The nation's vast needs can be filled. The saboteurs of production at 23 Wall Street can be scrapped, along with obsolete mills and politicians who pirouette between demagogy to the steel worker and subservience to the Iron and Steel Institute. The army of private po-

lice, spies, professional strike-breakers and "protection engineers" can be cashiered.

The steel magnates sneer at such ideas as the contentions of visionaries, but in the Soviet Union, now second in the world in iron and steel production, the men in the mills work lustily toward the proof that socialism is more efficient than capitalism. The ancient argument that socialism is Utopian and runs counter to human nature is breaking on the plain fact that a hunger for profits is not born in the babe. The creative and constructive elements of human nature, freed from the curse of privation and insecurity, can build a brilliant civilization. Humanity is not condemned to believe that Morgan, Taylor, Schwab and Grace are the end-products of evolution.

By the time the book came out, things had calmed down considerably in Pittsburgh. It was no longer the toughest town in the country. The governor abolished the coal and iron police and a union man could show his head without losing it. Once again, Jessie and I began to look for greener, or blacker, pastures.

Love Is
Something

Not long after I joined the staff, I got my first big—and very difficult—assignment. Harvey sent me to Gastonia, North Carolina, to cover the activities of the National Textile Workers Union (N.T.W.U.), which was formed by the Communist Party. The N.T.W.U. was trying to organize a big anti-union mill, Loray. When I arrived, in August of 1929, the energies of the union were absorbed by the defense of thirteen members charged with the murder of Chief of Police Aderholt. While in Gastonia, I always had the scary feeling that life was much too real and earnest. We Northern reporters were violently disliked by a power structure that stopped at nothing in fighting unionism. The workers lived precariously and wretchedly. Having returned so recently from the U.S.S.R., I couldn't help but compare the behavior of the Christian bosses of Gastonia with that of the atheist Bolsheviks. If Gastonia were any indication, the godless often came closer to Christian ideals than the god-fearing.

The Federated Press had assigned me to Gastonia to report on the trial and, in the process, I learned much of Southern unionism. The previous spring's attempt by the "contented, docile, Anglo-Saxon workers," as the Chamber of Commerce loved to describe them, had been met by beatings, bayonet proddings, kidnappings, floggings, mobbings, relief wrecking, and shootings. Though North Carolina had no law against unions, agencies of the law condoned all violence against unionists, and punished severely any violence incidental to unionists' efforts at self-defense. I had read Robert Barry's reports in the *Washington Post* and the *New York Evening World*, which described anti-union bitterness and violence as "community spirit," the reaction of a patriotic and religious city to Bolshevik agitators. As soon as I started interviewing Gastonia's workers, I realized that Barry had counted them out of the community. Avoiding all Gastonians I knew to be unionists, I talked to store clerks, carpenters, shoemakers, taxi drivers, and textile workers. All but one favored acquitting the unionists charged in the Aderholt "murder." Though phrased in various ways, all agreed with the sentiments of one man who said, "the union is the only thing that will help the people." The last was a minor bossman in the mill, the type described by a striker as "the kind that if the boss gives 'em an ice cream cone they'll do anything." Though hardly a strident unionist, even he admitted, "I'll join the union when they get it organized, but meanwhile I got to eat."

The ordinary workers in the Loray Mill didn't eat particularly well. Their whole diet consisted of fatback, beans, cornmeal, cabbage, canned milk, and margarine. On the basis of figures provided by the owners of the mill to the North Carolina Department of Labor and Printing in 1925–1926, I calculated that men's wages ranged from fourteen to twenty-four dollars per week and women's from ten to eighteen dollars—and this for a five-and-a-half-day week of ten-to-twelve-hour shifts. Moreover, Loray workers told me that these appalling figures were actually optimistic for, in reality, some men who had worked for years earned twelve dollars or less a week and women, seven to nine dollars. Women had an added handicap: the mill sometimes denied them full-time work even at these slave wages. The women's "days off" allowed the mill to string along "extras" to supplement the work force in the case of sickness or injury. Company houses, Southern mill owners argued, compensated the workers for low wages. Wade H. Harris, editor of the *Charlotte Observer*, declared that the "cotton mill operative lived amidst the best surroundings that medical science can devise and in all the comforts that money can provide, for it is the human element that dominates Southern textile industry." In the Loray village this meant houses like cigar boxes, only just heated and set on stilts. Built on poorly drained, mosquito-infested land, the houses were not even equipped with screens.

The company houses and stores gave the mills an almost feudal hold over the workers. The mills paid part of the workers' earned wages in the form of the house over which they retained control. If the worker joined a union, he lost not only his job but his home. A private home was out of the question to workers who earned so little. The company store graciously allowed the worker to buy on coupons issued against future wages. But company prices exacted high interest for this graciousness. I learned that the company bought wood from local farmers for six dollars per cord and sold it in small lots to workers at a rate amounting to eighteen dollars a cord. Given their wages, the workers quickly fell into debt to the company and were even more tightly tied to their place.

When the worker had a full-time job, the mill controlled him bodily most of the time—at least fifty to sixty hours a week. According to old Southern traditions the home was sacred and women's place in it, but not in the mill village. Low wages and the mill rule that families who lived in company houses had to furnish two hands pushed women out to work with their men. Often women chose night work so they could take care of children during the day. Exhaustion robbed the workers of the hours in which they were not actually on the job. The workers stood for their whole shift in an atmosphere kept damp and unventilated for the sake of cotton. They had no supper period, but gobbled their food on the job using one hand or foot to work, and the other to eat. With its right hand the North Carolina Department of Labor reported "industrial life in the South is happy and contented, healthy and prosperous." With its left, the Department announced a 50 percent increase in death due to pellagra—malnutrition—in 1929 over the same period in 1928. The demeanor of Southern mill workers belied the statements of the industrialists. I soon learned to identify the workers by the terrible economy of energy in their every motion. They moved their legs just enough to walk, threw their voices out just enough to be heard. They had an ingrained enervation, an all-pervading tiredness. It was this that the North Carolina Chambers of Commerce called docility in their advertisements.

But in 1929, the workers of Gastonia had grown tired of being tired. As I interviewed Gastonians about the trial, Southern labor conditions, and Southern unionism, I heard about the great textile strike of the previous spring. Villages untouched by unions across the state had begun to invite union organizers to come into their mills. Unions—A.F. of L. or more radical ones—received more calls for organizers than they could fill. The editors of the *Gastonia Gazette*, *Charlotte Observer*, and *Southern Textile Bulletin* insisted, of course, that "100 per cent American workers" would never have dreamed of being discontented with Southern conditions if Northern agitators had not convinced them they were unhappy. Southern mill operators, who had got into the habit of thinking themselves benefactors, were apoplectic at this turn of events. They had brought mountaineers down from the hills to civilization, given them all the amenities of cotton mills and company towns only to find the workers liked the hours and air better in the hills. People like Wade Harris had urged Northern industry to flee states with any union influence and take advantage of an inexhaustible labor force dominated by hardworking, rugged individualists of "Rooseveltian characteristics": unfortunately from Harris's point of view, when Northern capital arrived, leaving mill towns in New England idle, the Southern workers displayed totally other, unexpected Rooseveltian characteristics: a genuine desire to fight back.

Mill owners considered the idea that workers should have some control over their lives blasphemous. They were determined to give no foothold to any union. The bosses fired active unionists, whether A.F. of L. or N.T.W.U., as soon as company spies reported them. Then the unionists were blacklisted by all surrounding mills. If any particular mill were struck, the entire Manufacturers Association would back the mill, paying all the bills for union-breaking—especially if the struggle were long and the mill tempted to yield a little. This is what the Gastonia workers were up against when, on March 30, 1929, they had held their first mass meeting and formulated demands ranging from twenty dollars per week minimum wage with a forty-hour work week to bathrooms for company houses. When the company had fired twenty union members the following Monday, most of the mill had come out.

Tuesday evening the police had tried to stretch a rope across a street to keep strikers from the mill gate. The strikers grabbed one end and staged a tug of war, which the *Baltimore Sun* correspondent described as "no more than a scuffle." The Loray Mill used this scuffle to secure five companies of militia from Governor Gardner to "protect their property." The mill continued operations, at first, with a greatly reduced force. The bosses brought workers in from other regions. Some of the strikebreakers found conditions so bad that they joined the strikers. On the other hand, some of the strikers, "job-scared," drifted back to work. Many simply moved out of Gastonia.

The relief problem was acute, for many of the strikers had no more than a few cents in their pockets when they walked out. The Workers' International Relief erected a tent colony for those evicted. When sheriffs arrested picketing strikers on trifling or trumped up charges, the International Labor Defense (I.L.D.) handled their cases. The prompt aid of these organizations helped the union win the workers' confidence.

The bossmen had tried to scare the workers by reminding them that Communists advocate Negro equality and atheism. "Would you want your sister to marry a buck nigger?" they asked. But in spite of the traditions of the South, most of the workers refused to get excited. "What do we care what the union leaders think, as long as they stick up for us," they said. The local press played up the shocking fact that godless Communists were leaders of the union. I tried to sound out what some of the workers thought about that. "I suppose it makes a lot of religious people nervous to see a union like that come in and try to get shorter hours," I ventured. One of the men looked at me quizzically and said, "Lady, if all the religion in Gastonia was nitroglycerin, it wouldn't be enough to blow one man's nose."

When racism and red-baiting failed, Gastonia's anti-unionists had gone and thought up a new one. On April 18, about 2:00 A.M., a masked mob wrecked the union headquarters and raided the relief store. They threw food into the street and poured kerosene on it. The soldiers sent to preserve law and order quartered two blocks away somehow didn't hear the noisy chopping. They did not come till the mob was through. Then the soldiers arrested, not the mobbers, though a few were still on the grounds in their masks, but the strikers inside the headquarters. The soldiers had already gotten into the habit of prodding the strikers on picket duty with bayonets. When the Gastonia Grand Jury investigated, two of the strikers identified members of the mob as Loray bossmen. But the jury and Governor Gardner's special detective declared themselves "unable to find any clues."

Soon after, the state withdrew the soldiers, but special deputies took their places. Many of the deputies belonged to the "Committee of 100" organized by the company. This committee—mill foremen, "loyal" workers, and hangers-on—aided actively in breaking up picket lines with blackjacks and threatening the strikers. The city council passed ordinances against picketing and parading. Strikers walking two by two along the sidewalk were arrested and maltreated.

In May, the company began a new campaign of evictions that continued throughout the summer. The authorities dragged miserable furnishings out of the mill shacks. I remember a little girl, sick with running ears, moved out in the roadside. The Valentine family, whose four-year-old daughter was ill with smallpox, for which North Carolina had no quarantine law, was evicted with the rest. Truly it was "the human element that dominate[d] the southern textile industry."

Yet the strikers were undaunted. After the raid, the strikers had built a new headquarters near the tent colony. At the opening ceremony, Officer Gilbert shouted at a union speaker, "You'd better make much of it, big boy, 'cause it won't stand a week." Anonymous threats and menaces from the "Committee of 100" were frequent, especially in the early days of June. The afternoon of June 7, the union held a meeting on the grounds. A few members of the Committee of 100 threw bottles and eggs at the speakers. A scuffle took place and one of the Loray bossmen fired a pistol, but a union man knocked it down so the shot went into the ground. Officer Jackson, who was present at the time, walked away without making any arrest. In the evening the picket line went toward the mill. The strike committee had received word that 75 percent of the scabs on the night shift wanted to strike.

But that night, workers reported, every door in the mill was locked and guarded by a member of the Committee of 100. And police broke up the picket line before it reached the mill. They beat and choked Sophie Melvin, Vera Buch, and Edith Miller. They knocked down an old woman, Mrs. McGinnis. A group of them beat Earl Tompkinson across the railroad track. Many witnesses heard Policeman Gilbert say to the other officers, "Let's go down to headquarters and clean out the sons of bitches—now is as good a time as any." Officer Jackson, just returning from union grounds, said, "No use going down to headquarters—it's all quiet now." But the officers drove to the lot.

They rolled upon the grounds, jumped out, and started toward the hall. A union guard, George Carter, asked them for a warrant. Several witnesses heard Gilbert say, "I don't need no goddamn warrant, this is all the warrant I need," while he drew his pistol. Then he scuffled with Carter to take the gun away and knocked him down. According to the people who were returning from the picket line, the officers began the shooting. The officers—two of whom were already under indictment for a drunken shooting at the Catawba River— swore the unionists fired first. Anyway, union guards shot for they feared this was the beginning of a long-threatened raid. This time they intended to defend their headquarters and the tent colony of women and children on the hillside beyond. Chief Aderholt was mortally wounded, and Officer Gilbert, A. J. Roach, and a striker, Joseph Harrison, were injured.

Terror followed. Armed members of the Committee of 100 arrived immediately. Their promptness suggested to many observers that they had already prepared to raid that night. Till early morning they searched the tent colony and town. Some were legally deputized and some were not, but they all arrested strikers. They threw over 100 into jail, and treated them to beatings and tear gas. At first the state charged seventy with conspiracy to murder and assault. Finally, sixteen were charged with conspiracy to murder, and seven with felonious assault.

The *Gastonia Gazette* had cried for lynching and blood immediately. But there was no lynching. The *Gazette* did not have popular support. When the trial was called for July 29, Judge Barnhill ruled that a fair trial in Gaston County was impossible. Not only witnesses but even defending counsel had been threatened. A new trial, which Federated Press had assigned me to cover, was set for Charlotte, August 26. This attempt ended in a mistrial. After three days of hearing and seeing the state's evidence, one of the jurors went raving mad. I had never seen anything quite like this "trial." Yet certain phases were as significant as they were horrifying.

The state charged thirteen young men with "conspiracy to murder in the first degree." Conviction, in North Carolina, meant electrocution (mandatory), and the suave, genial lawyers of the prosecution, so careful of their rose boutonnieres, earnestly intended to burn all thirteen. They required all jurymen to state they would be willing to send a man to the chair on circumstantial evidence. The state reduced charges against three young women to second-degree murder, which carried a prison sentence of from two to thirty years. The lawyers did not want Southern chivalry to interfere with the conviction and electrocution of the men.

Mill officials always asserted that the local workers themselves bitterly resented union "interference." In picking the jury, however, the prosecution challenged (until peremptory challenges ran low) every talesman who had ever tasted the joys of working in a cotton mill—even some who only had cousins and uncles in the mills. The defense, with three times the state's challenges, could afford watchful waiting, and eventually secured a jury of one mill worker, two union men (a clerk and a carpenter), four other workers, four tenant farmers, and one grocery clerk, all young.

An outrageous feature of this trial, unique in the history of jurisprudence, was the appearance of an effigy of the dead chief, with sad, accusing eyes, in his own gory garments during the trial. The widow wept, six feet from the jury box. Judge Barnhill ordered the effigy out. But Solicitor John G. Carpenter of Gaston County, in his zeal, straightened its hat to show the eyes while he argued with the judge. Three times the judge gave his command before the dummy was trundled away. For a lesser man than Carpenter, this might have been counted contempt of court. The incident showed to what lengths the prosecution would go to secure conviction. As a matter of fact, however, the appearance of this gruesome figure precipitated the insanity of the juror, who, townspeople told me, "had not far to go." I interviewed five of the jurors afterward, who all declared, "We were solid for acquittal, if the state had no stronger evidence than what we heard." Even the *Gastonia Gazette* failed to find a juror for conviction. After hearing the sworn testimony of the flower of the Gastonia police force, without a word in defense of the strikers, the first jury favored acquittal.

While they appealed before the bar of law for the electrocution of union leaders, Gastonia's "better classes" had no shame about breaking the law to harry the union. Why should they? They had lawyers with them, and the county of Gaston was their playground. The night of the mistrial a group of them, angry at the postponement of legal vengeance and the expense of a new trial, took the law into their own hands. They lined up in about fifty to a hundred cars, damaged I.L.D. and union headquarters in three counties, kidnapped three organizers (beating one of them unconscious), shouted threats against defense counsel in the streets of Charlotte, and broke brica-brac in a hotel when thwarted. Local papers reported most of this, but did not seem to consider it a breach of the peace. Neither did the police. The deputies refused defense counsel's request for protection, and failed to mention the affair on the police blotter that night. The conservative *Charlotte Observer* reported casually that a car full of Gastonia "peace officers" accompanied the mob.

Unionists scheduled a mass meeting for the Saturday after the mobbing. Threatened by the Committee of 100 and warned by the press, the unionists decided not to yield to intimidation. On Saturday the way to the meeting ground bristled with guns. Hundreds of Legionnaires and Loray hangers-on were deputized "to keep the peace." Yet they did not interfere with the murder of Ella May Wiggins, in broad daylight on the public highway. Armed men in cars turned back the truck bearing her and other unionists to the meeting. They pursued the truck, edged it into a wreck, shot down Ella May, sole support of five little children, and hunted the other unionists "like rabbits across the cotton patch." The unionists of Gastonia did not believe Ella May's murder had been an accident. "The songs she made up were too good," they said. "Her singin' made folks think. She was a wonderful organizer, and they wanted to get her."

When the new trial had been set for weeks ahead, I had gone back to New York to work with my favorite editor, Harvey. The heartrending news of Ella May's death came the next weekend. I remembered her from rallies she sang at—a slight figure with brown bobbed hair, a firm profile, and a very thorough smile. Ella May would sing her "ballets," as she called them, from the stoop of deserted shacks while men, women, and children crowded around to hear her. Her full throaty voice gave the songs in mountain style, with an odd sort of yip at the end of each line that delighted her audience.

"Purtiest singin' I ever heard," said one woman, who stood throughout a meeting at which Ella May sang. This woman with feet firmly planted, baring her breast occasionally to nurse the baby in her arms, was typical of Ella's audience. People who often had the simple, far off look of peasants. People who were trying to see through life to the truth, but were not used to trying. People for whom the union was not just tactics, but their whole life, their greatest adventure. The workers would chuckle at Ella May's apt digs at the mill bosses, and kept calling on her for more favorites. They would not let her stop:

> Now listen to me, workers, listen to what I tell.
> Remember the textile workers, in their dirty cell.
> Now we must stand together, and to the boss reply,
> "We will never, no, we'll never, let our leaders die."

These songs spread over the countryside faster than literature or tracts. Listless and half-illiterate mill workers glowed to life as they heard them, grinned at the idea that instead of standing their conditions, they could get together and change them. As they agreed, the word grew in power. Ella May's death was not her first brush with hostile forces. Long before this, intelligent, steadfast, and talented Ella May had become a worker to be reckoned with. "Persons unknown" had turned their attention upon her immediately. They poisoned her well, and sent her several threats of death. But they misjudged their Ella May. She went to Washington anyway to testify against the mill owners in the Senate investigation of the Southern textile industry. Returning, she continued to give her unquenchable vigor to the union and the defense of the Gastonian workers on trial. Small wonder none of us believed that her death had been accidental.

The murder of a fleeing and defenseless mother was somewhat brazen, even for Gastonia. Protests boiled in the state press. Mob activity became somewhat more discreet again. Still, small bands of armed men visited and threatened practically all the union sympathizers in the county. Even in Charlotte, a car full of vigilantes waked the landlady of a reporter at 3:00 A.M. to ask if any union people lived at her house. The mobs hinted their disapproval to local, Southern organizers, beating Cleo Tessner and shooting Charles Blue in the ankle. Only two arrests came out of all this violence and intimidation: for the kidnappings and the murder of Ella May. But no one was ever convicted. The Committee of 100 in the Loray Mill could always produce airtight alibis. If fifteen witnesses swore they saw Loray bossmen in the mob, thirty Loray scabs swore the bosses were in the mill the whole time.

I went back to the harsh realities of Gastonia to cover the new trial of the unionists. I was glad in those tenuous circumstances that I had the company of more experienced reporters. In spite of her known labor sympathies, Mary Heaton Vorse had been hired to cover the trial for a sensational New York tabloid. We thought we might understand all the detailed testimony better if we went to look over the union headquarters where Aderholt died. I went with Eleanor Copenhaver, a Southerner studying the whole textile situation for the industrial board of the Y.W.C.A. She was petite, soft-spoken, and brave. As we approached the hall, a police officer rushed over and grabbed her roughly by the arm. "How dare you, suh?" she asked with calm dignity. His jaw dropped and so did his arm. He couldn't quite imagine how a white Southern gentlewoman got mixed up in Gastonia's union troubles! I enjoyed seeing him so nonplussed.

The September 30 trial amazed me even more than the mistrial. The prosecutor showed he could learn from experience. To keep the defense from getting a jury like the first, the state whittled down the number of challenges by reducing the charges from first- to second-degree murder, and dismissing some of the defendants. The state hoped the jury would convict more readily with the women and the less implicated boys out, and with the penalty prison instead of the chair. The procedure was loose. The state charged conspiracy, but asked punishment only for unpremeditated murder. The impossibility of conspiring to murder without premeditation troubled nobody in court. By entirely dismissing six men whom it had tried to electrocute three weeks before, the state seemed to confess to having sought six lives on negligible evidence. That admission aroused doubts about the whole case—outside of the prosecutor's office, anyway. These moves succeeded, however, in forcing the defense to accept a jury of nine farmers, one postman, one millionaire grocer, and one Ford worker, nearly all old and less sympathetic than the first.

The evidence was complicated. Witnesses on both sides (and often on the same side) contradicted each other. Local papers carried long accounts, but only the *Raleigh News and Observer* and the *Greensboro News* gave anything like fair play to the defense. The star witnesses for the state were Gastonia officers. Their credibility may be gauged from the fact that they swore they used no violence against the pickets. They also denied under oath offenses such as being drunk and disorderly and bootlegging, for which defense lawyers had affidavits or copies of the record of the court where the officers were convicted. Yet they were convincing enough to the jury and Judge Barnhill.

State witnesses reported threatening remarks by unionists. They said Beal told a bunch of unarmed men, women, and children on the picket line to "go into the mill" (guarded by armed men and a high wire fence), "drag out the scabs, and if anybody bothers you shoot and shoot to kill." They maintained the unionists fired first. If the deputies were to be believed, union guards shot fifteen to eighteen times, but the officers, of a more pacific disposition, did not fire at all. A. J. Roach admitted that he shot once from his pistol after he was wounded. The state, which could not say who fired the fatal shot, depended on the conspiracy charge to incriminate all of the defendants. The evidence for conspiracy consisted of a few knotholes in the side of the union hall and the strikers' stuffing up of a broken windowpane earlier in the evening in question to prevent two anti-union women on the next porch from overhearing strike plans. According to the state's picture, the unionists decided that killing an officer would further their cause and could think of no more anonymous way to do so than to lure him to their own grounds, at 9:30 in the evening, by sending out an illegal picket line.

Defense witnesses said union guards did not fire till after two or three shots from the officers. One witness intimated that the first shot went off accidentally when Gilbert struggled with the guard. The defense tried to show why the unionists felt they had to defend themselves. It brought out the unpunished raid on the old headquarters, officer's threats against the new, and the threats and violence against unionists. Strikers who had been pushed on the picket line testified to Gilbert's and Roach's whiskey breath, raising further doubt about the officers' credibility. The possibility that, in the dusk and the melee, Officer Hord, who was separated from the rest, might have shot Aderholt himself was suggested by lawyers in their closing arguments. But no defense witnesses had seen Hord fire. Defense lawyers did point out that the shots found in Aderholt were scattered from head to heel, and Hord alone had a sawed-off shotgun. Hord claimed his shot were a different size, and that he never fired at all.

Another interesting feature of the case was the cross-examination of defense witnesses about communism and religious beliefs. At the beginning Judge Barnhill ruled out all reference to communism, stating this was purely a murder trial. The prosecution loudly agreed, and ridiculed radicals for suggesting the unionists trial might parallel the Sacco-Vanzetti case. Nevertheless, the state seized every occasion to throw the word "communism" before the jury, and finally E. T. Cansler argued against the judge's repeated exclusions on the ground that it had been ruled relevant in the Sacco-Vanzetti murder case! Judge Barnhill withheld his decision till Beal came on the stand. Then he announced that while he would exclude mention of the word and the Party, he would allow the defendants' own beliefs to be shown. The defense counsel argued that, with the conservative farmer jury, this would virtually deprive the defendants of equal protection before the law. The judge remarked, "A Communist ought not expect to be tried as a loyal citizen."

He did not bar the testimony of atheists, but allowed the state to show that they *were* atheists "to give the jury a chance to decide how much to believe them," he said. "I think if I did not believe in a God who would punish me hereafter, I might be more likely to tell a lie to save my friends." He ruled out questions about race equality, however, on the ground that they were not really impeaching.

Edith Miller was the only Communist besides Beal who testified. Her testimony was needed to corroborate Beal's evidence that he and Miller were in the inner office all during the shooting and had no guns. All the other people with them in the office were or had been defendants, and they were Communists, too. The state kept Beal a whole day and Mrs. Miller a whole morning. Cansler, who cross-examined Beal, asked such exaggerated questions in such a bombastic tone that Beal could generally deny them. At the end of the day he had not elicited a real statement of Communist aims from Beal. But his melodrama undoubtedly disquieted the jury. Jake Newell interrogated Edith Miller more moderately and got more out of her. Asked about overthrowing the government, she answered calmly, "No great social change has ever come without the masses of the people using whatever means they had—just as this country broke away from England." Newell next forced her to admit her pledged word was as good on an almanac as on a Bible. He considered that very incriminating.

Newell also insinuated that Miller's marriage was invalid. Cross-examiners are allowed great latitude in North Carolina, and the prosecution lawyers seized the opportunity—eager as hounds on the hunt. For the lowest muckraking, they called on Newell, brother of the Methodist minister in Gastonia and deacon of the church. He asked quiet Dewey Martin about his trip north to raise union funds. "How many women did you go around with in New York?" "The girls in the union office," replied Dewey all innocently. "Aha!" cried Newell insinuatingly. "Now, Mr. Martin, how many women did you have in Chicago? How many women in Milwaukee? What, no woman in Milwaukee, and you were there a week?"

To discredit Paul Shepherd's testimony, Newell brought out a confidential letter handed over by his doctor, contrary to medical ethics. All's fair in love, war, and Gastonia. Shepherd, a young theological student, had had a false alarm about syphilis, a scare that he had caught it in a public toilet, which, of course, was not possible. Shepherd's frank, unruffled manner in court carried conviction. But Newell, the deacon, would not be cheated of his dirt. In his speech to the jury some days later, he said with an ironic leer: "You know a public toilet's a fine place to take a woman."

The lengths to which the lawyers went in their arguments to the jury were almost incredible. Cansler, slightly more ethical, still played to the prejudice of the nine farmers. "If the defendants are justified, then they have the right to organize unions of farmhands to dictate wages and hours." This after he had just finished objecting to a defense lawyer's statement that the real issue in this case was the right to organize. To convict these defendants, the state played both ends against the middle.

The solicitor, who supposedly represented a state seeking only justice, behaved most unfairly. He labeled the seven young fellows, who tried to organize workers against the sixty-hour week and speed-up, "fiends incarnate," "deadly assassins," "devils with hoofs and horns." He called incoherently upon "the flag of this great country, singing the song of emancipated minds." He got all tangled up in the yarn Gastonia spun: "Why, you could wrap it around the sun sixteen times, around the moon thirteen times, around Mercury, Venus and Saturn, stretch it from San Francisco to southernmost Africa and right back to Gastonia—before Beal crept into this peaceful God-fearing community on his belly, like the serpent crept into the garden of Eden." Carpenter lay on the floor and writhed in agony; he knelt and prayed as if at Aderholt's deathbed; then in a final burst of ranting he seized the weeping widow's hand and pledged the vengeance of the state of North Carolina.

Judge Barnhill objected at times, and in his charge two days later, he told the jury to disregard all emotional appeals—locking the door a little late. His charge was the epitome of fairness. He recalled the rights of self-defense, and reminded the jury that a killing might be only a manslaughter. He told them to judge the resistance of the defendants not only on what the situation actually was, but what the defendants feared it was. "A clear charge to acquit," said an anti-unionist behind me. But Judge Barnhill ran no such risk. He read his charge, full of monotonous legal phrases, rapidly for two hours while the jury dozed. Yet the charge had the value of protecting him from a retrial on grounds of bias.

After less than an hour of deliberation, the jury cut through all complications and pronounced the unionists guilty. Judge Barnhill of the fair-sounding charge made his sentence on distinctly sectionalist lines. He subtracted from seventeen to twenty years of the lives of the four Northerners, Beal, Miller, Harrison, and Carter. He gave McLaughlin and McGinnis twelve to fifteen years, and Hendrix five to seven years, though he had said, "If I had doubts about anybody, it would be Hendrix."

Most of the Southern newspapers hailed the verdict. "It will not be safe for any so-called labor agitators to be caught nosing around here any time soon," said the *Gastonia Gazette* in an editorial entitled, "Verdict Pleases." A few liberal sheets disapproved. The *Asheville Citizen* criticized Judge Barnhill's ruling to admit evidence of beliefs. "In the nature of things, his ruling let down the flood gates," it said. The *Raleigh News and Observer* agreed, and also regretted that Judge Barnhill had not repressed more of Solicitor Carpenter's oratory.

Criticism increased at the next events in Gaston County. The grand jury failed to return indictments for the Ella May Wiggins murder. When the chief of police was killed on private property, in the dark, Gastonia preferred charges, at first, against seventy men and women, and punished seven with long prison sentences. But when a poor mother was shot on the public highway in broad daylight, Gastonia could find no evidence even for an indictment. The grand jury "investigating" called only thirteen of the seventy witnesses who testified at the coroner's hearing, leaving out the most important.

When the grand jury released all the suspects, feeling ran high among the workers. These descendants of the revolutionists who first fought for American freedom spoke bitterly. "What kind of people are sore about it?" echoed a Gastonia taxi driver. "Why, most everybody except the rich and a few office workers. All the people I meet say it's a funny kind of justice that could find seven men right away who shot Chief Aderholt, but couldn't find anybody that shot Ella May." Another said, "The people here ain't naturally Communist, but the Gastonia government's been teachin' the workers as fast as it can that they can't get no justice in the courts. All it would need to start a rebellion here would be for two or three men with shotguns to begin."

"Talk about Communists overturning the government," said a strong-looking landlady, "if there was any, the bossmen sure turned it over the day they killed Ella May. And again when the grand jury wouldn't do nothin' about it. But the people are scared stiff. For weeks Loray has been working three or four days a week, and laying off hundreds. They said after the conviction business would be better—if only we could get shet of the union. But times are worse now than ever. Everybody who can is leaving town, 'cause they can't live on half a week's wages at Loray. People used to talk about the union and the boys in jail, whenever they got together, but since the conviction and the layoffs, they shut up like clams."

Gastonia workers were still brave, however. When Red Hendrix, convicted of murdering Chief Aderholt, drove to Gastonia on bail, two hundred of them gathered around him within plain sight of the Loray Mill and begged him to come back to talk union. They offered to arrange meetings and promised to protect him against threatened lynchings. The rising spirit of the "poor whites" was expressed by a Gastonia store clerk, who joined the textile workers' union because he believed all the working people should stick together. "If you saw a lot of little skinny monkeys in the jungle carrying nuts for one fat lazy monkey," he said, "you'd wonder why they didn't quit. Some day the Southern workers are goin' to quit. Some people say the union's dead. But *we're goin' to have a union*."

Sadly enough, the brave textile workers of Gastonia did not win the shortened workday or a union contract. Instead many lost their homes and their leaders, who were put in prison. But their resistance cost the industry a good deal, and in the days of Coolidge and Hoover, we counted that a kind of victory. The turmoil interrupted production and lowered profits and the bosses spent a good deal of money to crush the strike. Still more important, the men and women of Gastonia showed that there were limits to the amount of exploitation that those "contented" Southern textile workers would endure—that pushing them beyond that point was more trouble than it was worth. If I had been an organizer, I'm not sure that I'd have advised in favor of a strike in Gastonia. I might have had great doubts about inducing or encouraging those hard-pressed people to take such risks. Yet it was not ultimately the organizers' choice—the workers of Gastonia had had enough. And if risks had not been taken in the past, we would still have child labor, the twelve-hour day, and the seven-day work week. In any event, I was an observer-reporter. I resolved to keep telling people about the abominable conditions in which some human beings had to live. Harvey urged me to write an extended piece on Gastonia, and when I returned I did the pamphlet for a Progressive Labor Party on which this account is based.

I

I returned to the New York of the panic; the stock market, which had been going up and up, crashed October 29, 1929. We heard of rich men jumping out of windows, and one bank after another failed, taking away all of some people's savings. Workers, laid off by the thousands, had no unemployment insurance either to live on or buy with and business got rapidly worse. People urged President Hoover to do something. The man who had organized the feeding of millions in Europe after World War I replied that the nation had fallen into the grip of ineluctible economic forces that would have to run their course. Things got so bad that New York City decided to distribute food baskets to the neediest. Harvey assigned me to the story. "But that's a waste of time," I objected. "The whole thing is already written up in the *Times*—just how some of the different people looked when they got their baskets, and so on." But Harvey said firmly, "I think you'd better go out and see for yourself." I went, and what a surprise the big story was! Something had gone wrong and not a

single basket had been given, even by 11:00 A.M. The *Times* wanted
to get that story in the morning edition and had just taken a chance
that things would go off as planned. I relearned something about
newspapering that day.

This was only the first of stories I covered for Federated Press that
you couldn't read in the mainstream papers in the early days of the
Depression. In February of 1930, I visited the job sharks who constantly staked their power and information against the desperation of
the growing numbers of unemployed men and women. "How about a
nice little $4.00 job—it'll get you $40.00 a month—or would you
like this $2.80 in Brooklyn—it pays $7.00 a week?" The question
with slight variations was asked up and down Sixth Avenue by
leeches who could afford an office and telephone. The sharks lived
off human misery—they exacted from the jobless 10 percent of their
first month's salary. In return, the client received an address where
there *might* be a job. "Four dollars might look like big money to you
now, but remember it pays ten dollars a week," the shark said—with
a grin that was meant to be encouraging—to an uncertain young girl.
She stared at him as if hypnotized by the shine of his sleek hair and
ostentatiously false diamond stick pin.

Then her thin hands opened a worn purse and she fingered a few
bills. She wanted to be a waitress in a good restaurant, but whatever
you wanted cost money. You couldn't expect a swell ten-dollar-
a-week job hefting dishes ten hours a day for nothing. Four dollars,
then, she decided. But she had briefly forgotten that she would have
to wait seven days for pay. She gave up her ambition: "I can only
afford the $2.80 job now," she said apologetically, settling on waiting
tables in a lesser place. For the benefit of other customers, the shark
hastened to turn on a new line of sales talk. "Why, seven dollars a
week is just the beginning of what you'll get in this place. This ain't
no coffee pot, no counter job. You'll be waiting on table, girl. And
it's a corner, the busiest corner in Brooklyn. With a little friendliness
and good cheer, you'll be making all of thirteen dollars a week."

After the girl paid her fee and left with the address, I talked to the
shark who told me he was a "good deal of a philosopher." What were
the prerequisites for success? His business was, he said, 100 percent
bluff: "You've got to size people up and make 'em feel you know all
about it. Then you can't be softhearted. These people will rob you if
they get the chance. For instance, there was a woman last week who

said she had three sick kids, so I let her have the job on credit till payday. After she got the job, she said she wouldn't pay for it, can you beat it? Well, I hated to do it, with the kids and all, but I had to get the boss to fire her. It's the principle of the thing. She came back to me this morning, crying and begging to have me put her somewhere. But I told her I wouldn't handle her anymore. You can't be weak-minded in this business." It was a tough business for sure. The shark turned down another mother who came in hope of a factory job. She was thirty-four and had six children to feed, but she was too heavy for the shark: "She might be a very comfortable woman for a home, but she'd never move fast enough in a factory. Factories are keyed right up nowadays. If I sent her, they would just send her back."

But the shark wasn't completely heartless. Sometimes he even engaged in job training. I saw him put on a really talented exhibition for the benefit of a shy, pretty blonde. He wanted to teach her how a nightclub cigarette girl could increase her sales to drunkards. "We always coach our people—that's how we keep our job clientele—send people who can do the trick," he told me. "Now you can do it, girlie—all you need is confidence." Then he proceeded to set down an imaginary tray on an imaginary table and, with graceful gesture and fetching leer, pressed an imaginary cigarette into the mouth of an imaginary roué, saying coyly, "I know this will taste better than anything you ever tried before." The shark was not taken aback when, in spite of his best efforts, the young woman declined. "You'd make a lovely cloakroom girl but you haven't got quite the sans-gêne for a cigarette girl. Would you like that dearie?"

What exactly did these people get for their fee? Quite often, nothing at all. Some spent entire days tracking down leads to jobs that didn't exist. They got their money back only if they could outmaneuver or outshout the shark—no mean feat. At least, in this case, the law was technically on their side. Still more insidious were the jobs that lasted just long enough to "earn" the shark his fee— according to the law. The vamp-trainer had a spot of trouble while I was visiting his office. I heard a loud, complaining voice shrill with the weak intensity of outraged and thwarted hunger. "I want my money back. I paid you eight dollars for that job last Monday, and here they laid me off already. Just a week of work, just twelve dollars for my family, and here I got to go job hunting again. I paid for the job and I want my money back."

The shark tried to quiet him—such outbursts were bad for business. But the man only shouted louder. The shark then out-screamed, out-cursed, and out-argued him. With a final grand gesture, he led the man to the wall, where a copy of the New York law on employment agencies hung conspicuously. "You see?" he thundered. "If a man is discharged within a week he is entitled to his money back. After that the agent is not responsible. Is it our fault if you don't give satisfaction? Now get out, or I'll call the police on you for making a public nuisance." The shark's great, lazy slouch of an assistant, probably retained for just such circumstances, eased the betrayed one out. What could the man do? Law is law and its ways are mysterious. But he knew he had lost his eight dollars forever. Such was the working of those divine forces, competition and capitalism, in the employment racket.

The ink was hardly dry on the job shark series when I was reminded of other time-honored capitalist techniques for solving problems of unemployment. My experiences with the jobless not only increased my frustration with governments that acted only in the service of capital, but also my appreciation for the work of the Communist Party. I had never joined the Party. Like my father, I felt uncomfortable with its rigid orthodoxy. The devoted Party people thought that they and they alone had the light and they refused to tolerate any solution to a problem except their own. They sometimes attacked fellow leftists more mercilessly than they did the capitalists—at one point, they called all of the other leftists social fascists. In Russia I had not had much contact with the Party, but I had seen Bolsheviks admit to and correct mistakes of policy. The American Communists, on the other hand, insisted on being more Catholic than the Pope. They had never run a real, live government, had never been in or near power, and, therefore, their theories were sometimes divorced from reality. In fairness, the Communists were only slightly worse than the Socialists. Far, far too much energy went into internecine battles. I remember once drawing a cartoon of a giant named "labor" lying on the ground in chains with two minuscule parties fighting over who would lead him. For their part, the Communists suspected me of veering toward liberalism while the Socialists were certain I was a Communist in disguise.

Yet previously in Gastonia, at that time in New York, later in Harlan County and Pittsburgh, I saw the other side of the Communist Party people, too. They were wonderfully brave and devoted.

They went places nobody else would go and tried to organize those no one else could reach. They risked their lives in these very, very dangerous places—and some did die and others went to prison for years. Their commitment was absolute and their sacrifices inspiring. Nobody was doing anything substantial for the unemployed then, and nobody would as long as they sat quiet in their misery. Still, to organize these hopeless people was daunting. At that time labor could barely organize the employed—who could at least threaten to bring some fleeting pressure on their bosses by withholding their work. The Party called for a demonstration by and for the unemployed on March 6, 1930. In the sparkling sunshine of that New York spring day fifty thousand people stood in Union Square among five hundred policemen, red armored vehicles, green riot wagons, and mounted police, listening in orderly fashion to denunciations of the chaos and irresponsibility of a system that threw millions out of work and left them without a livelihood. For hours before, thousands milled in and out of the plaza. Perhaps as many as a quarter million witnessed parts of the demonstration between 11:00 A.M. and 3:00 P.M. That the demonstration was Communist-organized and that it attracted a crowd of this size probably accounts for the official response. Not since the days of the Palmer Raids in 1920–1921 had New York seen such an hysterical massing of police force to quell radicals. For the first time in history, the mayor ordered City Hall locked, barred, and guarded by machine guns. Though Communist tactics forbade individual acts of violence, the city's business element was clearly terrified.

When the word went out to march to City Hall, the heart-chilling shriek of sirens filled the square and riot wagons began to weave back and forth across Broadway. Mounted police backed into the crowd and foot soldiers charged like wild bulls. They pressed the Party standard bearers up against the walls, tore off placards that said "Down With Police Brutality," beat up any unfortunate, male or female, old or young, healthy or infirm, who came within range. Eight police cornered one worker in the entrance to a small shop, pounding him to a pulp with short, cruel blackjacks. One policeman paused near me: the little old man he was chasing had fallen just beyond me, but the thug was out of breath. I will never forget his heavy breathing and the feeling I had that I should grab his nightstick before he hit any more. I didn't though. I was too frightened

and confused to move. This man was in plain clothes wearing a big
sheep-lined jacket, but as he panted with it open, I saw a police
badge underneath.

The authorities transformed one of the greatest democratic demonstrations in the history of New York to its most vicious police riot.
Commander Whalen gave the main-line media the official version of
the day's events:

> So I told their committee that New York is a city of law and order, and
> that they couldn't march to City Hall without a permit. But they want-
> ed trouble, because their meeting had been such a flop, and they knew
> this was the only way they could make the front page. Boys, I hope you
> will give them a little squib in the back page; that's all they deserve.

Whalen smiled genially. He'd done a good day's work. "Nice job of
police work," one reporter said to another. "They had the whole
thing cleaned up in fifteen minutes." Sure enough, the business press
reported it the next day under the headline: "Police Quell Riot in
Union Square." The American press was free to repeat any lie the
police told them.

Harvey and I were married as soon as the divorce came through,
but we didn't take our honeymoon immediately. We kept right on
working. Life was real and we were young and devoted to the task of
publicizing harsh, and constantly worsening conditions that we
thought America needed to change. Two weeks after the wedding
Harvey sent me to try and take the place of our most distinguished
correspondent, Laurence Todd, who handled the Washington bureau. He researched, wrote, stenciled, mimeoed and mailed two le-
gal-size sheets every working day, and always looked cool and collected when he left the office at 5:00 P.M. Larry was gone when I
came but he left me some hints about where to collect releases and
check with labor people and other reporters. I still felt lost but did
my damndest. My ignorance of the city and slowness in writing
didn't help and it was often 7:00 or 8:00 P.M. when I went to bat with
the old mimeo machine, which performed so neatly for Larry. The
temperature was often over 100 that July and the sweat would drib-
ble down my nose onto the copy as I fought my inky battle with the
maddening "labor-saving device." Fridays were a heavenly relief:
Harvey would come down and with a few competent adjustments
and an hour or so of laughing and singing we would have the service

mailed. I had thought I was smart taking a place near the office at a very reasonable price. I soon found out why the room was so inexpensive—all the streetcars in Washington came in and turned at that very point. They squeaked more on the turns than on the ordinary runs, which were noisy enough. I moved as soon as I could and life became a little better. And I shouldn't complain. Perhaps the very horror of the weekdays made the weekends so delicious. I could look forward to seeing Harvey, my soul-mate both for fun and for purpose.

Back in New York after three weeks, I was relieved to work with an experienced editor—Harvey—and not be solely responsible for the service. With him I kept working and learning. Harvey's main aim was to have us get the facts firsthand. "We don't want to be like those radicals who just sit in an office and rewrite the *Times* from a different angle," he said. The Federated Press provided just a tiny trickle of a fact to refute the kind of journalism that called the police attack on the unemployed in Union Square a riot. We tried to keep our reporting fair and factual. We served all the groups on the left and in labor struggling for a better world in different ways. We must have succeeded because all kinds of papers took our reports: labor, farm, cooperative, liberal, Socialist, Communist, anarchist, and foreign-language. I couldn't think of any place I'd rather be—than at the heart of the important struggles of the day writing for Federated Press.

II

As difficult as conditions were in New York, they were easier than many other places in the country. New York had a large leftist and liberal community, at least in relative terms, and even leftist reporters had freedom of movement and the ability to get and print critical stories. My own experience in Gastonia had taught me that New York was definitely safely behind the front lines. We, at the Federated Press, couldn't escape that fact anyway because we received stories from all over. The news coming to us from Pittsburgh was particularly appalling. A nonunion town, run by the coal and steel industry for its own benefit, Pittsburgh combined abysmal living and working conditions with complete intolerance for reform-minded people and reporters. Harvey felt that the town needed a pro-labor paper to pressure the industries to change and I agreed. We decided to move to Pittsburgh and open a Federated Press office until we could start an independent newspaper.

In the meantime, we had a vacation coming up in August. We needed a little time to play hooky before we took on the toughest town in the country, as Pittsburgh was called then. When Dad invited us to join him for a sail, we agreed. I had told Harvey how I loved being on a boat and had wondered how he would like it. Fortunately, he took to it like a duck to water. We were sidetracked by one other trip before we hit Pittsburgh. Harvey was also eager to travel in the Caribbean and Mexico to learn Spanish and observe labor and political conditions in those areas. After Christmas we sailed south on the Ward Line, which made stops in Cuba and Yucatán.

Machado was the dictator of Cuba at the time. We got a taste of his methods very early in our stay: when we visited the student club of the Communist youth, blood from an attack by his guards still stained the stairway. We witnessed other ways in which Machado responded to dissent. About five weeks before our arrival some Cuban women had dared to demonstrate in the streets against him. These women had been protesting the unconstitutional repression of civil rights, the closing of the university, normal school, and all high schools on the island and the shooting of civilians in peaceful demonstrations. In general, Cuban feminists were not pressing for the vote. With constitutional guarantees suspended and Machado's habit of making deals with other nominal parties to present only one ticket in each district, the vote would mean nothing. Instead, these women declared that their first aim in organizing was to secure Machado's resignation. Following the demonstration, the women who participated were assaulted on the streets by male and female thugs, who not only injured them physically, but humiliated them. Time after time the women were beaten and their clothes completely torn off their bodies. Two blocks from where we stayed, I saw a young girl whose blouse had been torn to shreds revealing deep red gashes from the nape of the neck to her waist. The most conservative people I interviewed admitted that Machado had kept a group of strong-armed men for years for precisely this purpose—to attack any dissidents.

While Machado assured the United States that his regime was dedicated to law and order, he orchestrated the campaign against women at home. Government newspapers acclaimed the protesters' attackers as "fine women" and described the assaults graphically. Of all the loathsome devices of a terrorist, this undressing was one of the most disgusting. Machado knew that in Cuba, the victims would prefer to bear all in silence rather than admit publicly that they had been undressed. Several told me that they would have to leave the country if the newspaper mentioned their names. The fear of personal violation undoubtedly kept many women from speaking against the government, which was, of course, Machado's point. Long editorials in the daily papers advised women that since their whole duty was "piety and tolerance," they shouldn't trouble their brains, "none too large," with the coarser passions of politics. Following these strictures did not guarantee safety, however. Several women with no record of political activism were also attacked probably because they had been mistaken for someone else. I admired the courage of the feminists who risked so much with so little protection. All I could do to help was to send stories to Federated Press on their behalf.

I do remember one amusing and ironic event on our visit. Though Machado was no union man, he tolerated unions in some industries. The tobacco workers, experts at making a critical export, had secured a union contract. The contract stipulated that they could have a reader to while away the long hours as they wrapped cigars. The day we visited the factory, the workers were listening to *Das Kapital* by Karl Marx! The reader sat on a small raised platform in the middle of the room, and as he read this most subversive of books, no other conversation was going on. He had the workers' complete attention!

We stopped next in Yucatán. Because the water was so shallow the liner had to anchor far out and we had to wait a long time for the small boat to come out. We climbed a long way down a rather precarious ladder to the launch, and the crew let our baggage down on a rope. When we got to the dock, that seemed a mile long, too. Out over the shallows, we encountered the porters and spent another long time arguing with them. If I remember right, they wanted a dollar for each piece of luggage although they trundled it in on a cart. Harvey did not resist at all: he was pleased to see a well-organized labor force making the most of their opportunity. But this was at a time when twenty-five dollars was a week's salary for young college graduates starting with a publishing house, and I thought seven dollars for that little trip a bit excessive.

We went by boat and train to Mexico City, where we went straight to the pension of Chole (Soledad) Guzman. Besides general sightseeing and studying the history and conditions of the country, Harvey began studying Spanish and shorthand, and I was lucky enough to study photo developing and enlarging in the studio of Hugo Brehme. What a pleasure! He took magnificent pictures and graciously shared his knowledge with a complete novice.

Mexico City had several million fewer people in 1931 than now; the air was not blue with auto exhaust; the streets were not crowded. Visiting foreigners were not thick enough to be a nuisance, and thanks to Lalla Rogers, Harvey's old Seattle friend, and my Texas artist friend, Emily Edwards, we were well received by Diego Rivera and the American artist Pablo O'Higgins, who took root in Mexico. Land reform and the peasant cooperatives dominated our discussions. We learned how hard a time peasants had acquiring supplies they needed or the training to run a big place. But many kept up the good fight.

While we were in Mexico, Sergei Eisenstein, the Russian film director, arrived to make a film on the Mexican Revolution, which appeared in cut version in the United States as *Thunder Over Mexico*. I can't remember just where we met him, but he said he was using a real *hacienda*, on the high dry hills that surround Mexico City in the state of Hidalgo. The crop was maguey cactus, the source for *pulque*, the common drink, and the distilled drink, *tequila*. He invited us to come out and see the place where one of the owners was still living. "I have to go away on business just now," he said, "but my cameraman, Tishe, will show you around."

A train took us as far as the loading station of the big farm. A little carriage on small railroad wheels took us to the great red gate of the hacienda. We got an unforgettable picture of the life then of the wealthy landowner in the high dry hills of Mexico: a handsome but rundown house, plenty of money for meat and drink and generous hospitality, enough servants to cater to every whim. *But*—the landowner was still constrained by the constraints he put on his workers. A high brick wall and a locked gate confined all. Anyone coming to visit had to mount the unpaved road between two smelly rivulets of filth. The owner himself had to pass these as he went in or out. Long brick buildings, workers' quarters, as low as sheds, with no windows and only a slit in the bricks for a door, flanked his view on both sides.

Years later we saw *Thunder Over Mexico* in the States. Eisenstein took some stunning shots in that harsh place.

As much as we loved Mexico, and learned from it, Pittsburgh beckoned and we had to get home. I went via Winnetka to see my mother. Harvey hurried back to work in New York and packed for Pittsburgh, but he granted me another week. I settled in for a real visit with Mother, the first in two years. Always full of lively stories about her work for peace and world government, she also had a wonderful sense of humor. Soon, however, came a telegram from Harvey saying that our correspondent had just got shot out of Harlan. "Can you resist taking his place?" he asked. Mother was outraged. I wondered if Harvey didn't love me anymore. I had to phone. "You are the kind of person they wouldn't shoot," he said cheerfully. "Just go to Governor Sampson and tell the press about it and ask if a white Southern—or half-Southern—gentlewoman is safe reporting in his state. You'll be O.K. Besides," Harvey continued, "our man, Boris Isreal, wasn't shot seriously. He was just taken to the state line by two deputies and told to get going. As he left, his legs were peppered with bird shot. It's important not to let the coal companies think they can do anything they want to the miners because no one will know."

I agreed to go. Harvey thought I should head right for Kentucky from Chicago, the most direct route, but I had to see him again. So I went to Pittsburgh first, and then on to Kentucky. The Governor received me kindly saying, "You will certainly be safe if you obey the law. Stories from Harlan are greatly exaggerated." Still I felt so nervous I couldn't swallow anything but milk and even though the weather was warm for September, my feet kept getting cold. I stopped in Pineville before continuing on to visit a fine, brave lawyer who believed miners had the right to a union. As I asked at the bus station for my ticket to Harlan, a friendly soul advised, "I wouldn't go in there if I were you. They'd just as soon kill you as look at you." But I said, "I'm a woman." He replied, "Oh, it don't make no difference there." Scary, though I didn't quite believe him.

The sheriff of Harlan, J. H. Blair, had a reputation for tough anti-unionism. I decided to go see him, introduce myself, and kind of dare him to do something to me. I told him I expected to be treated like a human being. Blair gave me a wicked grin. "You'll be alright," he said gruffly. "Just don't take no rides with any of my deputies." His humor broke the spell of terror and I walked back to the hotel and ordered a steak dinner. I hadn't had anything but milk for two days. Just before dinner was served, the waiter brought a special delivery letter to the table:

Madam

You have been here too long already and remember two other red neck reporters got what was coming to them so don't let the sun go down on you here. If you do it will just be too bad.

100% Americans

We got your number and we don't mean maybe.

Luckily the sun had already set and I was not about to rush around in the dark. But I had to send the plate back and order another glass of milk.

The next day, I interviewed the people of "Bloody Harlan," as it was known on the left, and had my first personal contact with the lives of American miners. In early 1931, the full brunt of the Depression in the coal industry fell on Harlan County. The lives of the miners deteriorated from subsistence to starvation. Appeals for relief went unanswered—too many were hungry in that year already. When the miners sought the solution to their problems in unionism, calling in the United Mine Workers of America (U.M.W.A.) for help, the operators closed mines, fired and blacklisted miners. The U.M.W.A. organized a rally in March denouncing the increasingly unfair work conditions the bosses were forcing on the miners, but urging them not to indulge in any wildcat strikes. In the following months, as the bosses fired unionists and cut wages still further, the miners came closer to the brink, and, finally, struck without the approval of John L. Lewis and his U.M.W.A. Lewis had little stomach for hard fights in the early thirties when unemployment deprived miners of clout. He was a much more effective labor leader after the Wagner Labor Act guaranteed the right to organize. Unfortunately for these men and women, that was several years off. The U.M.W.A. refused to give strike support to wildcatters and the Red Cross would aid only victims of natural disasters. The striking miners, completely alone, saw their living conditions worsen daily. In May, blacklisted miners, who had moved to Evarts to escape harassment by the operators, received word that the bosses' gunmen were on their way to shoot up the settlement. When the deputies fired on the miners, the miners fired back. In a fifteen-minute rain of bullets at least four men died, including two deputies among the invaders. The state charged forty-three miners with murder and sixty-three others with criminal syndicalism.

After the Battle of Evarts, a radical union moved in. The National Miners Union (N.M.U.), led by the Communist Party, offered organizing skills and all of the material aid they could (though obviously not much). The Harlan miners could not understand the position of the U.M.W.A. They appreciated the militancy of the N.M.U., which they celebrated in ballads sung across the county. I heard them many times. One of my favorites went like this:

> The coal operator thinks it an awful thing to see
> The National Miners Union driving down the Main
> The miners look ragged and they look tough
> There is about 100,000 is doing their stuff
> They are called Reds, and they are called Blues
> If there was anything else, they would be called it too
> The N.M.U. the operators don't like
> They are putting up a darn hard fight
> When they cut the miners they cut them in the back
> And that is the way the miners is going to pay them back
> It looks mighty hard and it looks mighty tough
> Now is the time the miners got to do your stuff
> I see the sun comin' over the nob
> On the other side is a union job
> Put your shoulder to the wheel and put it over the top
> And then the gun thug operators will have to stop.

The U.M.W.A. tried to fight back, echoing loudly the red-baiting tactics of the bosses. In late July they published "Words of Warning" to the miners of Harlan, blasting the N.M.U. as a "red outfit" seeking "to create class hatred and discord, and get our people into serious trouble that will cause additional hardships." By the end of the summer neither the strike nor the division in the labor movement had been settled, and the intermittent violence continued.

I walked into that situation. I could feel the hostility as I went to the post office and did other errands. Two gentlemen offered me lodging in the jail. Another fellow predicted I would get my "snoot bashed in" and be run out of town like the other Northerners. A deputy told me, "You are brave. You walked alone last night, but your luck can't last. You are on the wrong side." One afternoon the loud, ominous heels of three deputies' wives tapped behind me wherever I went. Finally, I turned around. "If you are going to follow me, I might as well go with you," I said. They just glared and snapped, "You are making it hard for our men. We want you to get the hell out, or we will make it hot for you right here in the street." In all, I received five threats in ten days. But nobody took a shot at me. Still, the tension seemed to grow constantly. As one taxi driver told me, "This county is so on edge that if a kid was to set off a firecracker on Main Street, a dozen men would be dead before anyone would stop to find out what happened."

No one suffered more from the tension and violence than did the people of Harlan. One day I went with another reporter to a union meeting at the Wallins Creek soup kitchen. I remember a tall skinny woman with a sweet but terribly drawn face saying in her mountain drawl, "They call us reds. That's because we're so thin and poor that when we stand up against the sun, you can see red through us." I marveled at the courage of these people.

A few days later the local paper reported a disturbance at the new soup kitchen near Harlan. The report said the deputies had to shoot two miners to death in self-defense. Though the union raised the money for the soup kitchens on the outside, people who worked at them had a lot of nerve. The mine operators clearly believed that the food the miners got at these kitchens kept them on strike. I took a taxi to an evening meeting of the union nearby and had the driver let me out at some houses close to the kitchen. I asked what had happened at one house after another. Everyone gave me the same story. On Sunday evening, families were relaxing and talking in front of the kitchen—sitting on the steps were men, women, and children. The police came, shined their lights at the door, and ordered all of the women and children out of the way. Then they told the men to put their hands up. When the men obeyed, the police shot them anyway. At the scene, I saw the blood in the gravel. It gave me a feeling that has never left me. Those hard-working men, trying to feed themselves and their neighbors. Class struggle is not something I want to preach. It is something that happens to people who try to resist or improve intolerable conditions. The local paper said the police acted in self-defense so I called their correspondent and told him what really happened. I told him to check with the neighbors himself, but he never corrected his story. Back in New York I went to see the editor at Associated Press and he said, "Well, I have no doubt you are telling the truth but there's nothing I can do about it now."

In spite of the violence, the union idea was hard to kill in Harlan. Sporadic struggles continued for another decade. Even the disappointing behavior of John L. Lewis didn't shake the people's confidence. Most of the miners I talked to continued to support the Communist-organized N.M.U. The men's militancy came out in our conversations. "I was blacklisted," one said. "The boss told me if you'll keep quiet and not talk so much you can continue on your job. But I told him I would keep on working for the working class. And now, my fellow workers are taking care of me, little as they have, to see that organizing goes on. We have cried for freedom and now we have a chance to get it!" Most had little interest in anything but the N.M.U. As one put it: "The U.M.W.A. took our dollar, and when we got through we didn't have organization and we didn't have our dollar—didn't have anything. The miners were dumped in a ditch and the N.M.U. picked them out." I did occasionally hear miners frustrated by all the red-baiting of the local officials and the fighting between the unions talk about forming a third, local union unconnected to any outsiders, but none ever materialized. Even then, when I asked them what they expected to gain striking in a time of economic disaster, they said, "What's the use of going into the mine and working, and then having your family starve? We might as well starve out in the sun." What the union wanted was a living wage, not charity, but the relief coming in through the N.M.U., little as it was, beat nothing and the union told the rest of the country about Harlan.

Harlan fortified me for Pittsburgh. There miners and steelworkers suffered massive underemployment that affected all other workers who depended on their trade. Before Roosevelt and the social safety net, these people could look only to equally hard-pressed relatives or charity for help. With so many in need, charity couldn't raise enough money or food to go around. Harvey and I wanted to help, but knew only a few people in Pittsburgh. We decided to use the list of subscribers to *The Nation* to raise funds for relief. Most of the subscribers were professional people who could afford to contribute, and since they took *The Nation*, we hoped they would be sympathetic. I particularly remember one young receptionist in a doctor's office. When I told her my business, she said, "He'll see you, I know. The hunger around here is getting awful. We're going to do like they did in Russia if this goes on." I heard talk of revolution again and again in those years in Pittsburgh, sometimes mixed in with strike talk, sometimes out of the blue. Extreme poverty and total repression sparked frequent talk of the most extreme solutions—talk that I hadn't heard in either Gastonia or Harlan. When Roosevelt became President and his New Deal began putting people to work, most of the talk melted away.

In October of 1931, though, delegates from practically all the steel-producing areas of the country reported to the Metal Workers Industrial League Conference in Pittsburgh that men in their plants had reached the limit of endurance. The situation in and around Pittsburgh was miserable. Some companies cut wages every month or two by as much as 25 percent. The previous year men worked at least five days a week—in 1931 they were lucky to get five days in two weeks. One delegate said in disgust, "If we don't strike, pretty soon we will have to work just for exercise." The delegate pointed out that the Amalgamated Association of Iron, Steel and Tin Workers used to count eight hundred men in his mill—but that year, the local had sixty-five.

One of the reports that most disturbed me came from nearby Ambridge. There, the American Bridge Company put in a new shop called a beam shop that would produce more per week than five of the old shops did in months, and with fewer men. Almost half the former employees had been laid off, the Ambridge delegate said. The new riveting machine put in twenty-six hundred rivets in ten hours with only four men. "Yet the bossmen keep pestering us to move fast, or they'll get somebody else," he said. One of the bossmen, according to this delegate, told a worker who complained he was not earning enough to feed his children, "Why did you make children? It's not our fault; we didn't make them." This same bossman sang with the Salvation Army urging workers to follow Jesus and their troubles would be solved! Under these circumstances keeping a steady voice for workers alive in the Federated Press seemed more crucial than ever. In fact, in Pittsburgh and surrounding areas, Harvey and I often served as conduits for local labor news. We tried to foil the intricate spy system by carrying personal messages and news from labor people in one town to another.

One of the fascinating things about Pittsburgh was the variety of nationalities working there. The company owners thought that language differences and distrust born of past history in Europe would slow down organizing attempts. Poles, Hungarians, Czechs, Slovaks, and many others flocked to the great mills and mines. Instead, some of the most energetic leaders came from these groups. One of the happier excursions we made was to a Yugoslav neighborhood where Harvey spoke on civil liberties. Tony Minerich, an organizer for the National Miners Union, invited him. Tony, a Communist, had been charged with sedition against the state of Pennsylvania. We expected a small dutiful audience sitting on hard benches in the usual cheap, dingy hall. The hall was standard but the sound of happy music and the smell of good things to eat greeted us. A man played a little six-sided accordion on a small stage. People sat listening around the edge of the room, and in the center some—including a grandmother and a five-year-old boy—danced. Everybody had a grand time. When the accordion finished, a chairman came forward and announced a speaker from a brother union. After the speaker, two girls sang a duet. Then Tony called for Harvey, who received great applause. More dancing followed his talk. These Yugoslavs figured you could support a cause without boring yourself to death, a new angle on the radical movement. They spent their whole Sunday afternoon together, and enjoyed it! I was furious when local papers singled out the ethnics for attacks and red-baiting. While they claimed to be protecting the country against "un-American" elements, I knew good old-fashioned bigotry when I heard it.

In the meantime, I encouraged Harvey, who was writing his first book, helping with research when I could. As Harvey says, his book hit a snag with publishing houses fearful of libel suits, and we decided to go to the Soviet Union at the invitation of Anna Louise Strong. The *Moscow News*, published in English, reached thousands of American engineers and technicians (whose numbers rose as the Depression deepened). Strong felt that experienced American correspondents might make the *News* more readable and useful to its readers.

I had bought an apartment upon leaving Moscow in 1928. I knew claiming it would cause a tussle in 1932, so I left before Harvey, in August, for Moscow. Through the intervention of the editor, Mikhail Borodin, I overcame the red tape. Harvey and I got two rooms in a four-room apartment in a new building. We shared the kitchenette with the couple who lived in the third room, and a single person in the fourth. The couple's maid slept on a wooden bench in the kitchenette. Once, when her brother visited from the country, he slept on that narrow bench too.

As soon as I arrived in Moscow, I realized that some things had changed since 1927. Huge pictures of Stalin were plastered all over. Before, the Russians avoided such glorification of living leaders and Lenin had spoken out against "the cult of personality." Food shortages made rationing necessary. People on the streets looked glum rather than buoyant. Shopping—something I had not had to do in 1927 when I boarded with a family—took forever. We hired a woman to shop for us as we both worked all day and the stores closed evenings. Harvey and I had determined not to eat better than the Russian people. Therefore, we didn't patronize the *Tuzhek* stores where our American currency could buy luxuries and delicacies. The ordinary people of Moscow peered into the windows of these *Tuzhek* stores wondering at all the riches in there. We really regretted it, but we knew the government needed foreign currency to buy machinery and other imports. The Russian people were remarkably quiescent; they didn't smash the windows of those stores to loot the contents.

What a frightful winter! Stalin had ordered the peasants into the collective farms. Nobody would get credit for livestock or farm tools—all had to go in on an equal basis. Those who had been thrifty and hard-working and had a cow or two swore they would not go into the co-op with those they considered lazy. So many killed their cattle and feasted—in the short term. In the long-term all faced the food shortage and starvation, although we, in Moscow, had no idea just how bad things were in the south. I translated one of Stalin's big speeches that offered some hope of change on his part. He said before the Party Congress: "We are at fault, we made a mistake and should not have rushed so much. The people were not ready." When the Russians were the most hungry and angry, Stalin admitted that.

Perhaps the Russians' patience stemmed from the fact that Soviets still did good things. The evil doing of the Czars was a fresh memory. The participation of workers in industrial management continued to expand. I attended production conferences where workers criticized management openly and saw the work planning meetings in various shops in which workers helped set production goals for the following year. Soviet women got equal pay for equal work, not to mention maternity coverage and leave and day care. Many Russians argued that their Revolution was quite young—and that the gains had been impressive. Along with them, I hoped that the things that were wrong would pass. Given the conditions I saw in Pittsburgh, I was hardly in any position to preach.

Our working conditions were unpleasant. I had known our editor, Borodin, since my teens. Anna Louise Strong, the associate editor, occupied a little alcove off the main newsroom, insisting that the door be locked when she was away. Actually, we couldn't keep people out of her office for we were short of typewriters and people insisted on going in. When she discovered intruders, she would bawl out Harvey, the technical editor. But Anna Louise wrote powerfully and could concentrate on what she wanted to do. In the middle of typing furiously—no American was too proud to type—she would stop and say, "Jessie, what do you think of this?" She would read the story to me and I would open my mouth to reply. But she would be back typing again before I had a chance to say a word.

Theater and opera tickets were hard to find by 1932. They went in large blocks to workers and trade union groups. Only the leftovers were sold to the public. One day on the way to a story I saw a line forming at the Bolshoi Opera. I joined it, because I did not want Harvey to miss the unique way they performed *Boris Godunov*. I was playing hooky but I got a good story anyway. The young man ahead of me came from Vladivostok on the Pacific to see the Bolshoi's *Carmen*. He worked as a spotter for a crabfish fleet. The theater club on the mother ship planned to put *Carmen* on themselves. "We want to do it right," he said. The trip took twelve days by train each way, which left him just six days in Moscow. He had a spark of the same enthusiasm I had admired so much in 1927. "I studied at the Crustacean Institute. You had two choices for a major: either crabs or crawfish. I chose crabs," he said. That spirit was so rare in the thirties.

Before we left, we got tickets for a play by Tolstoy. Hearing Kachalov, the leading actor of the Moscow Art Theatre (Bolshoi), was one of the most beautiful experiences of our stay in Russia. Besides the actors playing the characters in the story, one came out on the side of the stage between scenes to give the audience the inside story. Kachalov, playing that role, simply stood and spoke, but we were transfixed. Harvey knew little Russian, yet he was as fascinated as I. The infinite modulations of Kachalov's rich voice, his perfect clarity of diction, and the expressiveness of his whole being were of a quality

I had never seen before or since. Sometimes he delved into someone's soul. Once he explained that the court's adjournment had nothing to do with the case at hand, only with an urgent private need of the judge's digestion. Whether sublime or ridiculous, you felt to the ultimate with Kachalov. His image is still bright in my mind after forty-five years.

All in all, the Soviet Union disappointed me. I still believed that, for all of its problems, the Revolution remained the best hope. I had not seen much of Sonia when I returned, though she did visit once. When I asked if she was living alone she smiled and said, "Not entirely." Depressed by the path the Revolution had taken, she was losing hope. Her writer friends who hadn't been arrested faced heavier censorship. It was very sad. (I wrote to her when I returned to the States. After a while, she stopped writing back. A Quaker friend, who saw her later, said that when her mother died, she went to pieces. The Quaker found her unkempt and distraught.) We were more than ready to leave when we got word that Harvey's manuscript had been accepted for publication.

III

Pittsburgh was a much more hopeful place when we got back from Russia. The New Deal, which guaranteed workers the right to unionize, had transformed the area. Forlorn, despondent people took on industry. Everywhere people spoke for unions and against the company-organized variety. With labor struggles in progress all around, it was a marvelous time to be a reporter for Federated Press.

During this exciting labor drive, I narrowly missed arrest in the town of Ambridge. I had gone to Ambridge to cover the strike of the Steel & Metal Workers Union, another Communist-backed organization. As a Federated Press correspondent in Pittsburgh, I found, again, that I could facilitate communication between local labor leaders—critical when so many contemplated or waged strikes. In a place in which one of the company towns was known as the "Siberia of America" by union men, helping the flow of information was critical. In the company towns, deputies met strangers at in-coming street-cars, cross-examined them, and turned them right around if their answers didn't please. Reporters headed the list of undesirables. At the union office, I asked about the conditions in the mill that had led to the strike. Along came a policeman, perhaps the chief, to tell the union people, "Get your pickets off the street or we will get them off." The unionists replied that they had a right to picket. The officer walked out. Next thing we knew, a bunch of deputies with ax handles started beating up the pickets. A candy store proprietor, who had let the pickets meet in the back of his store, was shot through the heart when he stepped out to look around. The officers arrested many of the leaders of the union, so I decided to get a lawyer to defend them. I had heard of a liberal one up the valley in Beaver, and I headed there. The lawyer sympathized but said, "If I defend the union men I would get no more business in this area from people who can afford to pay a lawyer. I'm sorry, but I can't. Get someone further away from here who can't be hurt so much."

Out of luck, I returned to the Ambridge police station to get the names of those arrested. The woman in the office showed me their cards. When I was reading the names with the cell numbers, I came to a card that had no number or cell listed yet. The cell was reserved for "Jessie O'Connor, small car, brown clothes." There I stood with brown coat, brown scarf, and brown hat and my knees shaking. I wanted to run, but asked the girl, "Who is this, Helen?" referring to another card. "Well, she was in the thick of it in that office so they pulled her in." I fit the description on my card to a tee but fortunately the police who had done the arresting were still out, mopping up maybe or celebrating their victory over the unarmed pickets. So I left as deliberately as I could, to where I had luckily parked my small car. A friend of the union told me where the main organizer was hiding. "Take him to the city," the unionists pleaded, "they might kill him." I did get to him and got him in the car without problems. He kept urging me to drive faster, but there were dips in the pavement at every intersection and going faster would make people think I was crazy or had done something wrong. I told him to duck his head down and be patient till we got out of town. We got there without further incident, I let him out, and went home.

By that time—around 9:00—it was quite dark and late. We rented our house from a couple who lived in a house back up the alley. The landlord, a pattern maker, very friendly and fairly well off, had his ten children posted on different corners to look for me. When I was a block or so away, one of them jumped on my running board to warn: "Turn down your lights, Mrs. O'Connor, the police have got your husband." The child told me to go to their family's garage where his mother filled me in. She said that the police had searchlights on our house and were waiting for me. Thanks to her children I had slipped by without being noticed.

I told my landlady later that I was going downtown to tell the reporters about this scandal. I assumed, as did much of the country, that Harvey had been arrested as revenge for embarrassing Mellon in his book. I only realized later that I had been the cops' primary object and Harvey a consolation prize. Our landlady dressed me up in a black silk coat, rouged my lips, and made a different woman out of me. She wanted to help me escape detection. When I went downtown to the newspaper office to contact a friendly reporter, he suggested that I turn around so that their police reporters couldn't see my face. They were thick with the police department. The reporter couldn't help much, so I got in touch with a lawyer. Next morning, we sat in court as they brought in Harvey, who looked quite disheveled from a night on a hard shelf in Allegheny County jail. The judge dismissed the case against Harvey and the police had lost interest in me. To my extreme annoyance, the police had stolen a nice little Swedish knife I had given to Harvey. I was all for doing something about it but the lawyer said, "You want to stay in Pittsburgh? Better leave the police be or they can make it tough for you." So Harvey never got the knife back. But we had a hearty laugh about the way those mindless Ambridge cops created nationwide publicity for Harvey's book. I felt a little sorry for Andy Mellon, getting all the blame.

If the outlook on the domestic front had improved somewhat, foreign affairs became bleaker. Frightening stories came out of Germany as the Nazis consolidated their power. In Europe, radicals and liberals joined to form the League Against War and Fascism. Some of the distinguished members of the European groups toured America to speak, and committed people formed chapters in many parts of the country. I was elected chairperson of the Pittsburgh League. I found the on-the-job training quite difficult. Organizing meetings or presiding over them and making speeches was a new experience. I sometimes felt like Kipling's Kangaroo, who developed stronger legs because Yellow Dog, "Dingo," chased him.

People jammed the hall for Hans Eisler, the German composer whose songs appealed to working people. Pittsburgh workers reveled in his strong songs, which expressed just what they felt. The workers cheered, stamped, and begged for more. Eisler responded and even convinced them to join in and sing along. The crowd applauded loudly for a song called "In Praise of Learning." I hadn't heard it before either, but I was touched by Eisler's delivery. He played the piano as he sang. Though his voice wasn't terrific, he projected his words right to the heart of his audience.

> You must learn, you must study
> If you don't understand, then you want it explained,
> Women in the kitchens, everybody!
> You must be ready to take over!

The powerful, triumphant chords—not to mention the message— stirred the audience. "We must have a copy!" many cried. Nights like that helped carry us through the hard times, of which there were many. The closer the country came to war, the greater the intolerance for our message. We kept fighting, nonetheless, for a firm, peaceful solution to complicated international problems.

═══ IV ═══

In 1937, Harvey's writing and research carried us back to the Middle West. I was happy to live in Mother's house in Winnetka for a time, but also pleased to be invited to move into Chicago in the fall of 1939. Charlotte Carr, the new head resident of Hull House, realized that Harvey and I were active in civic work and welcomed lively people at the settlement. Much progressive activity in the area centered around Hull House.

When I lived in Chicago I said that I worked for thirteen different organizations and wasn't doing justice to any of them. They still elected me to their boards—probably because so much needed to be done. The League of Women Shoppers urged American women to use their buying power for justice. Women, we reminded anyone we could reach, did 85 percent of the buying in America. Though individual shoppers' actions passed unnoticed, many shoppers organized could get results. We used our leverage to improve conditions in the workplace and wages for American workers. We pointed out that inferior conditions produced shoddy products, in addition to human misery; that higher wages meant increased buying power and a strong economy; and that many shoppers unwittingly supported sweatshops and child labor with their purchases. Above all, in those critical days of labor organizing, our League endorsed the right of workers to unionize. "In keeping with the democratic traditions of our country," our brochure read, "we believe in the right of men and women to assemble and organize to protect their own interests." I offered direct help to the labor movement when I could. At 5:00 A.M., one freezing, windy morning, I joined the picket line at International Harvester. Many prominent people came at that ungodly hour in the hopes of preventing the police from attacking the strikers as they had at the Republic steel strike shortly before.

At Charlotte Carr's suggestion, I joined the Metropolitan Housing Council. The Council aimed to clean up slums and to compel the city to enforce laws regulating rental properties. The conditions in which people lived appalled me. I encouraged friends from Winnetka to come see them. I hoped they would also get to thinking and start jumping up and down for change. But they responded, "What, go down there and track all those germs back to my family? I couldn't possibly." A color movie would show them, I thought, without subjecting them to germs.

I filmed some of the worst places I saw. In one, which had been a family home, each floor had been made into an apartment. The pipes had broken in the basement, the cellar was frozen in spots, and some of the water had seeped into the apartment, creating a sheet of ice on the floor. One tenant, a woman, had four little children packed in her dark and nasty apartment. On the top floor the balcony sagged and the railing, loose at one end, rocked back and forth. The apartment was more than an eyesore. With children living there, it was a deathtrap. In another building the plumbing leaked, the tenant had patched up holes in the wall with pieces of cardboard, and an overhead tank dripped into a dustpan the tenants had designed so their backs wouldn't get wet when they used the toilet. The tenants couldn't fix up the plumbing themselves, even if they had the money, because then the landlord could charge more rent and throw them out. Far too many Chicagoans lived in such condition to be ignored.

In the Women's International League for Peace and Freedom and the League against War and Facism, I continued to do all I could to avert the bloodshed of another world war. I remembered the last one too clearly to do anything else. We urged that the economic pressures be brought to bear against the aggressors—especially Hitler—early enough to stop him before he did too much damage. We brought in lecturers from near home and even abroad to report on what was happening, and we raised money for the victims of the fascists. Some of the fund raisers were held in our apartment at Hull House, where we had a very big living room.

My activities were probably never more diverse than in those days at Hull House. One day I'd be arranging for Eleanor Roosevelt to speak on civil liberties at the Civic Opera House (only to be undone by a Midwest blizzard that kept the audience at home). The next, as sponsor of the Stop and Go Light Mothers, I'd be agitating with Italian women to get more traffic lights on dangerous street corners. These earthy, friendly women gave the most memorable parties. Once or twice a year, the women brought delicious whipped cream cakes to Hull House along with their insignia—a pin with red and green lights that flashed when a chain was pulled. Once, they held a mock wedding with a lace curtain over the bride's head and a rolled, red bandanna in the proper place on the so-called man and then they paraded around the clubroom, everybody singing, "Here Comes the Bride."

I had begun to think about children while Harvey and I were in Pittsburgh. Harvey was such a good, gentle person that I wanted to bear his children. I remember asking Dad, "How much time does it take to care for just one child?" He replied, "All the time there is!" Still, I decided to try to have a baby. Harvey was a little worried about it but said, "Well, that is the way women are and you have to humor them." So we agreed. As it turned out, it wasn't possible. After numerous gynecologists and two operations, my mind began to turn to adoption. Many people thought we were brave to adopt. "You don't know what you'll be getting," they said. But, I felt, you never knew what you were getting anyway and you couldn't understand human life if you didn't have children. But all the agencies told us we would have to wait at least three years—and I was almost forty.

In the fall of 1942, my brother's wife, Mary, asked me if I still wanted to adopt someone and I said, "Yes." Mary told me she had friends who knew about a boy near Washington, D.C. His foster parents were breaking up; the father couldn't very well keep him and the foster mother didn't want him as he was too vigorous for her. She wanted a dainty little girl. In the meantime, some friends had taken the boy in, but couldn't afford to keep him.

Harvey and I went to Washington after Christmas to meet the child. A friend drove us out to Greenbelt and we arrived about 9:00 P.M. Polly, his foster mother, said she'd wake him. He was a good-natured child. At eighteen months, he walked in the room with a big smile and offered everybody a hammer toy, most genially. All the way out Harvey had been telling his friend, Ralph Winstead, how crazy women are when they want to adopt children. But all the way back to town Harvey said, "My son has poise, he doesn't get cranky when waked out of a deep sleep." So we adopted Steve. He already knew about twenty words. We went back to Chicago on the train at night time and suddenly another train roared by. Steve pointed to the window and said, "Happen?" I could see he was asking what it was and I gave him a full answer.

Steve's favorite toy was a white horse with a red and blue bridle and a music box inside. He loved Hull House. Although it was located near the center of the city (with three railroad stations nearby), it also had a lot of horse traffic. Peddlers kept their horses in a stable on the back of our block. When things were dull we would go down to the stable and Steve, overjoyed, would shout, "Da horse, da horse." I found out how different it was having a kid around and after a few days I got stir crazy. Someone came and spelled me and I went out and had lunch alone and liked him so much better when I came back.

I had always thought it was better not to have an only child so I made overtures to various organizations to adopt another. One agent said, "You've already got a child, why not give someone else a chance?" But I discovered another agency, the Chicago Children's Home, which preferred to settle children in families with other kids. After investigating us, the manager of the Home explained that she expected overcrowding in about a month. She would select a girl from the children coming who could hold her own with Steve, who had quite a strong personality. Soon the call came, "Kathleen—eleven months old, very outgoing, talks to everybody who goes by—if you don't take her, you'll lose her." As luck would have it, I had poison ivy at the time. I kept on a long-sleeved shirt in Chicago's hottest weather, so I could hold her. But once or twice, I forgot. Then I'd have to pull back when Kathleen extended her arms to me. I feared she did not understand my seeming rejection of her. What a sickly child Kathleen was when we adopted her. Kathleen's muscles were absolutely limp, like molasses. She wanted liver soup all the time and just ate and ate. Because the poor little thing had boils and some breathing trouble, the doctor said she shouldn't go in the water. So she couldn't join the crowd in the water when we went to the beach. But once she heard sounds of gaiety coming up from the lake and she was off—I only saw a little diapered rump going down over the bluff on all fours.

That summer of 1943 we lived in the Winnetka lakeside cottage that Mother and Dad had had when they were first married. Mothering two small children was as demanding as anything I have ever done. Unlike most women, I almost always had help with mine. One summer we had a wonderful helper named Blanchie from down near Maxwell Street who really knew how to handle kids. The next summer she worked in a shoe factory getting a lot more money. Blanchie told us that she led such a wild night life that the foreman often had to come by and beat on her door to wake her up to come to work. The summer we adopted Kathleen we weren't as lucky. Our helper, theoretically a quite serious-minded student, constantly left wet diapers in Kathleen's crib. I hadn't asked her to wash them, just to drop them in the basin outside so I could take care of them. When I kept finding them in the crib, I took the wet diapers and put them under her pillow. On the whole, I was fortunate with the women to whom I entrusted my children, and I think the children learned much from them. Though motherhood definitely did curtail some of my activism, their help allowed me to keep an oar in the water.

Adopting children was only one of the big changes in my family life during the war years. The last winter Mother lived on the ranch in Texas, she wrote, "Before one more revolution of this earth around the sun, I will need to have one of you staying with me here." I really believe that the constant horrible news about fascism and war hastened her death. She spent the last twenty years of her life calling for peace and world government. She could not bear even to read about torture—the descriptions would haunt her day and night. The horror of another world war was just too much. Yet Steve was three, Kathleen one, and I was struggling to find good part-time help while I still did some social action. I didn't know what I could do. When Mother came back north in the spring she was beautiful. I remember her handsome eyes, thoughtful face, and shining white hair as she attended a big meeting of the Winnetka Historical Society. Dad was in town for the first time in twenty-eight years and attended too.

Most of the town had looked askance at him over the divorce, so my sister Mary and I sat beside him to give him some support. Mother, we knew, had loads of friends. Dad was out on the steps smoking—he could never be long without a cigarette—when Mother arrived, but so far as I know they did not exchange a word.

Not long after that Mother took sick. Mary moved in with her, but she did not get better. In July, she went to the hospital. She soon insisted on coming home, and told us to call all her friends to come for an ambulance party. One friend refused, saying it was too silly, but all the rest came, and Mother had the fruit juice made deliciously. A few days later she died, with my sisters Mary and Georgia standing by. An autopsy revealed a big cancer in the pancreas, in a place where the X-ray could not show it. "Amazing she did not suffer more pain," said the doctor. We thought to ourselves, "Amazing that she suffered so much without complaint." Dad called about coming to the service, which was a small quiet one at home. He was in the East and I said I didn't think it was necessary. "You mean you don't want me?" he exclaimed, his voice shaken. "Of course we do, Dad," I said quickly. But I did think it strange.

No one had told me that when you lose a close loved one, you hurt all over physically as well as emotionally. And when I lost my mother, for the first time I felt really grown up. And I hated it. I moped indoors, brooding over all I had not done for Mother. Just when I was at the lowest ebb an old friend, Atlantis McLendon Marshall, came by with a big box of runners pruned off her prize strawberry bed that had to be planted right away. "What is she thinking of," I fumed, "at a time like this, they had to be planted immediately." But as I patted them into the warm black earth in the lovely sunshine, a feeling for life came back into my intense grief. Atlantis was wiser than I had thought.

Ironically, a few months after Mother's death, Harvey got a job in Texas as publicity director for the Oil Workers International Union. I was reluctant to leave all my Chicago activities and the good Mary Crane nursery at Hull House. I stayed in Pittsburgh when Harvey went to Washington, D.C., a few years before, and I thought I might do the same now. When Harvey called he sounded very pleased with the people, and said even the air smelled good in Fort Worth—quite a change from Chicago. I soon got used to the idea of moving. I asked Harvey about finding us a house to rent. Impossible in the war years, he said—so he bought the first one the agent showed him. It was nice—two stories on two lots, a rare thing on Clarence Street in Bird-ville. The neighborhood was full of hard-working people, and so informal that at any time you might see a housewife crossing the street in her dressing gown to share a problem or bring a toddler to play. With twenty-four children under eight on the block, Steve and Kathleen found it ideal. We had a throughway kitchen. I never knew when a horde of wild Indians might come whooping in between me and the stew.

The summer of 1945, I let Steve go to a nearby riding camp for a week while I took Kathleen with me to visit my aunt Rena Maverick Green in the Davis Mountains. Five thousand feet high, near a westerly bend of the Rio Grande, the mountains are handsome and cool. As our bus came into Fort Davis, I saw a fire truck weaving down the street ahead of us with a few cheerful men squirting hoses in all directions. "The war is over!" they shouted. It was V-J day, August 14. Learning about the horrors of the atom bomb came later. Either that fall, or early in 1946, I wrote a letter to the *New York Times*, short enough that I thought they might even publish it. It went about like this: "Creation of the vast destructive power of the atom bomb makes one wonder. Perhaps the Almighty is tired of the way the human race keeps fighting over all the lovely gifts he has given us, and has decided to give us one more: enough rope."

The *Times* did not print it. But peace has been at the top of my political agenda ever since. I felt that bomb very vividly in my imagination, just as I had the bombs at Guernica nine years before. In ensuing months, a phrase kept coming to me: "He hath loosed the fateful lightning," from the "Battle Hymn of the Republic," by Julia Ward Howe. That winter I concocted a "Hymn for the Atomic Age," using her first verse and adding three of my own about the teaching of one of humanity's great social engineers, Christ. I mimeoed it and sent copies to churches and church organizations. I got almost no response—then. The bomb seemed too far away to think about. In the eighties, though, three Episcopal churchmen in Rhode Island wrote me appreciatively. Our local United Congregational Church minister, Beverly Edwards, put it on a program.

Mine eyes have seen the glory of the coming of the Lord;
He is trampling out the vintage where the grapes of wrath are
    stored;

He hath loosed the fateful lightning of His terrible swift sword,
His truth is marching on.
  Glory! Glory! Hallelujah!
  Glory! Glory! Hallelujah!
  Glory! Glory! Hallelujah!
  His truth is marching on!
Two thousand years ago He told us how to heal our woes:
"To your enemy do good"—dissolve the hate that moves your foes.
Not practical, said we, and wrecked each other with our blows,
And death is marching on.
  (Chorus)
We have tossed the ball of evil back and forth without a rest;
Love could be a shock absorber, but we never made the test:
We did everything for Jesus save to follow his behest,
And war goes marching on.
  (Chorus)
Repent! Repent, or perish where the atoms sear and rend!
Fires of hell will come on earth if we allow the peace to end;
From our foes there's no escape, so we must turn them into friends.
God's truth is marching on.
  (Chorus)

That winter I decided to take the children to visit Dad in Jamaica, at his lovely and very original place overlooking Montego Bay. It had been almost impossible to get train tickets during the war and was still very difficult. Steve was five and a half and Kathleen was three and a half. What a trip. The train was filthy and overcrowded, the kids, bored, picked up anything they found including cigarette butts. Whatever sanity I had left that evening I owe to a nearby soldier, a kind, family man who amused them for a while. "Peace at last," I thought when we got our reserved berth at New Orleans. At midnight Steve still charged up, stood in the upper berth greeting everyone who went by. The train was late to our Florida connection. We made it by only a hair, but found our hotel room canceled. Our dear friend, Josephine Herbst, took us in in a pouring rainstorm, then put us back on the pushing-crowded train next day; at last, we boarded the plane at Miami, landing at Kingston, on the other side of the island from Dad. Dad had sent his chauffeur for us and put us up at a hotel seven miles away, the Manor House, since it was too late to drive over. I looked forward to having food brought to me in a good dining room—we were very hungry. The head waiter said, "Children are not permitted in the dining room." Seeing my face fall, he quickly added, "Your maid will give them supper on the balcony of your room." It would be the first time in three days I had been able to swallow a few mouthfuls without running after my two little monsters. The finely printed menu he brought me had fourteen courses. I ate all of them but the dessert.

We had a lovely time with Dad. The Jamaican helpers handled the children with kindness and imagination. I had a real rest. On his birthday, February 24, Dad let the children come up from their usual meal with the helpers to the big dining room for dessert, and they did a lot of spontaneous dancing to the pleasant music he liked to play on his big phonograph. The floor was mahogany, polished to a smooth rich brown shine by the floor maid. The children laid on their backs and pretended to be steamboats, pushing themselves around with their feet. Dad said it was one of the nicest birthdays he had ever had.

In the spring his wife, Madge, wrote us that a large, inoperable cancer had been found in his lungs, that he was feeling no pain and had no idea of his condition. He would be kept comfortable. Since she wanted him to be free of worries, she didn't want us all to rush to visit him. Better to keep writing him lots of letters about our doings and the children. Some time later he wrote me, "It may amuse you to know that I think I have athlete's foot of the lung." He died June 30, apparently without pain. Two or three days later the *New York Times* wrote with a two-column head that we had buried him secretly. I protested to the obit editor, saying in substance: "The widow did not get out a mimeographed release, but she called friends she knew on the *Chicago Tribune*. If you were not so insular you would have seen the notice next day, and would not have made his death sound like a whodunit." My siblings and I were oppressed again with that empty, too-grown-up feeling.

Harvey and I yearned to sail again during his August vacation. Jessie Fox, Harvey's kind and capable sister, kept the children for us. Two good sailors came along from New York: his old pal from high school days, Hays Jones, and Tom Wright, editor of the *United Electrical Workers' News*. As we sailed into Sakonnet, Rhode Island, I thought, "What a lovely place for my parents to meet!" I wondered why I visited so rarely. I met my cousin, Anne Maverick Weise, who encouraged us to rent a place. "Our children hardly know each other.

Why don't we rent a big place for next summer the way your mother did in 1914 and all get together?" The rents sounded fantastic even then. "But if you would consider buying," said the tempter, "there is an old house in Little Compton with eight bedrooms, a four-bedroom cottage, a cabin, and a barn, and the total price is just six times the summer rental of that last place we saw." Buy a house on the seashore? I liked the place, but with Harvey working in Texas and only three weeks vacation, it seemed insane. We went back on the *Volya*, taking one white rose and one pink rose out of the hedge between the front yard and the ocean. Sailing away to Cutty Hunk, I kept sniffing the roses and asking our radical friends what they thought of it. They did not say, "It's too bourgeois." They said, "It's an awfully nice place." By the time we landed at Cutty Hunk, I had decided I wanted it. I bought the property before returning to Texas.

We moved into the house in Little Compton in 1948, though we spent the summer of 1947 there also. We began entertaining countless friends and relatives, many of whom came for extended stays during the summer. One lovely summer afternoon as I slowed my car to round the jog into the Warren's Point private road, one of our most respected local ladies hailed me. "Mrs. O'Connor, people say you have fifteen house guests." I nodded with a smile. Actually, that very day I had twenty-five, and six more young people were coming from the Cape to folk dance in the barn and sleep in sleeping bags.

V

The peacefulness of Little Compton could not shut out the problems of the rest of the world. The Truman administration launched a witch-hunt with loyalty oaths and arbitrary lists of subversive organizations as early as 1947. The hysteria about the Communist peril reached such peaks that I wrote letters to numerous public officials in defense of free speech. My letter to the attorney general summed my feelings up:

Dear Mr. Clark,

The Star-Telegram said May 28th that you had given out an additional list of 32 subversive organizations, besides the 90 you mentioned before. It did not print what they were.

Two I have heard mentioned by the Un-American Committee (and I don't know whether you had them on your list or not), are the Joint Anti-Fascist Refugee Committee, and the Southern Conference for Human Welfare. I worked with the Joint Anti-Fascist Refugee Committee for years, and attended many of their meetings, and never by word or hint was any suggestion made by them to overthrow the U.S. Government, either by force or violence, or even by persuasion. They did not even discuss how to overthrow the Franco government of Spain—a clerical dictatorship which outlaws our Protestant sects, degrades women, and starves the Spanish people. All they did was discuss how to help individuals to establish a living again—Spaniards and others who had been hunted out of their countries for striving against Franco's or Hitler's or Mussolini's dictatorship. Some of those individuals were not of the same political persuasion you are. But none of them were attempting to overthrow the U.S. Government. We used to boast of American freedom to differ in opinion, as long as there was no incitement to violence. But maybe you and Mr. Thomas think democracy can't win in an argument. Frankly I have more faith in democracy than that.

Then I have worked with the Southern Conference for Human Welfare and never heard anything there about overthrowing the government. In fact they seemed to care more for the government than most Southern governors; they wanted the federal government to take a hand against lynching, the poll tax, the Un-Christian race discrimination, and help get the South better education and health services. You are looking in the wrong place if you are looking for anti-government people in the S.C.H.W.

So what I am writing to ask you is, if these two organizations are on your list of subversive bodies, and if they are a fair sample, please send me the complete list, or announce them to the country, so that if there are any other Christian, freedom-loving endeavors that we have not known about, we may send them some money too and do a little work for them.

The tone of the letter was consciously defiant. Tom Clark couldn't touch me and I thought that any suggestion of fear would only encourage him. So many have forgotten that the Red Scare was in full swing under Truman long before McCarthy arrived.

I wrote a letter that summed up my response to the whole disgusting witch-hunt in 1951 and it was published in part by the *New Republic*. Later in the year, I sent the whole, uncut letter to all my friends with my reasons and fears spelled out:

So far, the only penalties for unconventional thinking are economic and social. If we let those terrify us into acquiescence, we shall live to see, as in Germany, the harshest forms of physical torment applied for any expression of humane thought. The time to resist insanity is now. And in so doing we are the true patriots, because the course urged by the reactionaries in their ignorance will make America the focus of the world's hate, instead of what she was and should be again, a friend to all people aspiring for a better life.

If anything else were needed to seal my reputation as a "Red," that letter did it. I've always been glad I wrote it and, sadly, it is still relevant today:

This administration has assumed the right to state, without proof, that certain organizations are Communist fronts, that if you were in them and not a Communist, you were an innocent dupe. I resent and reject that term. In any organization I was in where there were Communists, I knew it. I also knew the organizations were making no moves toward dictatorship (except the indirect move of trying to become popular with the public) and that they were working for certain immediate aims which I wanted as much as the Communists did.

Look at the aims of some of these organizations. Race brotherhood—is that unpatriotic? No, it would win America millions of friends. Justice for the underdog— is that unpatriotic? No, that too would build our world influence, and boost morale at home. Better care of health, more wages and more food for the poor—is that unpatriotic? No, it would make America more powerful than ever before, by strengthening our weakest links.

But they say now, a Communist is a pariah, you should refuse to talk to him, no matter how energetic he is in good causes. That is not the way I figure it, and those who try to legislate me into figuring it that way will have to contend with my eternal contempt—and undoubtedly the contempt of the British and the Scandinavians, and all the other people who believe free speech is more than a word to hurl over the air waves.

The quaking little men and women who passed the McCarran monstrosity act as if Communists were witches— as unchangeable, and as powerful. But it is human beings who have become Communists, for certain reasons; also human beings, for reasons, have refrained or become ex-Communists. An American, brought up on the Declaration of Independence, embraces the idea of proletarian dictatorship with reluctance. He does it only because his judgment makes him at once less hopeful and more hopeful than the rest of us. Less hopeful, for he believes the present government machinery is so rigged that the poor will never get their rights; more hopeful, for he trusts that the machinery of despotism can somehow, in the hands of working people, avoid its usual injustice and social bitterness. Can you cure his beliefs by kicking him around? No, that merely confirms his distrust of democracy, and disaffects his family and friends, too. Repression defeats its own purpose, like other un-Christian—unkind—methods. Have our would-be patriots noted the fact that every country where Communists were harshly repressed is now either run by Communists, or has to contend with a powerful Communist minority? The only countries where Communists don't count, and can not drum up a following, are those that have maintained complete freedom. Then why abandon our greatest advantage?

A Communist is often a person of more than ordinary energy and organizing ability. I say it is far better to keep these talents working for generally acceptable aims in a front organization, than to drive them underground. If while he is working, some social improvement actually takes place—as it seems to, in spite of the Communist's pessimism— then I think I can convert him to democracy more easily than he can convert me to dictatorship. So I shall continue to work with a clear conscience for anything I believe for the public good, with anybody who will work for it; my decision will depend on what the organizations do, not on the private opinions of the members. Surely freedom of association is the right of all Americans; and the grown-up ones, who have faith in their own judgment, will wrestle against all the powers of darkness to keep it.

I refused to lower my profile or trim my sails in response to the hysteria. When I had an opportunity to visit Yugoslavia in 1951, I jumped at it. Though I still didn't realize the extent of Stalin's crimes—I learned that only with Nikita Khrushchev's speech in 1956—I knew enough about his alliances and purges to worry me. My interest in Yugoslavia, whose Socialists had different ideas from Russia's, deepened. My visit reinforced my hopes, though Yugoslavia was not perfect—any more than Russia had been twenty odd years before or the United States was then. At first, Belgrade looked poor and bedraggled. Bullet holes marred the buildings and, while the people dressed warmly, they had to patch their clothing heavily. I counted seventeen patches on one jacket, some on top of each other, all very neatly stitched. Yet the people walked with a vigorous, purposeful gait and I was surrounded throughout my trip with medleys of animated conversation in strong, pleasant tones.

In some ways, I found Yugoslavs and Russians alike, but there were some amusing contrasts. With the same Slavic roots to their words, I thought I could pick up some Serbo-Croatian. But it would have been easier if they used entirely different ones, because often the root I thought I knew from Russian would mean something very different in Serbo-Croatian. Yugoslav habits also differed from those of the Russians. The most striking was in the matter of getting up in the morning. Yugoslavs worked from 7:00 A.M. to 2:00 P.M.— straight through, except for a snack in the office. I asked my pretty young guide how she could stand to be on the job at 7:00 A.M. in the dark days of winter. "We like our hours," she replied. "There was one time when Tito thought we should try to have the same hours as other countries. Everybody felt worse and worse and finally Tito got on the air and said, 'Comrades, let's go back to the ways we like.' What a relief!" "What do you like about it?" I asked. "Well, you get all through, and then have a clear time for yourself. In summer heat we go right down to the Danube to go swimming. Then we go home and nap and eat and go out to the movies." Not all Slavs get up so easily. The book *Oblomov* describes a Russian whose efforts to get up take the first fifty pages of the book.

In Chicago the Yugoslav consul had given me the address of one of his countrymen who returned to Belgrade after many years in America. I found him satisfied in spite of the adjustments he had to make. He no longer owned a car, and had little choice in things to buy. But he enjoyed the goodwill and energy of the people. His health needs were taken care of along with his children's education. "I have much less luxury, but also much fewer worries," he summed up.

I returned home to find that that year the witch-hunt would spread. The government deported Communist labor organizers all over the country and passed the word to bail bond companies not to make bond for these people while their deportation hearings were pending. Any murderer, drug pusher, or white slaver could get bond from these companies, but not men and women whose harsh experiences while working to better labor conditions had made them believe in communism. An old friend asked me to bail out Eula Figuereido, a shoe worker who had been held a long time and who was ill. I knew it would cause me trouble, but I thought she had as much right to bail as a real criminal. I got my banker to raise five thousand dollars quickly so I could do it.

The news did not come out right away. I think my brother and his wife and four children were visiting in the cottage, on their way back from two years in Switzerland, and Earl Robinson and his family were there too. Two days before a town square dance I had arranged, the papers carried the story—"Little Compton woman bails out Communist." Lots of people were horrified. I got some irate phone calls. Worst of all, as I found on my way to the dance, somebody had put up hand-printed signs along the road: "Don't go to the dance. You'll contribute to the bail fund." The dance had nothing to do with the bail, of course, which was already deposited. In fact, I had told the town council that whatever we cleared over expenses would be given to them to help pay for the caller for another dance. But the signs must have been believed, because outside of the people in our compound—who amounted to about two squares that time—we had very few others. I was desolated. One of the local women took it as her duty to reprove and berate me very seriously. She phoned me often, even late at night. I would just say I thought Mrs. Figuereido had as much right to bail as anybody else. Her calls became rarer, and after a year or two she moved to Fall River—unfortunately not a toll call, but still her interests must have broadened. But after a lapse of two or three years, she started calling again. "Where is that Communist now?" she asked combatively. "I have no idea," I said. "Well, if I had five thousand dollars invested in somebody, I sure would want to know," she answered. (Actually, the bond was returned when Eula was deported.)

Throughout the fifties, I campaigned against war—conventional and nuclear. No sooner was the country out of Korea than Vietnam became a possible site of violence. Vietnam grabbed my heart the way Spain did in the thirties. Politicians and experts still argue about what we should have done in Vietnam. They miss the crucial point. We shouldn't have done anything. After decades of struggle against modern military power, the Vietnamese people had finally freed themselves from the French. As President Eisenhower said, "I have never talked to or corresponded with a person knowledgeable in Indochinese affairs who did not agree that, had elections been held in 1954, possibly 80 percent of the population would have voted for the Communist Ho Chi Minh." We could have lived with that as we did with Communist China and Yugoslavia, but we didn't. From the fifties to the seventies I wrote letters and joined nearly every demonstration against our Vietnam policy. By the end of the fifties, the Cuban Revolution had also gotten caught in the web of cold war tensions.

In 1961 Harvey and I went to Mexico for a couple of months so he could write, and we visited Cuba. Interviewing the president of the Cuban National Oil Company, Harvey and I noticed a conspicuous sign on the wall behind his head: "Please be brief—we have already wasted fifty years" (fifty years previously Cuba got free from Spain). "That's a great sign," Harvey said. "Credit the office help. They put it up," the president said, smiling indulgently.

We went out in the country to meet an American who had been conducting a model farm in Cuba for years and did not want to leave. But he thought the U.S. embargo against all trade with them was nonsensical and gave us examples of Cuban ingenuity in dealing with it. "They won't let us buy shingle nails. So the fellows drive an ordinary nail through a soda bottle top to give the extra width to the head. And brooders (chicken houses), we used to send $62.59 apiece for them to some firm in Michigan. Now we have to make them ourselves out of Masonite and keep the chicks warm with a plain twenty-five watt bulb. The chicks are just as comfortable and it only costs us three dollars. Fewer jobs in Michigan though. Too bad. Cuba needs a lot of development and if we would help we would find good friends here." As in Yugoslavia, I was impressed by the enthusiasm and spirit of the people in 1961. Young people working on the big push for literacy and doctors in newly established free clinics spoke frankly about their problems, but were full of hope that they could work together for a better Cuba. When I returned to Mexico, the trip gave me new food for thought. I was as convinced as ever that misdirected "patriotism" came from fear and ignorance, and I tried to write about it whenever possible:

> It seems time for a long straight look at what we are heading for. If a man cannot ask himself to take a live baby to his own kitchen and roast it to death, he should not ask to be defended by modern warfare. If such an act would be unbearable for him, there is no sense in planning millions of such acts. The fact that they will be done by remote control does not make them any more decent.
>
> Our planet must be a tragic and ridiculous sight, if anybody is look-

ing at us from the core of the universe. Here is America, having no quarrel, our leaders say, with the Russian people, simply preparing to defend herself against the ruthless dictators who have enslaved them. Here is Russia, with the friendliest feelings, her leaders aver, for the American people, merely girding herself against "the capitalist warmakers who have exploited and tricked them." Ah! Then do the military on either side plan any selective shooting at dictators or warmakers? No, that isn't practical. The practical thing, obviously, for this is what the "realists" are preparing, is to incinerate whole cities full of men, women and children.

Yet our years in Little Compton were spent in joy as well as activism. Since 1948, when we moved in, the chronology of what happened when is sometimes a blur but the things themselves remain vivid. I have always wanted to tell young radicals that it is important to dance and laugh and celebrate as well as walk picket lines and write articles. For instance, take dancing. We had a nice big living room and enough people over the years who wanted to do it. (Not that they all thought they did at first.) Most, after seeing how much fun we were having and how little we cared for perfection, would join in, and find out that it was easier than they thought. Years of timidity and inhibitions fell away in our house. And why not? Dancing must be instinctive: at least, it is done and well done in all "primitive" societies and the men are usually even more active at it than the women. In self-styled "civilized" societies men are the more reluctant, and I have several theories about that. Men feel they must look expert before they try: they have a foolish fear of looking foolish. Another hazard at more formal parties is that men are responsible for the choosing of partners, and may get stuck with someone too long. A Hungarian circle dance *Csankansa* is an excellent cure for that fear. The men form an inner circle and the women, an outer circle. The man grabs a partner, takes four steps side to side, and whirls with her for eight counts. Then everyone takes four steps backward slanting to the right and advances to whirl with a new partner. By the time the dance has finished, everyone has danced briefly with everyone else. At home we never worried about being responsible for partners. We just danced for the fun of dancing with any man, woman, or child handy.

Dancing is also great exercise. In my mind, there is too much sitting still in America, especially in the middle class. They sit still on the way to work, at work, at meals, and then if they go out afterward, they sit and talk and drink. That's not my idea of a party. Human beings have muscles and they were made to be used. If they don't use their muscles and put weight on the bones, the substance tends to be taken for current upkeep, and the bones get softer, the muscles weaker, and the blood doesn't circulate right all over. Sounds as if we have to exercise, so why not dance? Follow the ancient urge, move to lively music with jolly people. Roll up the rug! Wall-to-wall carpeting is the curse of America.

Shyness did not persist in our house. Sometimes when we got inspired we would put on a Beethoven symphony and improvise to it, or "The Ritual Dance of Fire"—that really set us going. Our favorite came from an album of Vracha gypsy songs. Its fierce rhythms and sudden stops inspired dramatic action. Steve and I used to get everybody convulsed with laughter. Other people, who might have been shy their first day, would soon try their hands too. "Abandon inhibitions, all ye who enter here."

When the Newport Folk Festivals were in full flower, we used to get a few calls like, "Can my daughter and some friends stay in your yard?" Or my nephew, or my grandson. "They will bring their own sleeping bags." So in the early mornings the lawn would be strewn with these shapes. Once we counted forty-five. Luckily our big old porches could have accommodated them in case of rain. But it was really no trouble—they would be off to the festival all day and evening, and you'd never seen them on the hoof. I was sorry when they stopped the folk festivals. The rowdyism Newport had was from the jazz festivals at that time. But I think they stopped the folk festivals too because too many good antiwar songs were sung there. I particularly liked the lyrics of Phil Ochs. His sensitive soul a few years later led him to suicide. What a loss!

During the daytime the festival provided workshops on how to play every folk instrument, how to make some of them, and how to write songs—a rich menu. Most of the teachers were real country people, some brought from places as far away as Appalachia and the deep South. Their workshops were just canvas-separated alcoves on a big grassy field, and their admirers could gather close around, or try one after another. The artists could swap experiences and jokes with each other between times, and enjoy playing to a large crowd in the evening.

===== **VI** =====

In a time when liberals are edging toward conservatism, I am still a radical. Not in the sense of wanting to do things harshly or violently but in the sense of going to the root of the problem. Millions of people are a lot more miserable than they need to be in this wonderful country. That is what I call "the waste of joy" and it hurts me to the core. Giving them handouts, no matter how generous some of the rich might want to be, is only mopping up spilt milk. As long as a few people are in a position to make money out of making food scarce and housing scarce and automobiles scarce, there will always be shortages and poverty.

A man from Mars, looking at this scene of unmet needs, unemployed workers, and underused productive capacity, might say, "Why don't the unemployed take hold of it and start making the things they need?" Well, that would be competing with private business. It would be anticapitalist and, therefore, to some people, unpatriotic. I deny that it is unpatriotic to want to give the American people a chance to be strong and healthy. On the contrary, our country would be stronger than it is now.

People sometimes ask me how I get the courage to keep on struggling for what I believe when the majority disagrees. There are several angles to that. For one thing, the fact that the majority disagrees with you is usually a good sign. Every change that we call progress was greeted at first with ridicule or fierce antagonism. But, more important, it doesn't take much courage to be brave when you have an assured income—as I always have. The men and women I admire are those millions—black, white, all kinds—who, through the ages, have braved job loss, eviction, even bullets to organize for a better life.

In this cause, virtue is its own reward. What a joy to work with brave, far-seeing people, who are not concerned with the fashionable or financial climb, but with the future of the human race. And most of them keep a lively sense of humor too. The friends we have encountered here and in every country we have visited are the treasures of my soul and a rich pleasure to remember. I wish I could do a page on each one but that would be at least four hundred pages more. One thing I conclude is that national distrust is stupid. There are wonderful people everywhere and we should work to build bridges to them, before our governments get us into more trouble. As Malvina Reynolds once sang, "Love is something when you give it away—you just have more and more."

Solidarity
Forever

I had been typed in New York as a fat-cat biographer of great fortunes. Convici-Friede offered me a $500 advance to do a book on the Guggenheims, the copper and smelter kings. As $500 was a good chunk in the thirties, I accepted. We invested part of the money in a fearsome old trailer, heavy as lead, with expanding sides, which we hitched to our Plymouth roadster. Though we remained based in Pittsburgh, Jessie and I lit out on a cold day in the winter of 1935–1936 on a cross-country research trip. At all the Guggenheim mines and smelters along our way we viewed operations and talked to workers (or whoever else had useful information).

In some ways the Guggenheims handled the press better than the other robber barons. Daniel Guggenheim certainly talked a better game than the likes of J. P. Morgan. In one instance, Frank P. Walsh of President Woodrow Wilson's Industrial Relations Commission asked him if he believed "that workingmen should have a voice in arrangement of work conditions." Dan rose beautifully to the occasion:

> The workman should not only have a voice—he should have a compelling voice. The Workman's Compensation Act was won by the working man. He will win more legislative victories. And legislation that will benefit the many is desirable no matter what that legislation is . . . You may call me socialistic, if you like, but it is a job of the United States to look after its people.

Neither the Socialist Party nor the Mine, Mill and Smelter Workers Union offered honorary memberships to the beneficent Mr. Guggenheim. My research made it clear why the offers had never been forthcoming. Whatever Guggenheim said about the need for humane work conditions or cooperation between capitalist and worker, the conditions in his smelter and mines were as barbarous as anything I had seen or written about elsewhere. No wonder his workers were so prone to strike.

Studying the Guggenheims allowed me to investigate a new avenue, the forerunner of what is now called the multinational corporation. The Guggenheims had been among the first North American capitalists to invest in Latin America. Taking advantage of the likes of General Bernardo Reyes—men ambitious for themselves as well as their nations—the Guggenheims secured spectacularly valuable concessions at bargain-basement rates. Whatever minimal concerns they might have felt for American workers disappeared below the border. Dan Guggenheim saw himself as another Hernando Cortes, coming almost alone, to knock on the gates of proud Chapultepec to demand that the wealth of Mexico be laid at his feet.

Guggenheim, in his single-minded pursuit of the greatest profit, assisted unwittingly in the birth of the Mexican Revolution of 1910–1920. Guggenheim and his ilk developed, in Mexico, a proletariat completely divorced from the soil. The peasants had initially worked for the capitalists to supplement their income. But the peasants considered it inhuman and outlandish that they should be expected to work from dawn until dusk. For centuries they had lived by tilling their corn patches on the mountainsides, by fishing and hunting. The miners and smelters, annoyed by the absenteeism this fostered, caught the peasants in a trap of debt and alcohol and soon forced them to live in swinelike huts away from their land. The Guggenheims relied on the local constabulary to deal with dissenters. Strikers or complainers were summarily executed. The miners were treated like slaves.

On the eve of the Revolution one Mexican complained:

Mexico . . . [has become] a land of adventurers without religion, or family, whose God [is] gold and who, like the gypsies, pitched their tents on the spot which Mercury designated as propitious . . . The monopolization [is] so wanton that it [is] no longer possible to find a piece of land as big as the palm of one's hand that [does] not belong to some American, German or Swiss capitalist.

This stranglehold was the strength of the capitalists à la Guggenheim, and the weakness of the Mexicans. Even when revolution came, economic realities limited its potential. The Mexicans could change presidents, but could do little about international capitalism. Daniel Guggenheim, always the realist, did not join the pack of small producers calling for United States intervention. He knew that though Guggenheim profits had dropped a bit with Mexico under new management, they were still stupendous. What the Guggenheims did to Mexico, they and others repeated across the globe. Theirs was the story of American business abroad in the twentieth century.

The Guggenheim book was a modest success and Knopf offered the usual $500 advance for one on the Astors. The Guggenheims had been personally interesting and historically important. Old Meyer, the immigrant who peddled lace in the anthracite regions, striking it rich with an investment in a Colorado silver mine, and his son Daniel, one of the canniest, if most ruthless, of capitalists, kept one's attention. For several generations the Astors had done little more than collect rents in Manhattan and rather dimly adorn "Society" in the United States and later, England. Nevertheless, the name of Knopf was something. I thought it indicated I had reached the top rung in the publishing world—my own vanity did the rest. We had to move to New York and visit London to do the research. Against the paucity of material on the Mellons, I had to sort through too much with the Astors, most of it chaff.

After our return to the States, we moved to Winnetka, to the beautiful house of Jessie's mother. Frank Palmer asked me to become managing editor of *People's Press*, the labor paper. I had worked for the paper as a contributing editor in Pittsburgh while I finished the Guggenheim book. It was a genuine slave pen—twenty or thirty editions, with mail coming into Chicago from hither and yon, the editing done by an overworked staff, the printing done in Chicago and mats then rushed by air to Philadelphia, where they were put on the press and then mailed out. A crazy operation, made no easier by the fact that planes were more subject to the vagaries of the weather than now. They paid me seventy-five dollars a week and the rest of the staff much less, which didn't improve matters any.

I soon leapt from the hell of *People's Press* to the luxury of *Ken* magazine. Dave Smart, the publisher of *Esquire*, operated *Ken* as a flashy, progressive antifascist magazine, perhaps to salve his conscience for running *Esquire*, the snob mag. I don't know just how he got my name, perhaps through Meyer Levin, a staffer on *Coronet*, another of his productions. In the late thirties I belonged to the League of American Writers, a leftist outfit with a strong branch in Chicago—Nelson Algren and other local notables being in its ranks. Though the League broke up after the Soviet-Nazi pact, it brought a lot of young writers together and perhaps accounted for Smart's knowledge of me. Smart's offer rescued me from a dreary job. Knopf or some other publisher had inveigled me into doing a book on the Chicago meat packers. I wanted to get shed of it, so I bargained with Smart to pay someone else to continue the research.

I had a large office overlooking Lake Michigan in which I spent a good bit of time admiring the changing hues of the lake from morning to evening. The routine was simple—a bunch of manuscripts were turned over to me each morning. These I winnowed through, discarding most, and sending those with possibilities up to Arnold Gingrich, the editor. After lunch the accepted manuscripts returned with notations. A week before press time I would be asked into the great man's office, where he would be pacing down alleys between hundreds of photos. Smart disregarded nearly everybody's advice, including mine, but still it was exhilarating to see how a great mind worked. I saw one of his explosions; some poor creature sent *Esquire* a story explicitly describing how a lady was laid. What indignation— to think that the wretch would believe *Esquire* would contaminate itself with such-like! Nowadays it would be considered almost *de rigueur* to have such an incident in the story.

Smart's brother, the business manager, ran a sweatshop several floors below. Meyer Levin, Lawrence Martin, and I became interested in the plight of the young people who did the bookkeeping, circulation, and advertising drudgery. We got a charter from the United States Office and Professional Workers, then a left-wing union, but I can't say we had much luck with the terrorized workers. We had less with ourselves. In the summer of 1938, I believe, Jessie wanted to accompany her mother on a trip through Sweden via the Gota Canal, and I decided to tag along. Smart granted a leave of absence only too eagerly. Upon my return I found that Levin and

Martin had been fired. As for me, we'll call you, don't call us. Another cushy job down the drain.

Charlotte Carr, the head resident of Hull House, invited us to live at the settlement. We had a penthouse on top of one of the many dilapidated buildings that constituted Hull House. The Astor book had just come out. But the bloom was off that sort of book by then, and fewer copies sold. Freed for the time from writing books or working on *Ken*, I had more time for extracurricular activities. My reputation made me a hot ticket at fund-raisers up and down the Gold coast for the Spanish War Relief. Though we raised a lot of money from middle-class Jewish people, we could never crack through to the majority of the population of Chicago—Italians, Czechs, Poles, and others—with our message.

Being only a mile from the Loop and in the midst of Hull House's activities, Jessie and I led hectic lives. Jessie was on the board of thirteen outfits, more or less, and busy as a hen with ducklings. On one occasion we must have had nearly a hundred people in the penthouse at a reception for Harry Bridges and other notorious characters. Jessie gave a weekly dinner with some distinguished person as speaker, and other notables came and went. In time I became chairman of the residents' committee, which acted as a buffer between the residents, probably some twenty to thirty people, and Charlotte Carr. Charlotte, a heavyset person, was considerably more progressive than her board. Hull House always faced financial problems and even the sacred name of the late Jane Addams couldn't jar some of the heavy fat cats in town from their surplus wealth. Charlotte had a trying job, partly because the reputation of the settlement far outran its ability to be of service in the community.

I was elected to the board of governors of the City Club, an organization of do-gooders in a town that didn't have much use for do-gooders. I had previously served as chairman of the education committee, which engaged in perpetual warfare with the superintendent of schools, an ancient troglodyte out of the nineteenth century. The board met once a week at luncheon and the problems of the big city furnished plenty of food for thought and action. From time to time we issued reports, but the *Chicago Tribune* couldn't have cared less for our efforts.

I also served on the board of the Chicago Civil Liberties Committee, a considerably livelier body than the City Club; the committee regularly went up against the city machine and the infamous police department. Our board had folks destined for distinction—notably Arthur Goldberg, later a Supreme Court justice and ambassador to the United Nations. The police constantly went around beating up left-minded folks and the committee always had cases plodding their weary way through the courts. We also engaged in desperate efforts to mobilize public support against the outrages committed by the Red Squad roaming the city. Chicago was as bad as Pittsburgh at its worst. Our chairman, the venerable Dr. John A. Lapp, a professor at the University of Chicago, was an exponent of Jeffersonian liberty, pure and simple. He could not tolerate the attitude of the American Civil Liberties Union, which was already tossing Communists off its board—notably Elizabeth Gurley Flynn, a woman who had fought more civil liberties battles than all the members of the national board combined. The Great Witch Hunt began long before Joe McCarthy made a profession of it.

During the Spanish Civil War, I became chairman of the Chicago branch of the American League Against War and Fascism, later known as the League for Peace and Freedom, and even later as the American Peace Mobilization. The Spanish Civil War was the most horrible experience leftists of my generation faced. The Italian Fascists and the German Nazis backed the rebel generals in Spain who fought the young Socialist Republicans. Hundreds of young leftist men and women joined the Abraham Lincoln Brigade to help the Spanish Republicans and were obliged to sneak out of the country to fight for Spanish democracy. Most of them never returned; many of the others who managed to get back were wounded or sick. Theoretically the United States remained neutral, but, in fact, the government looked the other way while American conservatives and capitalists supplied weapons and materials to the fascists. And when the brigade's survivors limped home, the American government attacked them viciously. Instead of greeting them as heroes, the attorney general put the brigade on a list of subversive organizations and blacklisted its members. Even after the United States went to war with fascist Germany, the members of the brigade were not rehabilitated. The government continued to punish them, labeling them as "premature anti-fascists." It might have been funny if it weren't so tragic.

Our League Against War and Fascism devoted major attention to work for the Spanish Republic and for mobilizing public opinion against Hitler and his Nazis. On one occasion we filled the Chicago Stadium in a show of solidarity. Generally, we saw the growing international tensions and war fever as a dispute between capitalists for which the workers would pay in blood and lives. Initially many shared this view and Russia's unwillingness to join the war fever increased her prestige among people who opposed war. The League fell upon bad days when the Soviet Union invaded Finland. Many saw the invasion as an outrageous assault upon a poor little nation. Later in World War II, when the Nazis encircled Leningrad, it became obvious why the Russians had gone to war to push back the Finnish frontier. But the crowning blow was the Soviet-Nazi peace pact. Our Peace Mobilization—as it was then known—fell in ruins. Once again, the divisive force of foreign affairs ruined a domestic organization that aimed at social justice at home and abroad—the same had happened to the I.W.W. and the Socialist Party a generation before. When the Nazis invaded Russia most of those (all of them leftists) who had stuck with the Peace Mobilization became ardent warriors and after that little was heard of peace. I also came to support the war; with the Soviet Union, the world's only workers' state, under attack, I felt the war could no longer be dismissed as a capitalist game. For the workers' sake, fascism had to be defeated. We had tried to do it peacefully by embargoes and similar notions; but now we could do nothing but fall in line and work for the defeat of Hitler. Agitation for causes was *de trop* during the war—all energies had to be plowed into the war effort. For my part, I organized the American Labor Planning Association. Actually, I was the association and my principal effort was sending out news releases to labor, farm, and progressive papers. I operated from a tiny office in the Loop, backed up by a mimeo machine of ancient vintage. I hoped planning would be some sort of back door to socialism—another way I justified support of the war.

Nevertheless, with no new book in sight, the letup in agitation and my own uneasy support of the war led to a general malaise that drove me to stamp collecting (which a psychiatrist friend said denoted anal-mindedness) and, perhaps, Jessie to yearn for motherhood. I thought she was singularly ill-equipped for the role, what with her incessant business with the ills of Chicago, the nation, and the world; who would take care of the children? But Jessie told that part of the story.

===== **I** =====

My friend Irwin Elber, a whirlwind organizer for the United
Federal Workers, knew O. A. (Jack) Knight of the Oil Workers International Union-C.I.O. and introduced us. The union, Jack said, was
going great guns, and he wanted me to start and edit a paper and be
the union's publicity director. In 1945, the offer was compelling: I
was restive in Chicago and jumped at the opportunity to get back
into union work after so many years. There was probably never a
more exciting time or place to do it. The New Deal, as I said, had
given great hope to American workers. The Supreme Court's attack
on the Roosevelt administration, particularly its decision that the
N.R.A. was unconstitutional, had put a damper on the new enthusiasm. But the men once aroused were not easily discouraged. Men
hungry for the protection of unions responded enthusiastically to the
C.I.O. organizing campaign.

The new C.I.O. unionism succeeded where the A.F. of L. had
failed. Perhaps the biggest difference between the two lay in the
word "planning." The old A.F. of L. way of rocking along, meeting
situations as they arose, would never organize a basic industry dominated by hostile employers. The new streamlined unions in the
C.I.O., which, by 1945, had smashed through to amazing victories,
did so on militancy and knowledge. They had education departments
that energized the thinking members who were the union's fighting
edge; they gave them facts, ideas, and ideals to fight with and for.
Publicity departments kept the members and the public informed.
Research departments studied the industry and the union and could
give fingertip information to the officers. Meetings of the executive
councils judged the facts submitted by the union's best brains,
devised strategy for the conquest of nonunion positions, and planned
for the improvement of the conditions of the organized.

Jack Knight had been the leading organizer of the militant Hammond wing of the O.W.I.U. and had supported the insurgency
against the old O.W.I.U. tactics in the mid-thirties. The insurgents
had pushed for retooling and streamlining the union and putting
most of their funds into rank-and-file organizing. Though the
O.W.I.U. still lagged in tactics, by 1937 it shared in the liberation of
labor that went with the successful C.I.O. drive. The O.W.I.U. also
faced the same problems as the rest of the C.I.O. The A.F. of L.,

jealous and threatened by C.I.O. victories, joined employers in fighting the C.I.O. In the old days the A.F. of L. yelled Socialist or Red at I.W.W. organizers. Now they employed a new smear word—Communist—against the C.I.O. They often tried to disrupt conventions or encourage division in C.I.O. unions, sometimes even trying to take the unions over.

More significant than the virtual scabbing of the A.F. of L. was the malignancy of the Depression in 1938. The C.I.O. was forced to lay off many organizers, including those lent to the O.W.I.U., the numbers of new members dropped, the funds to hire new organizers fell with membership numbers, and foes in Congress, cranking up the un-American Activities Committee, took advantage of labor's weakness to start an anti-labor witch hunt. It was a depressing cycle, indeed.

The O.W.I.U. had faced the crunch along with other C.I.O. unions, but felt it more deeply as its organizing techniques and strategies were not up to speed. In the bitter winter of 1939–1940, the O.W.I.U. found itself in a crisis created by depression and antiquated tactics. O.W.I.U. was losing the strike at the Mid-Continent Refinery in Tulsa, and with it, the organization throughout Oklahoma and all vestiges of credibility. Many locals stopped paying dues, which further worsened the situation. In 1940, Jack Knight became the union president at the head of the insurgency and transformed the union along C.I.O. lines. The union funneled all funds into recruiting, learning strategy from star C.I.O. organizers like Mike Widman, who, in 1941, had just smashed the Ford company's resistance to unionism. From the beginning of 1942, the union went toe to toe with Standard Oil, the Dies Committee in Washington, and the A.F. of L., organizing workers throughout the industry. In 1944 alone, membership had risen 40 percent.

By the 1944 convention, the union began to look at postwar strategies. Above all, Knight wanted to hold on to all improvements and push beyond to better wages and greater security for workers. One problem loomed large. The O.W.I.U. was probably the least known of all the C.I.O. unions. The only international with headquarters in the South, it was far removed from the national centers of communication. Worst of all, the international wasn't even well known by many of its members, and this led to lack of interest in union matters farther away than the local union hall. Some said the O.W.I.U. was just a collection of locals.

Since 1935, except for sporadic editions of the *C.I.O. News*, O.W.I.U. had no international newspaper. The union had no way of reaching its members directly. At last, in 1944, the O.W.I.U. could support a paper. The *International Oil Worker*, in the best tradition of the union, was to "mirror the lives, hopes and ideals" of the membership. That's where I came in. I edited the sixteen-page monthly from its birth in March of 1945 to June of 1948. By specializing in news of the locals the paper built up interest and became a great unifying force in the postwar period. My decision initially threatened to strain my marriage. Jessie was aghast at this situation. She informed me she hadn't the slightest intention of pulling up roots in her native city and venturing into the uncouth precincts of Cowtown. I left for Fort Worth saddened, but hoping that things would work out somehow. They did. I hadn't been in Fort Worth for a week when I got a phone call from Jessie asking me if I had bought a house yet. I was flabbergasted! I hadn't even looked. An associate found me a real estate woman who took me out to Birdville, a working-class suburb, where I settled for the first house she showed me.

Things weren't all roses with the new job either. Jack Knight and Bill Taylor, another veteran of the victorious Ford strike, were already at loggerheads. Bill would sweep through the union offices about 10:00 or 11:00 A.M., spreading as much suspicion and dissension as possible. He had an easy task because the union's secretary, E. C. Conarty, hated Knight's guts, and vice versa. The vice president, Sarge Kinstley, balanced himself neatly between opposing forces. Things weren't all bad. Taylor would disappear for a week at a time on organizing business and I must admit, he often returned with the company's scalp dangling from his belt. The companies were tough, which made Taylor's life easier. The tougher they were the harder they fell, for their opposition solidified the ranks of the workers. Only Standard of New Jersey (Humble) had a wiser policy, concessions around the fringes, meeting the union scale, and holding the center line. This was true from coast to coast in Standard refineries, which after all accounted for perhaps a third or a half of oil output in the United States. I tried to hold aloof from the internecine strife. Though I was everybody's friend, I found myself under the cloud of being Jack Knight's protégé in the eyes of Conarty.

My job was to get the paper started—a neat trick without newsprint. The government forbade new publications during war time. C.I.O. operators did some fancy footwork in Washington at the War

Production Board and after several weeks I got a newsprint quota. I doubled in brass as editor and cameraman. The printshop was quite ancient and the press phlegmatic. Often my pictures appeared as dark blobs; on one occasion the vice president, reflecting prejudices all too common, accused me of making him "look like a nigger." At first the union occupied the second floor of an abandoned school building; later we moved to an air-conditioned building—a real improvement in Fort Worth's heated summers. After work I boarded the Birdville bus, an antiquated vehicle held together with bailing wire, which had been sitting in the hot sun for an hour or so.

I saw, firsthand, the union's success in organizing the refineries—a real tribute to both the organizers and bands of good ol' country boys who were tired of being kicked around. The local conditions were particularly unfavorable. The Texas legislature, owned by the oil and gas interests, was implacably hostile to unions. A bill introduced to provide the death penalty for Communists did not pass as the more moderate legislators thought it too extreme. Lefties weren't comforted when the moderates amended the bill to provide twenty years in the pen instead. Some years later a cocky little fellow, John Standard, put his head in the lion's mouth. In a memo statement he declared he was a member of the Communist Party and proud of it. This he distributed to the newspapers, radio stations, and the fuzz. The cops descended on his home and lugged out loads of books, Party literature, and equipment. Mrs. Standard, a keen young woman, phoned the newspapers and radio stations and soon squads of reporters and cameramen were there to record this invasion. The popular reaction was disgust; after all, many Texans still regarded a man's home as his castle. He sued for return of his property and won (although he commented that a good bit of his treasure was missing). Texas was a bastion of "anti-communism." Martin Dies, the head of the House Un-American Activities Committee, represented Jefferson County. His diatribes against communism and the O.W.I.U. so angered his constituents in Port Arthur, Beaumont, and neighboring oil towns that many were relieved in 1946 when Dies contracted an illness and decided not to run for reelection.

Racism also weakened the union. District 4, on the Gulf, was our most important district. I tried to attend each of their district council meetings. The first one was an eye-opener, through no fault of the council. It was one of those hot evenings in Houston and I went out for a breath of air and a late coffee. A young black person came into the open-air coffee shop. The proprietor ordered him to take his cap off. The young fellow refused. Thereupon the proprietor jumped over the counter and the young man fled with the boss in hot pursuit. All things considered, District 4 wasn't this bad on race, but it fell a long way short of perfection. In the Houston local the blacks sat at the back of the hall and kept their mouths shut. In Port Arthur and Beaumont there were Jim Crow locals, and all the efforts of the national union—not too strenuous—to dissolve them met with stony resistance from whites and blacks. The black local had their own hall, officers, and treasurer, albeit across the inevitable railroad tracks, and they didn't mean to give them up for seats at the back of the hall in a mixed local. The locals were in constant trouble with the E.P.A. or whatever it was in those days that took care of racial equality. The basic problem was that promotion for blacks was only in the dirty jobs of the refinery, digging ditches, maintenance, and cleanup. A compromise eventually was worked out so that one department had upward seniority but blacks had no access to the mechanical trades. Some unions would have solved the problem by jerking the charters and ordering assimilation. That was impossible in the O.W.I.U., a rank-and-file union, in which the rank and filers were especially jealous of efforts of the national union to order them around.

Nevertheless, shortly after I arrived, the O.W.I.U.'s new C.I.O.-style organization and tactics got their first test. Workers had piled up grievances that the companies, secure in the government's war-time no-strike edict, had refused to settle. Workers feared a drop in working hours (during the Depression, some had been reduced to working a few shifts a week) or a precipitous drop in wages. The rallying cry was "52/40 or strike." Workers had been taking forty-eight–hour weeks during the war—forty at straight time and eight at time and a half. They had been paid for fifty-two hours, though they worked forty-eight. Their postwar aim was to keep their pay levels and their fulltime jobs—hence 52/40. The companies fought every inch of the way against concessions in the contract. We moved the union headquarters from Fort Worth to Hammond, Indiana, to be in the center of the Midwestern industry, and ordered a general shutdown. We closed nearly all the refineries except Standard, and the strike was the big story of the week. The government stepped in with the military, "seized" the refineries, installed the superintendents as federal deputies, and temporarily broke the strike.

The time right before the strike had been hectic. The executive council of the union was in session and Jack Knight was off in Chicago or somewhere meeting with federal bigwigs. Emmet Conarty engineered a general strike motion with the unanimous backing of the executive council and instructed me to send out the orders to the local unions, which I did. When Knight returned, he was furious that his authority as president had been overruled by the rank-and-file executive council. While Conarty smirked in victory, Knight ordered me back to Fort Worth, "to get out the paper." He wanted a more dependable minion around. Nevertheless, the strike and the publicity surrounding it scared the companies and negotiations resumed, with notable improvements in wages, seniority, and grievance procedures. After a brief detour, strikers had gotten the best first-round postwar contract in the C.I.O. And the victories continued through 1947.

I had a blast the next time I was in Hammond. All the refineries at the end of Lake Michigan were organized except Standard of Indiana in Whiting and all our efforts there came to nothing. Standard met the union scale and had a company union setup for grievances. The attitude of Standard workers was that the union should fight for better wages and conditions and the Standard employees would benefit automatically. Why pay dues, they asked, when you guys are willing to do the fighting and striking? The union men, fed up with this, decided if Standard couldn't be organized on the inside, then it would be on the outside. So barricades were set up one wintry morning as thousands of oil workers patrolled the entrances. Many rescued derby hats from the attic padded with toweling to soften the blows of the police clubs. Trucks kept running coffee and doughnuts to the heroes on the line. Whiting was closed tighter than a cat's ass.

On the second day of the barricade the Army brass turned up at the union office, pleading for permission for employees of some secret atomic bomb project to be relieved as the operation required twenty-four-hour attention. I relayed the request to the secretary of the Hammond local, a one-eyed guy by the name of George Hoffman. He cocked his good eye at me and said, "Tell the bombastards to go to hell." And the brass waited. That evening the word got around that the governor was sending in troops. The union made a virtue out of necessity by calling off the barricade and next day the Whiting refinery resumed normal operations. And it remains unorganized to this day.

By 1948, the prospects of the unions were beginning to dim. Texas passed laws making unions financially liable for strikes and putting union treasuries at the mercy of the legislature and courts. Standard of California handed to O.W.I.U. its first and most disastrous postwar defeat, breaking the newly organized locals in El Segundo and Richmond. Though the government had been little help in 1945 and 1946, the political climate forced it into some semblance of neutrality. But now the courts rained down injunctions against the union including damage suits of $28,000,000, the Feds looked the other way at Standard's Taft-Hartley strikebreaking tricks, and a hysterical press played up "back-to-work" movements.

Within the union divisions were deepening and becoming even more embittered by red-baiting. Now that the union had achieved national organization, albeit with some setbacks, the leftists, progressives, and Communists who had helped to organize it were considered persona non grata. President Truman was whipping up the postwar Red Scare that played into the hands of long-term conservatives in the union. As the progressives were expelled or left in disgust, the union became that much more conservative. Many were suspicious of me and my background as a "fellow traveler."

I was more and more discouraged. Then, along came 1948 with Harry Truman running for President. As publicity director, I was supposed to pump up enthusiasm for the candidacy of a red-baiter who had dropped the atomic bomb on two Japanese cities. That wasn't my cup of tea to say the least. I knew I had to go and, when I informed Jack Knight, I think he was relieved. It was a tradition of the O.W.I.U. for all to leave publicly on good terms, and so it was in my case. I left ostensibly to write a history of the union.

II

The house in Little Compton was not winterized yet so we were fortunate to get a nice house in Westport, which lies just over the state line in Massachusetts. In the fall of 1948, Henry Wallace ran for President on the Progressive Party ticket. That campaign was part of the reason I had left the union. I couldn't turn down the Progressive people in Fall River when they asked Jessie and me to manage the campaign there. Fall River was and is a rundown old textile town that had lost most of the textile mills to the South or countries abroad that pay low wages to ununionized workers. Low-wage industries now occupy parts of the old abandoned mills. We rallied a curious coalition of Jews who didn't care for Truman's stand on Israel (for what reason now escapes me), Russians who seemed to be more nationalists than Communists, and a handful of Portuguese, the lower class of southern New England. We never convinced any Anglos though we searched through the hay for these needles. Our own lack of previous contacts in Fall River handicapped the campaign and we couldn't use the C.I.O. tactics there. The Democrats had the Clothing Workers and Ladies Garment Workers all sewed up and Fall River had no left-wing unions. Our big affair was a luncheon for our vice presidential candidate, Senator Glen Taylor of Idaho, which didn't compare with that of the Democrats. Just before election Eleanor Roosevelt breezed into town for Truman, and the proletariat turned out en masse for The Lady. She pretty well cleaned up our campaign. We got around five hundred votes. The campaign had cost about twenty-five hundred dollars so we figured our votes cost us five dollars a head.

I didn't intend to sit in Westport all winter and spring admiring the scenery. So I got working on the history of the Oil Workers Union I had promised Knight. I wanted the locals to write their own history while I took care of the national organization. My research took me back through the oil fields of Oklahoma, Texas, California, and other areas and then back to Little Compton to do the tedious work of pulling it together. I was satisfied with the final product though I made no pretentions of objectivity and slanted my analysis toward rank-and-file struggles rather than toward the officials. Jack didn't object either and I got a warm welcome at the 1950 or 1951 convention of the union.

By 1949–1950 the Little Compton house had been winterized and we abandoned Westport. Our house had been known as the Withington house for years but this family had fallen on hard times and so we came into possession. It had the name of Land's End, which we never used. At the end of a peninsula, its third-floor tower room looked upon the ocean to the north, east, and south. The news got out and soon in summertime we had scads of people around, old friends and their children. Since we also had a cottage on the property, a cabin, and a large two-story barn with a finished room, we always had space for visitors. We were able to cope with the invasion of the hordes through the services of Iris and Phyllis Harvey. Iris had worked for Jessie's father in Jamaica and wanted to come to the States, and later we were able to wangle her sister's entry as well. In the evenings Jessie occasionally arranged folk dancing with all hands invited from near and far. The children organized plays for which they charged a modest sum of a nickel each to begin with, but soon greed forced the price up to fifteen cents, which I suppose went for candy. Among the star guests were Hays Jones, my old friend from Tacoma days, his wife, Rosamond, and their two daughters. So many came that we converted the back room, the former servants' room I suppose, into the children's dining room—if you can call it dining. Once the children rebelled and insisted on eating with the adults. We agreed on condition they cooked the meal. Even the children found it pretty terrible and did not bother us with any more rebellions. In addition to my friends, Jessie had scads of relatives, aunts, cousins, brothers and sisters, and whatnot parading around the premises. It became pretty rough on the Harvey sisters—summers were hard work and winters lonely with no Jamaicans within miles. So Iris finally flew the coop and went to work in a shirt factory in Fall River; a year or so later Phyllis also decamped. That pretty well ended the mass invasions as Jessie and I were not willing to do all the work involved. She had help in the kitchen from time to time when lucky enough to find someone capable of carrying on.

I had discovered sailing in the summer of 1935 when I was substituting for Laurence Todd in Washington. Jessie had always thought sailing was great sport but in 1935 I hadn't known anything more nautical than propelling a boat by car. As it happened, the Navy was selling off a small fleet of 26-foot sloops used by the Naval Academy midshipmen for training on the low seas. I had just gotten a check for royalties on *Mellon's Millions* and felt quite flush, so when they asked four hundred dollars for this carpenter's job of a boat, I did not blanch. The boat was delivered to a boatyard in Baltimore. When we came to claim her, the catwalks to the boats were under water. Our little boat was also half drowned. It had been raining pitchforks all day. I had wanted to name the sloop the *Watermellon*, in

honor of old Andy but Jessie forbade. We thought of the word in
other languages. The Spanish *Sandia* was out of the question for
being nonhailable. One evening we went to a Japanese restaurant and
the waiter informed us that the Japanese word was *suika*, which
quickly became *Suki*.

Jessie's father worried about our safety in heavy weather on our
little boat and decided to present us with a new one. *Volya* was built
in the winter of 1935–1936 at the Casey yard in Fairhaven, opposite
New Bedford. She was a thirty-six-foot yawl, with a roomy main
cabin, fore cabin with two bunks, and a large cockpit, self-bailing, of
course. Jessie's father designed the layout with all the gadgets and
conveniences he had thought of in years of sailing. With the mizzen
acting as a kind of rudder, it was a safe type of boat for novices and
also a lazy rig for those who don't care for the rigors of reefing in a
high sea. She sailed fairly well under jib and jigger and was as fast as
any comparable boat under full sail although she had a roomy beam,
ten and one-half feet. Jessie chose the name *Volya*, which is Russian
for freedom or will, and has a good sound for hailing.

My years with the O.W.I.U. had stimulated my interest in that
industry and I thought the available books on it quite inadequate.
Several, critical of the industry, pointed out its callousness to the
public interest but these were dated. Back in the 1890s, Jessie's
grandfather, Henry Demarest Lloyd, had written the first denunciation of the oil monopoly in *Wealth Against Commonwealth*. The University of Texas library had a room filled with books on the industry,
all technical, and only a handful were critical examinations. So after I
finished the union history, I decided to write an up-to-date analysis of
the nation's most powerful industry.

I had only begun my research on oil when I spent a few months in
Jamaica with the children while Jessie made a foray to Yugoslavia to
see some of her favorite Slavic peasants. We stayed at Jessie's father's
place—*Bu Saaba*. It should have been heavenly and was—almost.
Iris Harvey as governess took good care of the children. Every morning we were down at the Doctor's Cave beach where the children had
a great time swimming, diving, boating, and eating. But I saw the
contrast between the luxury of our own life there and the misery of
the countryside when the children developed continuous vomiting
for several hours. I knew that "vomiting sickness" was rampant in
the hills behind Montego Bay, where people were dying and the little

hospital was jammed with patients. But our doctor took one look at our children and laughed off that disease in their cases. "They are too well fed," he commented.

Eventually Jessie showed up, via the Azores and other stopping points, and I shoved off for Venezuela to take a look at America's premier oil colony. I traveled quite a bit for that book, which mentioned the international industry, but really concentrated on the domestic. I found the oil industry of the United States to be dominated by ten billion-dollar corporations that responded to no direction but their own. Even the stockholders found the corporations beyond reach—theirs only to ratify decisions made by the corporation. Standard Oil of New Jersey's annual revenue of nearly six billion dollars was greater than that of the government of Canada, and six times that of its relatively affluent South American dependency, Venezuela. Most of the companies were congeries of subsidiaries—Standard of New Jersey had more than three hundred—doing business around the world, producing in out-of-the-way places, and selling to all who needed their wares. The preeminent position of these companies in United States foreign policy followed from their $5.1 billion investment abroad—then 20 percent of all foreign holdings by United States nationals.

These intermingled companies controlled the major oil resources of the world—outside the Soviet Union—and, though they objected to the harsh word "cartel," they were hard-pressed to find another word to describe their entente. Production and prices throughout the world moved together in majestic concord, above the controls of such sovereigns as the United States and British governments.

The dominant companies built on a solid political base. Internationally they worked with any party or group willing to do their bidding; domestically, they preferred the Republican Party and kept a restraining hand on distasteful Democratic policies by control of ruling cliques in the Southern states. To shape public opinion, they spent freely, through the Oil Industry Information Bureau, through advertisements, through subsidies to schools, colleges, molders of public opinion, and organizations in touch with farmers and others critical elements of the population. They had erased all the petty risks of "free enterprise," but they were always aware of one overshadowing risk they could not exorcise—the rise of peoples, nations, and ideas. This risk they met resolutely out of the public treasury of their government, heaping arms upon arms until the earth groaned under the burden. And yet they were always a bit uneasy. In their deepest fears were my greatest hopes, as I wrote in the book.

I felt pretty good about the book when I finished it and started looking for a good title. One day my eyes lit upon Louis Fischer's *Oil Imperialism*, which dealt with the division of the swag in the Near East by the victors of World War I, an excellent book, written back in the twenties. Why not put "oil imperialism" into simpler form—*The Empire of Oil*? And so it was.

Sadly inflated by my own importance, I handed the manuscript to a literary agent in New York. I knew that the Red Scare was in full swing, and that people like me were under suspicion, but I thought my reputation would protect me. Leo Huberman, editor of *Monthly Review Press*, a Socialist publishing house, wanted the book, but I was above having a Socialist house do the book. Huberman bet me a good dinner that no commercial publisher would touch it. How right he was! After a year of rejections I bought Huberman a dinner. Came the day of publication, and the silence was deafening. The *New York Times*, which had favored *Mellon's Millions* so highly, wouldn't even list the name of my latest book. The reason? It was not published by a commercial house and the *Times* did not recognize Socialist publishers. As nearly all the avenues of communication were closed, the public couldn't know that the book had been published. As it turned out, however, I was fortunate. A commercial publisher would have printed three thousand copies and that would have been the end of it. Happily, *Monthly Review Press* had foreign connections and editions of *The Empire of Oil* and the subsequent volume, *World Crisis in Oil*, appeared in various countries around the globe: three in Spanish (Mexico, Venezuela, and Argentina), two in Portuguese (Brazil and Portugal), and British, French, German, Polish, Swedish, Russian, Hungarian, Arabic, and Japanese editions.

I can't say whether this fame or notoriety got me into the worst jam in my whole life. In other times I would have been given some credit for writing books that had gotten around and been well received, but in the early fifties it was nothing but jail bait. It happened this way. There was a Senator Joe McCarthy of Wisconsin, head of the Government Operations Committee, charged with overseeing the federal departments. He had a special subcommittee on investigations, which he also conducted, and at the time, in 1953, he was warring with Dean Acheson, the Secretary of State. Acheson was one of the most conservative and anti-Russian of all our secretaries of state but nevertheless McCarthy called him the Red Dean and in meetings across the country charged that he had in his hand a list of fifty or a hundred card-carrying Communists in the State Department—never any specific names and no proof. Kingpins for McCarthy's "investigations" were two gumshoe artists, Roy Cohn and G. David Schine, who went overseas to get the dirt on Acheson. So they investigated the overseas libraries of the State Department and what did they find but books by me! These libraries, aimed at acquainting foreigners with American culture, were scattered around the globe. The State Department sponsored the libraries but the American Library Association furnished the lists of books to be included. I was delighted to discover that my books were in collections in many an obscure city but I had never been consulted about their inclusion.

One fine summer day I was sitting on our front porch with friends, enjoying the sight of the sea and listening to a poet recite her latest poem. She had about reached the climax when our son Steve slipped out and whispered I was wanted on long-distance. I told him to ask the person to call later. When he did, Roy Cohn informed me I had been subpoenaed to appear in Washington in a day or so. I asked Cohn, a lawyer, if this telephone call was equivalent to a subpoena. He said yes, the committee had so ruled. I doubted Roy's and Joe's interpretation of the common law and called the Emergency Civil Liberties Committee in New York. I spoke to Leonard Boudin, the committee's counsel, who told me my suspicion was right. So on the day that was dedicated to my destruction in Washington I was at home admiring the scenery and hobnobbing with friends. When I didn't show up McCarthy emitted his favorite cliché, "You're in contempt." Later McCarthy reconsidered—after all, he had been a judge back in Wisconsin and must have known something about serving a subpoena. A couple of deputy marshals came down from Providence with the proper documents, and after the formalities one turned to me and said: "Mr. O'Connor, I'm glad you put up a fight for that subpoena. Serving them is how we make our living." I had hardly put up a "fight" for the wretched paper, but I was determined not to go to Washington without one.

In Washington I had a private session with McCarthy and his aides. When I refused to answer his fool questions, he called off the private inquisition and we proceeded to the Senate caucus room, the biggest in the building. The Senator, at the height of his notoriety, played to a full house. Dozens of reporters, radio and TV crews, and the public crowded the room. I was a little stupefied but when Mc-Carthy kindly inquired if I wanted the Klieg lights turned off, I answered, "*No.*" I was perfectly willing to let the public see what went on in the latest Inquisition. Attorney Boudin was at my side. McCarthy set the tone for the hearing by asking him to identify himself. "So you are the attorney for Judy Collins, the convicted Russian spy!"

After I was duly sworn I was asked the sixty-four–dollar question, "Were you or have you ever been a member of the Communist Conspiracy?" Another question: "Did you deposit the funds given you by the State Department for your books in the Communist coffers?" I hadn't received a penny from the State Department; in fact, I didn't know my books were in the overseas libraries until that day. On one question, I was baffled as to how to say "*No*" to shut him up. Boudin whispered some sort of legal mumbo jumbo that I duly recited, and the Senator immediately announced: "You're in contempt, step down." In his annual report, McCarthy wrote that I was "the most contumacious witness ever to appear before the Committee." I would like that as an epitaph on my gravestone.

I based my defiance of McCarthy on the First Amendment, which stipulates that Congress may pass no law abridging freedom of expression or association. My commitment to civil liberties made it impossible for me to answer McCarthy's question. To answer him would suggest he had a right to ask, and I could never do that. As far as McCarthy or any governmental agency was concerned, my politics were my own business, not theirs. When they run for office seeking votes, we are naturally concerned about their politics and affiliations. But when a "public servant" demands to know a citizen's politics, democracy has been subverted, turned topsy-turvy.

McCarthy had victimized so many people that I wanted the First Amendment tested again in the courts. The Hollywood Ten had made that test in the late forties and lost, and they went to jail. After that those subpoenaed began taking the Fifth, which protected them from self-incrimination. They didn't go to jail but usually they suffered discharge, blacklisting, and similar penalties even more severe than jailing. I believed that union activists, teachers, and workers with families were fully justified in using the Fifth. But I had to take

a stand—I could afford to. I knew how political prisoners were treated in American jails and didn't look forward to a year of it. But I was
willing to face it for this. And I had the luxury of knowing that my
family wouldn't suffer. If I landed in jail my family would be better
off financially and a stretch in the pen might even be enlightening to
an old-time radical.

I was duly cited. Only a half dozen or so Congressmen participated
on the floor and four were reading the morning funnies. It was unanimous—nobody raised a voice for the First. It was like that in the
Cursed Fifties. Then came the indictment and later the trial. I. F.
Stone and others in our little gang held a skull conference before the
trial. Izzy's thought that when I was asked by the district attorney if I
was now or ever had been, . . . I should turn to the judge and ask
him, as a matter of my conscience, whether I was obliged to answer
the fool question. It looked to me like a hundred-to-one shot, but
why not try? McCarthy testified to my contumacy. Asked by my
attorney, Leonard Boudin, if he had ever read any of my books,
McCarthy answered with great contempt that he had never bothered
to and couldn't care less about my writings. When the big question
came, I turned to the judge and I asked Izzy's question. To everybody's surprise, and to the consternation of the D. A., the judge said
as a matter of conscience, I need not answer. Score One for Izzy and
his strategy. The judge, a Cincinnati Taft appointee, nevertheless
found me guilty, suspending the sentence of one year. My partisans
wrung my hand in joyous acclaim, but I didn't feel victorious. I was
trying to test the First Amendment and had failed. So I appealed. I
liked the title of the appeal—*Harvey O'Connor* vs. *the U.S. Government.* How much better than the previous one, *the U.S. Government*
vs. *Harvey O'Connor*! It restored my self-confidence.

On appeal the full bench of the Appellate Court reversed the verdict and threw out the case. It was a curious business. The court
based its reversal on the Sixth Amendment, which provides among
other matters that a person cannot be convicted unless charged with a
crime. Their decision was a testimonial to McCarthy's sloppy way of
doing business. On the ninth and final question he had asked me if I
was a member of the Communist "Conspiracy" and directed me to
answer. But the Court of Appeals, looking through the Criminal
Code, could find no reference to such a crime as belonging to the
Communist Conspiracy and so I was let off the hook. The sad com-

ment on American law in the fifties is that, had McCarthy asked me if I were a member of the Communist Party, I would have gone to jail. The Smith Act declared that such membership was indeed criminal. So I won on the Sixth and not the First, as I had hoped.

So much for the legal aspects of the case. I spent much of the next decade or so bringing the issue to public attention. I made sure I fought publicly in groups that included Communists in their ranks. I felt public cooperation with Party members was a critical repudiation of McCarthy and the Smith Act. Whatever my differences, I had had cause over the years to have great respect for the work of the Party and I wouldn't deny that now. Even if I hadn't, people had the right to make that choice without harassment in a country that called itself a democracy. The Emergency Civil Liberties Committee came back to life with Clark Foreman as director. We decided to hold a public meeting in New York to see if interest could be aroused. In spite of the rather dismal fraternal hall near Times Square we held it in, the turnout was good. The E.C.L.C., the *Monthly Review* crowd, and many victims of the Inquisition showed up. Matthew Josephson, the author of *Robber Barons*, opened up with a learned discourse on civil liberty.

I recounted my experience, interspersed with a good bit of humor. The humor was intentional—it was a way of breaking the spell and seeing McCarthy for the miserable wretch he was. I refused to regard him with awe or fear, and closed with some beautiful quotations from the original civil liberties battler, Thomas Jefferson. Then I went to Boston, where the Liberal Citizens of Massachusetts, headed by John Howell, hired a hall in a downtown hotel. By 8:00 P.M. it was evident the hall was far too small and we shifted over to a bigger room. Things went so well in the New York and Boston meetings that E.C.L.C. decided to tour me nationally. On to Pittsburgh, where we still had many contacts, Cleveland, Chicago, and points west. Since Jessie bankrolled the operation, there was no O'Connor Defense Committee begging for money. Little did I realize when cited by McCarthy that I was beginning a new career in public speaking.

This whole affair also got me thinking about the state of the American "left," so to speak. We were, frankly, much better at speaking out against domestic attacks on civil liberties than on those that occurred regularly in the Soviet Union. It wasn't possible to raise these questions publicly during the Red Scare—the McCarthy types would have seized upon them and manipulated them. I did privately urge fellow radicals to do some rethinking. I remember writing to Claude Williams in February of 1953:

For my own part I believe the anti-Soviet propaganda has been so effective as to have blanketed us. The bad part about it, from my own point of view, is that we have made little effort to dissociate ourselves from the more unpalatable aspects of the Soviet system—the unending witch hunts, persecution, etc., which put our own McCarthys to shame as mere amateurs. The quick blotting out of the Prague miscreants was a shocking example; apparently nothing was to be left to chance or fate.

It seems to me that the Soviet people are on the horns of a real dilemma: how is it that such scum is attracted to the Communist Parties and is able to rise to the very top; what becomes of all the talk about comradeship and "Soviet Man" in such circumstances; or if they are not scum, what is it that seems to breed so much treason in the Soviet system?

I realize very well our own responsibility for sharpening the severity of the dictatorship; the Red Terror in the French Revolution arose in similar circumstances. However that is merely equating the evil of both sides, and I had thought one side was better.

My own belief is that we are going to make very little headway either as a Progressive Party, or in infiltrating any other party, so long as we carry such a trail of suspicion behind us.

It is time in other words to make it clear that we are for the Socialist part of the Soviet system and against the excrescences bred by unmitigated dictatorship. It is time for us to speak of what is needed for America's good, and not just for the Soviet's, not to engage in sly maneuvers and tactics which leave the unmistakable impression in people's minds that we really are un-American.

For my part I am willing to admit that I have glossed over the shortcomings of the Soviets, the more so as I have felt no keen responsibility for what they did as the Communist Party never held many blandishments for me. I saw Lovestone from a worm's eye point of view and saw too much of what makes the wheels go around to get fuzzy-headed about it. It is much easier not to criticize a friend when you think he is headed the wrong way and so I kept my mouth shut.

This has led to my own political inactivity; I have not been able to summon any enthusiasm for the Prog. Party since 1948 and saw it out during the recent campaign for lack of any cause which I though worthy of rallying behind. Nor do I intend suddenly to begin working within the Democratic Party because that is the current line. I'm tired of lines that turn and twist and prefer the stait and narrow, even though it's mighty solitary nowadays.

Nor I am trying to build any non-Communist movement. I got trapped in New America and drew the conclusion that movements such as that wind up as anti-Communist. Not being anti-Communist but merely non-, I am leery of joing groups which seem to develop some kind of dynamic toward anti-Communism. So there's another dilemma.

So I merely continue working on my book on oil, hoping that perhaps it will make some contribution.

Actually, I was more active than this letter suggests, but not in the ways urged by the Party or even some other leftists. Still, there was much to be done.

When the McCarthy episode ended, the concurrent travesty on human rights being played in Washington continued—a fact many have forgotten. The House Un-American Activities Committee (H.U.A.C.) continued well into the sixties, harassing activists in progressive causes from labor to civil rights. As McCarthy drifted away into alcoholism, H.U.A.C. took the center of the stage. I later found that as early as 1939 H.U.A.C. had taken my name in vain. Benjamin Gitlow, a high official in the Communist Party, defected and "told all." He told them that I was a Communist because I worked for Federated Press. Gitlow didn't know me, had never met me, and was dragging his statements about me out of the clear blue sky. Nevertheless, I became an "identified Communist," so referred to by H.U.A.C. and McCarthy on every possible occasion. Like other victims I had no recourse. The identification appeared in documents bearing the honorable shield of the United States Government and were what is known as privileged—no libel or slander suit allowed. In 1958, H.U.A.C. descended on Newark, New Jersey, with subpoenas for a score of school teachers (the most defenseless creatures on earth) and union activists. Just why H.U.A.C. chose Newark I know not for it certainly would not make the juicy headlines of the forays into Hollywood. The Emergency Civil Liberties Committee placed ads in the Newark papers and scheduled a meeting at the Robert Treat Hotel in defense of the new victims of H.U.A.C.. As chairman of E.C.L.C. I was one of the speakers. As I entered the lobby a deputy marshal stepped forward with the bright news, "I have something for you, Mr. O'Connor." I knew what it was and turned on my heel. The subpoena fluttered to the floor like a wounded bird. Once again my privileged financial position allowed and required me to resist where others simply couldn't. I was told later that it summoned me to an inquisition a day or two later, but I was not to be present at their exhibition. I am told a couple of marshals went out on the front steps of the Federal Building there and bawled out my name. But I was not within earshot.

Ignoring a subpoena is serious business, as my lawyers agreed. As agents of the court they could have no part in counseling me to treat a subpoena, as a friend said, "with ignorance." But Leonard Boudin and Morton Stavis, a Newark attorney, got their heads together to figure a way out of the impasse. In a maneuver as imaginative as Izzy Stone's at the McCarthy hearing, they decided to counterattack; they subpoenaed the H.U.A.C. records pertaining to my being subpoenaed. The judge in Newark granted the subpoena and now H.U.A.C. was in the hole. What records could they have that I knew anything about communism in New Jersey, when I had never lived there or been active there, and knew none of the defendants? So H.U.A.C. did the next best thing—they rushed a resolution through the House forbidding the committee to produce any records. That produced a stalemate. Nothing happened. My name was on the court docket in the northern district of New Jersey for years. I even at one time advanced to the number one position on the docket, which included the names of other malcontents accused among other things of pushing dope on school children. What company one keeps in these cases! After several years in which we did nothing to arouse the sleeping curs to action despite my constitutional right to a speedy trial, the district attorney dismissed the indictment. Later the news drifted across the Hudson and my attorneys informed me of the disposition of the Newark case. We were all happy.

In the summer of 1959, Anne and Carl Braden, civil rights activists, visited us at Little Compton and joined a conference on our front lawn. The subject was First Amendment defendants. Since my use of the First against McCarthy, more and more people had been using that amendment instead of the Fifth, and all faced prison. We decided to organize a First Amendment Defendants Committee to rouse public attention. We hadn't consulted the defendants. As it happened, many did not want to be organized: they wanted to be left alone by H.U.A.C. and everybody else. Nevertheless, a score or so of sturdy souls agreed and we cranked up our publicity campaign.

H.U.A.C. busted loose again, this time in Atlanta. One of us had mentioned the front lawn conference in a public meeting, which caused H.U.A.C. to allege that we were part of a "conspiracy" to abolish the committee. Conspiracy was H.U.A.C.'s long suit. We had started a campaign, to be sure, for abolition that very summer. Frank Wilkinson came east from Los Angeles and we formed the National Committee to Abolish H.U.A.C. (N.C.A.H.U.A.C.). I resigned as chairman of E.C.L.C. to assume the chairmanship of N.C.A.H.U.A.C.. Wilkinson ran a taut ship, much to my liking, with no fancy salaries, rock bottom wages, plenty of volunteer labor suitably organized, emphasis on education and agitation. That first year the returns were rather meager—one lone congressman, Jimmy Roosevelt of Los Angeles, introduced a repealer but got no support.

H.U.A.C. responded vigorously to our campaign. They got out a pamphlet, *Operation Abolition*, with the usual name-calling but not the slightest effort to meet the arguments and issues we raised. The pamphlet produced dossiers of all our officers and sponsors to "expose" our records. We had no objection to that for we were rather proud of our records. H.U.A.C. made an incursion into San Francisco and the Bay Area in 1960, and there was a terrific uproar in the marble lobbies of the City Hall where the hearings were held. Cameramen recorded the disgraceful scenes of demonstrators being swept down the marble staircases by high-pressure hoses. A film was made and widely distributed. This stung H.U.A.C., which prepared its own version of the events. This really launched our abolition campaign on a national scope.

The battle was on, and Frank Wilkinson and Carl Braden were the first casualties. They went to Atlanta to organize resistance to a H.U.A.C. hearing on communism in the South. For Wilkinson this meant a transcontinental trip. But hardly had they arrived when Frank and Carl were served with subpoenas. On the witness stand they stood on the First Amendment and were duly cited, indicted, found guilty, sentenced to one year. The Supreme Court, by five to four, upheld their conviction, the swing vote being that of Felix Frankfurter, the erstwhile valiant champion of liberalism. With our champions in the jug we went to work on the fight-back. Sylvia Crane in New York and others had organized a special defense committee; there were large ads in the *New York Times* and hundreds, perhaps thousands, responded. In the next Congress we increased our abolition vote by 600 percent—namely, six Congressmen had the guts to vote our way. After that it kept snowballing, up to fifty or so. But it took Watergate to shake things loose. After the Watergate scandal and the election in 1974 of a lot of younger Congressmen, we finally attained our object all sublime—H.U.A.C. was abolished. It had taken fifteen years and the leadership of Frank Wilkinson, a supreme organizer, tactician, and publicist, to achieve the goal. I understand the archives of H.U.A.C. have been sealed for fifty years. I wonder what scholars and historians in the year 2030 or so will think of this disgraceful period in our history.

H.U.A.C. having been abolished, we changed the name of our organization to the National Committee Against Repressive Legislation. We immediately had a big job on our hands. The Nixon legal crowd had revised the Criminal Code so that the choicest excrescences of H.U.A.C. and McCarthy were installed in the revised code. Our job was herculean for the code ran more than six hundred pages, beyond the comprehension of the layman. With a renewed campaign of publicity and organizing, we also succeeded on this. The bill died with the end of Congress and a newly revised version was introduced in the 1976–1977 Congress with some of the worse features removed but with still plenty of the Nixon-Mitchell influence in it.

The other important way of fighting the red hunters was to refuse to be daunted by them. And so, as I noted in my letter to Claude Williams, I began the research for *World Crisis in Oil* in 1953. This book concentrated on what the industry had done to the rest of the world—stripping nations of natural resources without paying a fair return. Indeed, in South American countries the rise of oil revenues often led to a further impoverishment of the people. Where countries like Venezuela had fed themselves before oil, afterwards, so much land was taken out of cultivation that people were hungrier than before. And virtually none of the profits reached the peasants—the rich lived extravagantly while the poor starved. Yet, as I pointed out in my book, the crisis for oil was already beginning. Some countries in the Third World insisted on control of their own resources. In other places—Cuba and parts of Africa—revolution and revolutionary ideas made it hard for America, with or without the multinationals, to govern the empire. I felt, in the late fifties and early sixties that McCarthy and H.U.A.C. and their ilk were part of a passing world—Cuba belonged to the future. When I look at current events in Nicaragua and Latin America, I think I was correct.

At loose ends after finishing *World Crisis in Oil*, I returned to an old ambition, to relive the stirring days of Seattle in the World War I years. Thus was born *Revolution in Seattle*. The research was a labor of love—talking to old-timers, digging up old newspapers, uncovering hitherto unknown publications. Marvin Sanford in San Francisco was an invaluable ally in the search. For years he had collected radical publications of the Pacific Northwest and I was able to get many of them into the University of Washington archives, along with material and letters of other old-timers. Sanford, a printer by trade and an inveterate collector by choice, boasted that all his grandparents had been Socialists. He was publisher of odd little magazines, many of which threw light on the Puget Sound communities of a half century ago or more. Sanford had a file of the little magazines that Thor Mauritsen of the *Daily Call* had published, many of which contained that episode. I thought the book a good way to wind up my career as an author—I hadn't planned for this memoir.

III

All my life fortune has been on my side. At various junctures fortune could have failed me, but it didn't. Result: a happy and fulfilled life. Consider:

(1) My unknown parents, God bless them, endowed me with a sound constitution that has stood me in good stead for more than eighty years.

(2) I was brought up in a working-class family where the choice was work or starve. This saved me later from an agonizing search for my identity; I never had much time for scrutinizing my navel.

(3) In my formative years I was lucky to grow up in Tacoma and Seattle, at that time cities with a dynamic radical movement. What if I had had to grow up in Indianapolis or Columbus!

(4) I am eternally grateful to the Socialist Party and the Industrial Workers of the World for my education. From those men and women I learned a wholesome understanding of social reality, the relation of

an individual to his fellow men and women, and an ideal greater than myself. I also acknowledge that society provided me with an excellent academic education in Tacoma High School. As a result of these circumstances I was spared the waste of college years. And my mother worked her way into an early grave to see that I got that education before I had to work full-time.

(5) By inclination and by good fortune I was led into radical newspapering, which matured my education. Especially I acknowledge my indebtedness to Anna Louise Strong and Harry E. B. Ault, who gave me the opportunity of training in daily newspaper work.

(6) Most of all am I indebted to Jessie Lloyd, my constant and unfailing companion. Not the least, she made it possible for me to write the books and to wage those battles for civil liberty and social justice that alone give me a claim to service in the cause of human freedom.

In our hands is placed a power greater than their hoarded gold;
Greater than the might of armies, magnified a thousand fold.
We can bring to birth a new world from the ashes of the old.
For the Union makes us strong.
Solidarity Forever!

Index

255